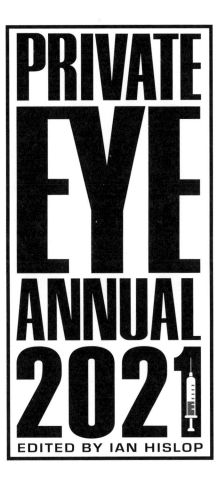

PRIVATE EYE ANNUAL 2021

EDITED BY IAN HISLOP

"I'm sorry, but due to Covid, we've decided to be rubbish"

Published in Great Britain by
Private Eye Productions Ltd
6 Carlisle Street, London W1D 3BN

www.private-eye.co.uk

© 2021 Pressdram Ltd
ISBN 978-1-901784-70-1
Designed by Bridget Tisdall
Printed and bound in Italy
by L.E.G.O. S.p.A

2 4 6 8 10 9 7 5 3 1

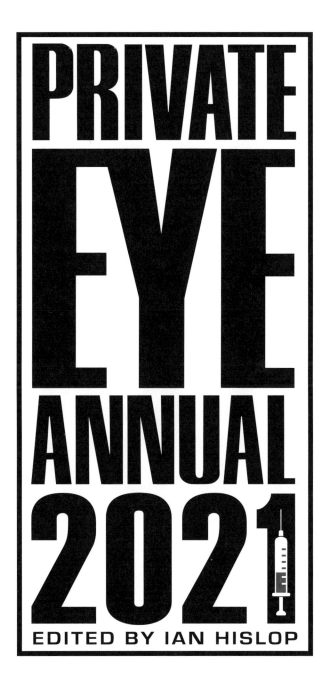

PRIVATE EYE ANNUAL 2021

EDITED BY IAN HISLOP

*"I really must apologise about my husband walking through
in the background"*

Boris Johnson

Home   Create

Boris Johnson MP
● Live   385,000,000 Views

Prime Minister's Question Time Live on Fakebook

👍 Like   💬 Comment

0 people **like** this

People of the United Kingdom

Never before in our island story have I had to use so **much** sub-Churchillian **rhetoric** to so many of you, with so **few** details. We have fought Covid on the **beaches**, we have fought it in the **streets** at 10pm, we have fought it in the **students' halls of residence**. We shall **never** surrender. It is not the beginning of the **end** of my Premiership, but it may be the **end** of the beginning. I promise you **nothing**, particularly not **sweat** and **tears**, as they may be **infectious**. And certainly not **toil**, unless you are toiling at **home**, in which case you should continue and only use the Clapham omnibus when **strictly** necessary and with a **mask**. This will be our finest **hour**. Or **weeks** or **months** or possibly **year**.

Cummings: Get on with it, fat boy, no one's buying the Churchill guff!

Boris: Fair enough, you're the **boss**. So, first question. Ah, it's from Miss Poke. I remember **you**! Runner-up in the Miss Henley **beauty** pageant, 2003, at which I was **honoured** to be the sole judge. **Phew**! Queen of the River! In-out, in-out! **Cripes**, those were the days! Does that answer your question?

Cummings: She's not asked it yet, fatty-puff!

Boris: **Hasn't** she? Oh, thought I'd dealt with that one rather **well**.

> What are the current lockdown regulations in the North East?

Boris: Right, yes, very **simple**. Rule of **Six**, that's **six** of one household and half a dozen of another. Unless you're having **tea**, in which case it's tea for **two** and two for **tea**. Unless you're **outside**, in which case it's 2-4-6-8, who do we appreciate? **Boris**! And then of course, it's slightly **different** in the North by North West, if you're meeting up with Cary Grant in a cornfield, in which case you'd better start **running**. This doesn't include the **Four Horsemen**, who are perfectly

free to organise the **Apocalypse** so long as it is **not** in a hospitality venue in **Liverpool**. So it's **yes** to the **Famous Five**, which includes Timmy the dog **obviously**, as one of your five a day, but **no** to the **Secret Seven**, because there are **seven** of them and we don't know what they're up to. Couldn't be **simpler**.

> I'm more confused than ever.

Boris: Don't worry, you're not **alone**. These regulations **are** possibly too complicated for your average Prime Minister in the street. So, let's try a different tack. If you want to know what the current regulations are, just see what my **dad's** up to, then do the **opposite**. Masks in shops? Masks in airports? What's Stanley doing? **Not** wearing one. So, obviously the law of the land must be the **opposite**.

> You're not helping at all.

Boris: OK, I'll have **another** go. That's the Rule of Six – I have **six** guesses as to what the regulations might be at any one moment. So, I think you're currently allowed to meet with your **grandchildren** at a **grouse** shoot in your halls of residence, but **only** after 10pm if neither of you is over **90** or having dinner with Jeremy Corbyn.

Cummings: For pity's sake, next question!

Boris: Right, **this** one is from someone called Lindsay Hoyle. Oh yes, **Lindsay**, I remember **you**! Miss Chorley, 2007!

> No, I'm the Speaker of the House of Commons.

Boris: Oh, **shame**, I wondered why you never returned my texts.

> When are you going to stop treating Parliament with contempt?

Boris: Oh **come** on, Lindsay. It's one thing having a **girly** name, it's another being a girly **swot**, pretending anyone gives a toss about all the **bores** on the backbenches. Holding the Government to account? **Yawno**! Scrutinising policy? It's none of your **business**, you great girly girl's **blouse** with a girly girl's **name**! Leave it to the scientists, like **me**! Boffo Bozza's **back** with his brilliant **bantz**!

> Are you sure you haven't got long Covid?

Cummings: No, he was always this shit. You've just forgotten.

Boris: **Nexteroony**! From Penny Less, who's a **student** in Manchester. Hi, Penny, what are you up to?

> I'm staring out of a window, wondering what you're going to do about this mess?

Boris: Oh, come on Penny, it's **not** like you'd be going to the lectures anyway. **I** never did! So, you're lying around in **bed** all day watching Neighbours and Countdown, with a **hangover**. This is student life! There's **nothing** new.

> Apart from the fact I'm paying for it.

Boris: Fair enough, **good** point, Penny. Trust me, we'll sort this out so you can have a university experience **every** bit as good as **mine**. Getting **bladdered** with fellow OEs, **trashing** restaurants, **burning** fifty-pound notes in front of **tramps**, and **debagging** James Delingpole before throwing him in the **fountain**. I'd pay nine grand just for **that**!

> Actually, I came here to study.

Boris: Why? What's the **point**? There aren't any **jobs**. Dido Harding's got them **all**.

Cummings: Wrong again, lard-arse. We're launching a new initiative to train people up for jobs they don't have the skills for. Like we should with you. Grab this trowel, it's time for a photo-op.

Boris: **Here** we go!

I'm not bricking it! Just rebuilding the Red Wall!

Boris: You see, Penny, a bit of **fun** there, just to **lighten** the mood. You students are all a bit **po-faced** these days, what with your 50-grand debts and your blended Zoom tutorials. You think **you've** got money worries? Wait till you've got **alimony** to pay, a **new** wife and kid number God-know's-what. And a **rubbish** job which pays **only** 150k. You can't even knock off a **column** for the Telegraph or do a **quick** after-dinner speech for Kazakhstan Konkrete Co! Money **trousered**, questions not asked. **Bosh**! So stop **moaning**, Penny. Just remember the new **slogan** which I have just thought of. **Act Fearlessly** but with **Common Sense**... or **Act Recklessly** but in a **Sensible Manner**... or **Act Like an Idiot** but **Don't be Stupid**... hang on, not sure these on-the-hoof slogans are quite as **boffo** as normal... anyway, must **dash**... time to go and **blather** my way through the Andrew Marrathon... **usual** technique... **blah blah blah**, Andrew... Oh dear we have run out of **time**... Which we have! **Bye**!

TRUMP COVID CRISIS

Trump in virus hoax embarrassment

THE world's most powerful virus was last night red-faced when news came out that it had caught President Trump.

Covid-19 was on record as believing that President Trump was "a hoax", and had refused to take him seriously. Back in March, Covid-19 had said, "This Trump guy is totally unbelievable. Nothing about him is true. He's a complete phoney. He's not a serious figure. He won't last long. We'll be rid of him by Christmas."

However, much to the virus's discomfort, it turns out that Donald Trump does exist and is the President of the United States.

Said a chastened Covid, "'I now realise Trump 2020 is a very real threat, and is capable of destroying the world with his dangerous policies."

The virus further conceded that Trump is more infectious than he thought, and has already spread through large swathes of America.

President Trump dismissed Covid's outburst as complete lies, saying, "It's Fox News."

(Rotters)

Late news

Virus goes for controversial drive-by to spread message. Thousands of supporters turn out.

"What have I told you about drawing on the walls?!"

The Eye's Controversial New Columnist

The columnist who has been stockpiling rusks since June

This week I am in total agreement with Esther McVey, in that teachers indoctrinate pupils with "left-wing" ideas and, furthermore, I completely support the government's policy of removing books that have a "left-wing" bias. I would go further and say this sinister propagation doesn't begin in the schools. Far from it! In my nursery there is already indoctrination. I have come across material which is obviously anti-government propaganda smuggled in under the guise of children's literature. In one of these books there is a character called "Mr Bump" who is coloured blue (not subtle!) and who makes an utter catastrophe of every job he does. This is somehow seen as a bad thing and not a good thing, as, instead of being promoted to Foreign Secretary and then Prime Minister, it is decided that he is only qualified to walk around orchards and knock apples out of trees. This is just the start! Another character (Mr Mean) is a tall, thin creature who hides all his money away in a box. Presumably, this is just petty cash and the rest is in offshore accounts and an Irish hedge fund. Mr Mean is tortured by a kindly old wizard (obviously an ex-Labour leader) for having the temerity to be savvy about his considerable fortune. I have organised a book-destroying programme, which involves sucking the corner of these books into oblivion. If Esther would like to help me suck, she could join me after milk and biscuits to *(cont. p94)*

Ronaldo tests positive

THERE was shock throughout the world of football as Cristiano Ronaldo, the world's top footballer *(apart from Messi, surely? Ed.)* tested positive for coronavirus.

Said Ronaldo's club doctor, "We knew something was up when Ronaldo displayed no symptoms whatsoever. If he'd been rolling around on the floor screaming in agony, then it would have been obvious that nothing at all was wrong with him. Especially if nobody had come anywhere near him, like, say, within two metres."

It is hoped that Cristiano Ronaldo will soon be back to 110 percent fitness and will resume his position as the world's top actor *(apart from Sir Anthony Hopkins, surely? Ed.)*

(Rotters)

Those Covid fines in full | HM Government

- Shaking hands with everyone at height of pandemic: **fine**
- Driving with your ill family across the country when it was in full lockdown: **completely fine**
- Messing up and leaving thousands of vulnerable people dead: **totally fine**
- Not knowing the rules you set: **100% fine**
- Wrecking the prospects of a generation of children: **fine, fine, fine**

Your Covid lockdown questions answered

Q: Can I...?
A: No

Q: Can I...?
A: No

Q: Can I...?
A: No

NEW GOVERNMENT WARNING
'R's LEVEL: STILL HIGH

Meanwhile, at the Vivaldis...

They've commissioned a second season!

Pearsall

GNOME PRESENTS *THE* VIROLOGY ARMCHAIR

ARE YOU enjoying giving your opinion about how the world should be dealing with coronavirus? Are YOU sure that if only you were in charge, this devastating pandemic would be sorted out in a fortnight? *Then you need the VIROLOGY ARMCHAIR!*

Just sit in it (no expertise required) and start sounding off! Comes with comfy armrests, inbuilt "reverse" feature to do a 180-degree swivel and with 94 pre-recorded opinions stored in armrests, ranging from, "It's our responsibility to cough on the elderly to make them immune" to "We should all be allowed out for ten minutes a day and no longer". **Buy now!**

Price: £2,994

The Free Speech Society's Toby Young says: "There won't be a second spike and this chair proves it."

THAT HISTORIC PRESIDENTIAL ELECTION DEBATE

Biden: You smell!

Trump: No, you smell!

Biden: Not as much as you do, Smelly!

Trump: That's rich coming from Smelly Joe!

Biden: You're the smelliest President ever!

Trump: Don't use that word 'smelly' with me!!

Biden: Smelly! Smelly! Smelly!!!

Trump: You're top of the class when it comes to Smelly!!

Biden: The only people who can't smell you are the people you've given Covid to!!

Trump: You would have given it to more people, who would then be dead and then really smell, but still not as bad as you!!!

Moderator: Gentlemen, I'm not sure this is the level of debate the public were hoping for.

Both: You smell too!!!

Trump: But not as much as Mr Smelly over there!!!!

Biden: Just shut up, President Smelly!!!!!

Trump: No, you shut up!!!!!

(Continued for 94 minutes...)

School news

St Cake's.

Lockdown term resumes after half-term on October 26th. Possibly.

There are 37 pupils at school, and 490 at home in isolation, due to the Spanish supply teacher, Señora Corona, testing positive after her break in Madrid. All pupils in years 1, 2, 7 and 94 are receiving blended learning which, as parents will know, is a mix of online and online tuition. It will include educational YouTube videos, a selection of informative Netflix box sets, and creatively-inspiring TikTok memes. Due to popular demand, Britbox is not included. Games will be held every afternoon, where pupils will have a chance to play each other at Assassin's Creed 94, Fifa 21 and Fortnite (Quarantine version). Games will end promptly at 3am. School catering will be outsourced to parents. There will now be tests for all staff and results should be in just after the end of term. Please rest assured that key school facilities, including your wallets, are still open for business. The bursar remains hard at work, tracing and testing your liquidity. Carols by Zoomlight (December 12th) has unfortunately had to be cancelled, as the school computer now also has a virus. The headmaster would like to wish all parents a very happy Christmas holidays, with all their family around them. It should be just like most of this term.

POETRY CORNER

In Memoriam Gerald Shur, founder of the US Witness Protection Program

So. Farewell
Then Gerald Shur,
You are dead.
Or are you really?

Or are you in
Suburbia with a
Moustache?

And known to all
Your neighbours
As Frank?

Perhaps we will
Never know.

E.J. Thribb
(17½ identities)

OH NO! I'VE LOST MY SENSE OF TASTE — THIS IS BRILLIANT!

EL JAMES THE MISTER

BRITISH BUMMERTIME CONTINUES

Don't forget to put your clocks back – to March

Three tiers for Boris!

AT LEAST THINGS ARE BAD IN FRANCE TOO

AS THE Covid-19 pandemic rages on across Britain, out of control in many areas, wreaking economic devastation and robbing people of their lives, as we head into an unknown winter of misery and isolation, it remains clear that one fact at least is to this nation's credit: things are also really, really bad in France.

The defeat of this disease is obviously a great human endeavour, one to which we must all devote ourselves. The disease is no respecter of national boundaries. A successful vaccine will be an achievement for all mankind.

Still, we can at least say, God, the French have messed it up too, haven't they? Not so clever now, are you, Frenchy? Think we might have been right in introducing a quarantine for you, eh?

There is no pride in seeing anyone else fail in the face of this deadly new challenge. Nonetheless, seeing just how high the numbers are in France, we can only say: hahahahaha [*continue until things in Britain get so bad we have to shut up again*]

Pandemic forcing people to rethink their retirement plans

by Our Aged Correspondent
Tone Deaf

A LARGE number of the over-60s say the coronavirus pandemic has made them rethink their retirement plans, from spending a relaxing 20 years dining out at local restaurants, enjoying foreign cruises and taking short breaks in the UK, to dying suddenly in their beds.

Said one expert, "The prospect of dying suddenly from Covid has changed the way many over-60s see their retirement years, in that they no longer see them at all, as they will be dead.

"Being dead clearly has a major impact on how people see their quality of life in retirement."

"*Alexa... make me happy!*"

ME AND MY SPOON

THIS WEEK

DANNY DYER

Do you have a favourite spoon?

Yeah – it's greasy. Because some of us didn't have a silver spoon shoved in our gobs when we were at Eton!

Do we need more greasy spoons in the Cabinet?

Well, one would be a good start.

Would you like to throw your spoon into the mix?

Leave it out!

What if the cutlery drawer at Number 10 was opened for you?

Shut it!

So you're saying "no" to any spoon role in the future?

I'm too busy. I've got a proper job – Eastenders, a new Podcast with my daughter, Dani Dyer, not to mention a game show called "The Wall". Not the Eton Wall, 'cos I'm not posh like all those muppets.

But you do rather keep banging on about how you're related to royalty?

Yeah – Edward the Third.

Is that cockney rhyming slang?

Get off my manor!

Oh – you've got one of those as well, have you?

■ *Mr Dyer stormed out at this point, claiming to have an appointment with the Queen Vic, before we could ask him whether anything amusing had ever happened to him in relation to a spoon, to which he would no doubt have entertainingly replied "Naff off, you privileged twat".*

Keir Starmer
WRITES

HELLO! As you know, we in the Labour party have adopted a 'three-Keir' approach to the coronavirus.

So far we've been through 'Keir one', (respectfully supporting the government in everything it does regarding the lockdown), and we've done 'Keir two' (urging the government to ease the lockdown, stop worrying and get all the kids back to school), so we're now entering 'Keir three' (screaming at the government to have another lockdown!! Don't you know there's a pandemic on, you idiots?)

As you saw at Prime Minister's Questions, it's no more Mister Nice Guy!

Yes, I've "taken the gloves" off at last – although I do still want to remind the nation that removing gloves is dangerous and we should keep our gloves on at all costs!

So, after many months of support, I've broken with the government and I've come to the conclusion that we need a "circuit breaker". This is a technical term, but just look on it as a short, drastic procedure we can effect to "shock" things back on the right track.

If you're still confused, let's find an analogy that I like to keep in my mind: Let's say the virus is a crusty, unpleasant union leader, and we need to make it harmless before it kills off the host, in this case the party.

So we implement a "circuit breaker", or for the purposes of the analogy, a sudden lockdown on the union leader and all his old friends which "breaks" the pattern of transmission of dangerous views and keeps the public shielded from all that virulent stuff that used to go round the "circuit" of Labour members.

When this "shock" action works then the virus is rendered harmless and anything it tries to do, like pretending it has mutated into a different virus, or no longer wants to give the party any money from union funds, is no use! The result, thank heavens, is that the nasty old leader – I mean virus – is no longer a menace to anyone and together we can unite and beat him – I mean it!!

Sincerely, Keir.

DIARY
CHARLES MOORE: MY TELEVISION

ATTENBOROUGH, SIR DAVID: I am sure Sir David knows a great deal about furry animals, fish, lizards, creepy-crawlies and so forth. The BBC certainly allows him a disproportionate amount of its airtime to boast that he does. There is, I suppose, no legal reason why he should be forced to wear a suit and tie or dinner-jacket, to present programmes from the jungle or the Antarctic. But it must be dreadfully galling for the Queen, who is known to watch his programmes, to have to witness a senior presenter in such a state of undress.

BAKE OFF, THE GREAT BRITISH: If friends kindly invite you to their houses for afternoon tea, you expect to be offered scones and cream if you are privately educated, or an Eccles cake, if you happen to be working-class. Last week on The Great British Bake Off, one contestant baked a Spanische Windtorte, and another a loaf of prosciutto and manchego soda bread in the shape of the Eiffel Tower. Are we witnessing the final push by the Establishment to nullify the referendum result in effect, though not in name?

DAD'S ARMY: Private Walker, the only character wholly committed to the values of the free market and the rule of law, was depicted as seedy and untrustworthy. Likewise, Mr Hodges, the air warden, was scorned for attempting to get the assorted subversives, adulterers and welfare dependents to obey the law. Has there ever been a BBC programme more overtly and catastrophically Bennite in its outlook?

EASTENDERS: Has an investment banker, a corporate lawyer, an hereditary peer or a hedge fund manager ever been spotted in Albert Square? This is the BBC, so the answer is, of course not. Friends tell me that these days the real East End is full of such worthwhile people. Yet they are never allowed a look-in.

FAWLTY TOWERS: It is more than likely that Basil Fawlty is a Liberal Democrat councillor. Many minor public school people are.

GARDENERS' QUESTION TIME: There is nothing inherently wrong with the fuchsia. Some consider it a useful stand-by in small-to-medium-sized gardens of under five acres. But it is unremarkable, to say the least, and tastes unpleasant. Why then do the powers-that-be at Radio Four devote so much time it? Is it because it is so clearly a left-wing plant, and unashamedly red? Last week, the panellists on Gardeners' Question Time, two of them from the North, one bearded (or so he sounded) spent well over three minutes expounding on its virtues.

LEWIS: Every week, Lewis features three or four unseemly murders taking place in Oxford. After protracted investigation, these murders are found to have been committed by tweedy academics or local grandees, many of them pillars of their local Conservative Association. Would television executives ever sanction a similar detective series set in Manchester, say, or Birmingham, with left-wing and/or Islamic lecturers unmasked as the killers? Silly question.

MRS BROWN'S BOYS: It soon becomes evident that, beneath the ill-fitting frock, the protagonist – "Mrs Brown" – is in fact a transgender male, barely halfway through whatever procedure the NHS has authorised. Needless to say, his/her entry is always greeted with prolonged applause, doubtless orchestrated by the Thought Police.

ONE SHOW, THE: A reader writes in to tell me that, in over 3,000 episodes, The One Show has still never contained an item in praise of General Pinochet. Yet it regularly features such inconsiderable characters as Amanda Holden and Basil Brush. Why?

PEPPA PIG: Is Miss Pig a Remoaner? Her general attitude – jumping in muddy puddles and so forth – suggests as much.

QUESTION OF SPORT: Those tuning into BBC's Question of Sport, hoping to hear a question concerning two of our most popular sports, will be disappointed. At a hunt dinner last week, I spoke to someone who had monitored every programme for the past 30 years. After all that time, he has still not heard a single question on hunting or shooting.

SONGS OF PRAISE: Still denied a proper daily hour-long showing on the BBC between 6pm and 7pm by the corporation's managerial Dawkins lackeys.

TOP OF THE POPS: It is a great benefit to civilisation that Top of the Pops is no longer filmed – I imagine because the majority of its performers and all its presenters are in prison, or awaiting charges. But the BBC has got around this by screening old episodes.

UPSTAIRS, DOWNSTAIRS: Broadcast by ITV, of course. Decades later, the question remains unanswered: why does the BBC continue to refuse to film a similar reality series reflecting the true nature of contemporary Britain?

WOMAN'S HOUR: Three mentions of Greta Thunberg over the past month, and none whatsoever of the Princess Royal. Why does this not surprise me?

Z-CARS: A neighbour – a well-respected figure locally – informs me he witnessed a hooligan speaking ill of a police officer on Z-Cars. I have no reason to disbelieve him. Forty-five years on, the BBC has still not issued an apology. We should bear this in mind when they next start bleating about the licence fee.

As told to
CRAIG BROWN

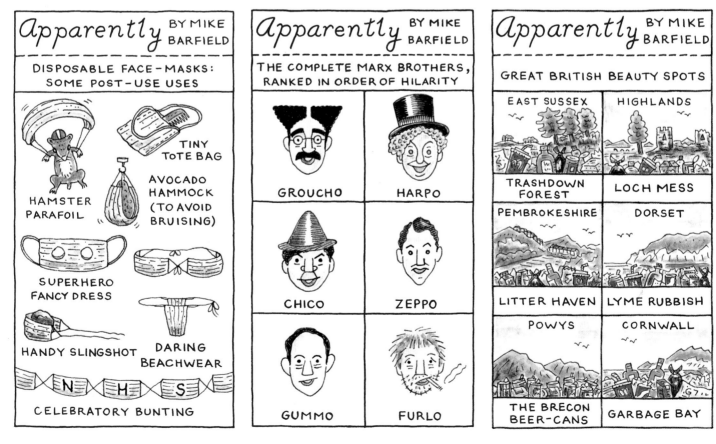

9

THAT TRUMP RELIGIOUS RALLY IN FLORIDA IN FULL

Donald Trump enters to a selection of Village People hits: YMCA, Nacho Man, Not in the Navy (or the Army).

The Reverend President Trump:

"I'm not saying that I'm the Messiah, and that God raised me from the dead. Though it was three days I was in the hospital, just sayin'! And I was dead – so dead. Then I rose again!

And the doctors came to my room and they found just a bed sheet, a shroud – with an orange stain on it. Because I had vanished! I was out of there! Driving around, visiting my disciples. Who were all saying 'Hosanna', which is a town in Texas, 'Heysanna', who's a lady I've never met or paid any money to, and 'He is among us – stand back, well back!'

And guess what? Now I'm IMMUNE! Totally immune! They should take my blood and give it to my followers. Maybe with a wafer or, better still, with a burger!

Because you know what? In the next couple of weeks, I'm gonna be all over the place – that's me! I'm gonna be EVERYWHERE! Everywhere at the same time.

Ring any bells? Just sayin'. I'm Omnipresident. And another thing – I know EVERYTHING! Nobody's better at knowing everything than me. FACT! Of the type I know, because I'm Omnisciosexual.

I don't know nothing like that Sleepy Joe. He's not rising again. He's just dead.

And by the way, nobody likes him. He's NOT NICE! He can't remember anyone's name.

Poor old Sleepy Fred. And he's NOT GOD! I'm not saying I am. But on the first day I said, 'let there be sunlight'.

As a cure for Covid. And there was. And it was good. SO GOOD! And, lo, on the second day I named all the cures: Regeneron!"

Hydrocloxy-moxydoxy-fluification! Kryptonite! They said there wasn't a crowd of 5,000, but there was. I counted them all! And there were 5,000 at the rally. And I only had five McDonald's Filet-O-Fish, and yet behold – I fed everyone.

So either there were only five people there or there were 5,000. It won't be reported in the failing mainstream Bible, that's for sure. So only two weeks to go. Can I perform a miracle? YOU BETCHA! Take up your bed and walk, Loser!

All the way to the polls. The only cross this all-American SonofaGod wants to see is the one next to the word 'TRUMP'! Bless you! Unless you're sneezing. In which case you've got the virus, LOSER!!

FOUR MORE YEARS – OF COVID!!! May Trump be with you! Hallelujah!!"

This rally got a 94 percent infection rating amongst the evangelical group 'Republicans Against Masks'. The other 6 percent were already classified as officially dead. But may be born again in time for a postal vote.

LENNON AT 80
How he would have looked today

CORBYN DINNER FOR 9 BREAKS RULE OF SIX

I'm eating with the many, not the few

Dacre surprise choice for head of regulator

by Our Media Staff **Ivor Pottymouth**

There was considerable shock throughout the broadcasting industry at the proposed appointment of the former editor of the Daily Mail, Paul Dacre, as head of Ofcom.

As his first act, Mr Dacre plans to change the name of the regulator to 'Fuckofcom', and then to concentrate on the problem of bad language on television.

"There's not nearly enough of it," said Mr Dacre. "And I'm going to fucking change that!" He proposes sweeping alterations to the TV schedules, which will shake things up as never seen before. Including:

● 'The Great British Bake Off' to become 'The Great British Fuck Off'
● 'Peaky Blinders' to be renamed 'Peaky Effers and Blinders'
● 'Songs of Praise' to be 'Songs of Bollocking'
● 'Blue Planet' to become 'Extremely Blue Planet'
● 'Judge Rinder' to be renamed 'Enemy of the Fucking People Rinder'
● 'Call the Midwife' to be 'Call the Midwife a Lazy Public-Sector Fucker'
● 'Countdown' to be renamed 'Cuntdown'
● 'Countryfile' to be 'Double Cuntryfile' (*Yes, we get the fucking idea. Ed.*)

What You Missed

BBC
All Channels

Nick Robinson on Radio 4: Now, minister, I have to ask you this, as devil's advocate and not because it is my opinion you understand, not at all, I have to put the contrary view which some people might believe to be right but not me certainly not...

Emma Barnett on Radio 5: …Obviously, minister, I have no views on this subject, and indeed no views on having no views, which you would be the first to agree is the right view to have on the vexed issue of having views…

Andrew Marr on all other stations: So minister... we have to maintain a strict impartiality on all matters, including the need to be impartial, so there are clearly arguments on both sides and it is our job to present both the case for balance and the case for lack of balance with equal weight…

(Continued on 94 MHZ until presenters are happy that their jobs are safe...)

HS2 GOES OVER BUDGET

IN OTHER NEWS

■ **Pope goes to Catholic Mass**

■ **Bears go to wood for...**
(Yes, we get the idea. Ed.)

LATE HS2 NEWS

■ **Worry over delay to link up major cities**

The latest postponement of completion of the high-speed link between London, Birmingham, Manchester and Liverpool has been met with concern. "We're worried that this delay is not long enough," said the Chief Medical Officer. "The last thing we need is a high-speed link for the virus to travel along!" However, HS2 assured him that once the track was built there was a safety system in place to prevent this. Namely – leaves.

LATE US NEWS

Presidential Race Hots Up – Both Candidates Still Alive

GLENDA SLAGG

She's Fleet Street's Fieriest Firework?!!!

■ HATS AND KNICKERS off to Lily Allen!!! She's the sexy songbird who has just launched her own vibrator?!!!??? She is one liberated lady!?!?!! And does it work?!!? Yes yes yes yes oh yes yes yeeeeeeeeeeeees???!!

■ LILY ALLEN??!?!!?? What a disgrace!!!!?!! Can't you shut up about your smutty sex toy?!!??? We're all sick of your porny publicity seeking so why don't you just buzz off?!!??? Geddit??!!!

■ JOHNNY DEPP?!! You're depply unpleasant in my book (coming out in time for Xmas, *In Depp Doo-Doo*, £9.99) and now the judge agrees?!? You are guilty Captain Jack (Sparrow in the film) and should be made to walk the plank and keel-hauled (like a pirate in the film, geddit)?!!?!! And poor old Amber has been HEARD at last?!??! Three cheers for the brave Sun newpaper and top crusading journalist Dan Wootton. *(Is this right? Ed.)*

■ SHED a tear for poor old Johnny Depp???!! How could Justice have been so blind????!? She is a good actress that Amber and she should be up for an Oscar for that performance in court?!??? Still, in my book (coming out in time for Xmas, *Heard Immunity*, £9.99) Amber should be seen and not HEARD?!!!! And Dishy Depp should have won his libel case against the scumbag Sun and Desperate Dan Wootton. *(Is this right? Ed.)*

■ JOHNNY DEPP and Amber Heard – why couldn't they both lose??!? They deserve each other in my book (*Acting Very Badly*, coming out in time for Xmas, £5.99) and they *(You're fired. Ed.)*

■ IS IT "Love Actually" for acting legend Bill Nighy and Vogue fashion supremo Anna "Nuclear" Wintour???!? Is this the Wintour of our Content!!?? Geddit?!!? Or is it well Nighy Impossible to Believe!!? Who Knows???

■ FAY WELDON and her hubby Nick?!!!! She Devil!!? He Devil??? Me don't care!!!!!

Byeee

News in brief

Tory MPs call for Boris removal

■ Tory MPs who demanded in 2019 that weak, ineffectual Theresa May be removed from office and replaced with the bold and charismatic Boris Johnson have today called for the weak and ineffectual Boris Johnson to resign and be replaced by the bold and charismatic Rishi Sunak.

"Just as Boris Johnson had everything the ineffectual Theresa May didn't have: style, charisma and the ability to connect directly with voters, Rishi Sunak similarly has everything the ineffectual Boris Johnson doesn't have: style, charisma and the ability to connect with voters," said one pink-faced Tory backbencher wearing a bow tie.

"We look forward to Rishi grabbing the reins of power and to us then deposing him deep in the recession of 2022 for some backbencher no one had heard of five minutes ago, because he comes across like a half-decent human being in an interview on the Andrew Marr show."

POETRY CORNER

Lines on the 80th birthday of Sir Cliff Richard, singing legend

So. Happy Birthday
Then Sir Cliff.
You are
80 years old.

If only there was a
Song of yours
That would seem
Appropriate for such
An occasion,

But *The Young Ones*
Doesn't quite do it.
And *Bachelor Boy*
Seems a bit mean.

No, I still can't
Think of one.

But, anyway,
Congratulations.

E.J. Thribb (17½
but still looking older
than Sir Cliff)

From The Message Boards

Members of the online community respond to the major issues of the day...

This post has been shortened by the moderators for breaching forum rules

Pub controversy

Guys, I see that London dominatrix Lydia Chadwick took a client on an ill-judged trip to a Lake District pub for 'public humiliation'. Said client identifies as female (but was described by witnesses as 'a man dressed as a woman') and was stripped to her lingerie before being tied to a beam and spanked with a paddle. Responding to criticism, Ms Chadwick riposted: 'People should get out of the Dark Ages and accept this sort of behaviour.' Ouch! –
Bogbrush

ignorent young person's know nothing of the passed. i studded the dark age's at uni it was a name invented by winston churchil for when hitler ruled the world, followd by what he calld the iron age when josef starling built an iron carton to keep russia safe. now its happening again with putin and trump. learn from history ppl!
– ***Jace 91***

Adieu au vice anglais! 😞 The purse-lipped poseurs have prevailed! Vale Jimmy Edwards and his comedy caning show 'Whack-O!'. Vale the Bognor Cane Company, driven out of business by the bolshy teachers' unions. Vale the Curly Horley, brass-handled leather strap banned by the Education (Governance) Act 1965. Vale Rhodes Boyson, no-nonsense headmaster-turned-politician, who declared, 'If you can't teach it into 'em, beat it into 'em.' Vale the 'Six o' the Best' caning machine, once-popular attraction at the British seaside. This post has been shortened by the moderators for breaching forum rules. – ***O tempora! O mores!***

We enjoyed that caning machine every summer at Rhyl! But does anyone remember that sound effects record? Track 1: 'Boy receiving six strokes of cane for slovenliness – chaffinch at window.' Track 2: 'Boy receiving four strokes for persistent lateness – passing locomotive with eight carriages.' Track 3: 'Boy receiving four strokes for insolence – cricket match in nearby playing field.'. The final one was 'Boy receiving 24 strokes for apple-scrumping – workmen drilling road in distance, light aircraft passing overhead, police van approaching, peal of church bells, bomb squad conducting controlled explosion at distance of two miles.' 😊
– ***Taffy Meg***

It was called 'School Days' and I was the boy who was beaten on the record! My dad was an engineer at the British Phonograph Company and they told me it meant that other kids wouldn't have to be caned in plays and films! I was paid two bob an hour, but some of the tracks took dozens of 'takes' and I must have had 6000 of the best! It was part of a series with 'Morning in the City', 'Sounds of the Sea', and 'Factories, Shipyards and Mines' but it was the only one that made the charts!
– ***Christopher Cross***

Great stuff guys! –
Bogbrush

"Be careful with this, the seagulls round here are very clever at nicking food"

BORIS WELCOMES THE NEW PRESIDENT OF THE UNITED STATES

The *Eye* is delighted to publish the two letters that Boris wrote to the White House on the eve of the presidential election.

Dear Donald,
I always knew you were going to win, and we were all rooting for you. Thank goodness good sense prevailed and they didn't put that senile old lunatic Biden in the Oval Office. What a disaster that would have been for the special relationship.

Yours,
Boris

PS. Looking forward to some great post-Brexit deals. NHS still on the table, and would love a chlorinated turkey for Christmas!
PPS. Love the no mask!

Dear Joe,
I always knew you were going to win, and we were all rooting for you. Thank goodness good sense prevailed and they didn't put that senile old lunatic Trump in the Oval Office. What a disaster that would have been for the special relationship.

Yours,
Boris.

PS. Looking forward to some great post-Brexit deals. NHS still on the table, and would love a chlorinated turkey for Christmas!
PPS. Love the mask!

CONSPIRACY UPDATE
AMERICAN ELECTION SPECIAL

CONSPIRACY UPDATE: We've got a bulging postbag this week, which is already suspicious because most of our contributors use e-mail! Perhaps I should investigate that postbag full of "letters" next week!

But first, let's try to get to the bottom of what REALLY happened during the American election! Regular contributor and Qanon fan MAGA435 says on his Facebook Page that the coronavirus was a scam to make republican voters trick themselves into dying before the election.

He says: *"They new that the plage was a reel thing so they sed it was a reel thing nowing we wud think it was a hoax, so we wud all not wear our masks and catch it and dye."*

He adds:*"We demand that the votes of our dead brothers and sisters be counted NOW before its tooo late!@!!!"*

TRUTH-IS-OUT-THERE4356 strongly disagrees, positing the theory that the missing Trump voters are all being kept under the ground in secret underground bunkers.

His twitter feed reads "Wake up sheeple! Giuliani's press conference in front of the garden center next to a sex shop and a crematorium was NO ACCIDENT. It was a SUBLIMINAL message! If we don't take shovels in our hands and DIG DIG DIG until we free our Trump friends from their incarceration by the Marxist FBI! Then we are SCREWED and DEAD, guys!'.

But I'll leave the wackiest theory until last! None other than 'realdonaltrump', a big fan of our column has written in, with the suggestion that the Democratic party had the organisational skills to secretly fake five million votes more than the Republican Party on the day and create tens of thousands of falsified ballots in key states with no one spotting them – creating the entirely bogus impression that they'd won!

Nice one 'realdonaldtrump'! Keep that tinfoil hat crammed tightly on your head now!

The mystery continues...

INTERNATIONAL CONDEMNATION OF US ELECTION

by Our Moscow Correspondent **Alexis Meerkat**

RUSSIA has joined a number of countries, including China, Belarus and North Korea, in refusing to accept the result of the US election, saying the election was flawed, as the votes were counted after they were cast.

"What sort of an election is it where the votes are not counted weeks before the election takes place?" asked a bemused Kremlin official.

"We're sure that had the vote been conducted properly, President Trump would have secured 87 percent of the votes, just as President Putin will here in the elections in 2024.

"Allowing votes to be illegally counted after the election takes place is a disgrace to despotic autocrats everywhere."

President Putin said he still recognised Donald Trump as president, mostly from that video of Trump in a Moscow hotel room that he keeps in a safe in the Kremlin.

THE DONALD TRUMP GUIDE TO GREAT VICTORIES IN AMERICAN HISTORY

THE BATTLE OF LITTLE BIGLYHORN
General Custard won a huge huge victory. HE WON BY LOTS! Lamestream Indian Media tried to fake the number of dead soldiers, but if they'd counted correctly, the US Cavalry won and the loser Redskins were LOSERS! FACT! Should have been orange!

PEARL HARBOUR
Big win for US Navy! Japanese bombs all missed. By miles. Observers weren't allowed in to witness it, so the Demojaps claimed victory. FAKE NEWS! Court will prove that Pacific Fleet intact and Demojaps sunk!

VIETNAM WAR
I was there. Bayoneted several gooks with my bone spurs. US suffered zero losses. RECOUNT 'EM! Paving way, after smooth transition period, to victory over democratic communism. Agent Orange WINS BY LOTS! ie Me! I love the smell of bleach in the morning!

9-11
Failing Loser Demoterrorists completely missed the Trump Tower...

WARNING!
These claims of victory by President Trump have not been substantiated by the Eye Moderator.

who did you vote for?

I hate Mexicans, women, and everyone who takes coronavirus seriously

Kesler

This week I am very angry because I was unable to throw my toys out of my pram. There I was, building up a good head of steam, ready to give my toys a good hurl and pitch them right over the side and onto the nursery floor, when I realised that they were all missing! It was only later that I remembered that I had given prior agreement to lend my toys to President Trump in case he would need to throw toys out of his pram on an international, nay, global scale. I learned later that two shadowy figures in dark glasses and wearing shoulder holsters visited in the dead of night with a requisition order approved with the presidential seal and took away my talking "Bob the Builder" and my chuckling "Postman Pat" with detachable cat. I do not blame the President for needing my toys to throw out of his pram. If the people of America had done the sensible thing and given him what he wants, which is to be President of the United States for ever in perpetuity, then I would not have had to put up with this no-toys-in-pram inconvenience. In my opinion, it's the ridiculous refusal of the left not to give in to Mr Trump's every whim that leads to polarisation of the political system. Now I will have to chuck out my Winnie-the-Pooh blanket instead, which is not an acceptable substitute because it won't land with a satisfying "Can we fix it?" or a "Ho, ho, ho, time to empty my big sack, Jess", which is hardly the *(cont. p94)*

TRUMP CLINGS ONTO POWER

I am ahead in every state… including Denial

Fresh appeal as Nazanin Zaghari-Ratcliffe back in court

by Our Iran Correspondent
Miss Carrie Justice

As she is summoned back to court in Tehran, the family of British-Iranian Nazanin Zaghari-Ratcliffe has begged the UK prime minister not to intervene, in the hope that this may spare her some additional jail time.

"We're begging the prime minister to pretend he's never heard of this case," said a source very close to the family.

"The last thing Nazanin needs is Boris standing up in the Commons to once again give credence to the jumped-up charges against her, meaning he gets her sentence doubled.

"This is one lockdown that Boris doesn't have to make worse."

Nursery Times

·············· From the Nursery Mail on Sunday ··············

THE FANTASTICALLY SILLY MR FOX

Exclusive interview with Lord Evgeny Luvvaduck

THE day I interviewed the Fantastic Mr Laurence Fox he was fizzing with ideas. "I know," he said, fantastically, "I'll set up a fantastic party to defend fantastic free speech. It's going to be… I don't know… Fantastic!"

But later he heard someone saying something that he disagreed with. It was a superdupermarket spokesman who told all the boys and girls that they were going to celebrate Baa Baa Black History Month.

The Fantastically Outspoken Mr Fox didn't like that idea at all, and began to dig himself into a hole by using his freedom of speech to tell everyone not to shop at the superdupermarket.

But a spokesman from FelloffStonewall, Mr Humpty Dumpty, thought that was silly and said that the Fantastically Misguided Mr Fox was a Fantastic Twat. So the Fantastically Offended Mr Fox was Fantastically Rude and used his freedom of speech to call the man from FelloffStonewall a "paedo".

The man from FelloffStonewall then used his freedom of speech to call a lawyer so that he could sue the Fantastically Libellous Mr Fox, soon to be the Fantastically Penniless Mr Fox.

Then, just when the hole he had dug himself couldn't get any bigger, along came the Fantastically Embarrassing Kelvin MacKenzie to offer his support.

Oh dear. Everyone thought that Poor old Mr Fox was Fantastically Fuxed! But not me, though! As a leading Lord Luvvieduck and famous newspaper proprietor of The Indebindependent, I could see that the Fantastically Deluded Mr Fox was in fact Fantastically Fantastic and was going to be Prime Minister of Neverland one day!
© *The Fantastically Impressed Lord Luvvieduck*

DRAMA AT RED RIDING HOOD GRANNY COTTAGE

By **Virginia Wolf**

EXTRAORDINARY scenes unfolded yesterday in the woods when a passing Woodcutter rescued an elderly Granny, who was shielding in isolation in her cottage.

The Woodcutter caught Little Red Riding Hood trying to embrace her Grandmother and expressing surprise at how big her Granny's ears, eyes and teeth were – because she had not seen her for so long.

In the nick of time, the Woodcutter stepped in with his axe, and despatched the miscreant hoodie child before any regulation-breaching hugging could take place.

"Don't worry, our family's fortune didn't come from slavery – it was made from sending children down mines"

Boris Johnson MP
● Live   385,000,000 Views

Address to the Nation from the People's War Room

👍 Like   💬 Comment

0 people **like this**

Boris: Sorry, I'm a **bit** late everyone, **just** the two and a half hours, I 've come **hotfoot** from a very important **Quad** meeting and I had to get here **pronto** before any of the others **leaked** it all. Put on **Statesmanlike Serious Face** and look **earnestly** down the camera lens... Now, you know I said last time that the **one** thing that was **never ever ever** going to happen, cross my **heart** and hope to **die**, was a National Lockdown? Well, there's been a **slight** change of plan. As of **Thursday** there's going to be a National Lockdown. So without **further** ado I'd like to introduce the **Boffins**, Professors Doomster and Gloomster, who will present a whole series of incomprehensible **graphs** in the hope that you will switch off and forget that I have done a **massive** u-turn. Or rather a massive **flu**-turn. Sorry, **no** time for jokes – apart from **these** two.

[THE TWO PROFESSORS PROCEED TO CLARIFY THE EXACT EPIDEMIOLOGICAL POSITION BASED ON THE LATEST STATISTICS]

Professors: ...so in a nutshell, our best case scenario is that YOU ARE ALL GOING TO DIE!!!!

Boris: **Good**! That clears **that** up. **Now** I'll take some questions. Laura Coronaberg from BBC News...

Coronaberg: Why didn't you do this ages ago, as all the scientists suggested?

Boris: It's always a very **difficult** balance, Laura, between doing things **very** late or far **too** late. And you have to weigh up **all** the arguments before coming to a **decision** that is bound to be a **compromise** and will satisfy **no one**. Which is why we are going into lockdown **immediately,** or rather on **Thursday**, and we will come **out** again on December 3rd. Next question – John Snowflake, Channel Four Horsemen News...

Snowflake: Are you relieved that this second lockdown has taken the focus away from your school meals fiasco ?

Boris: What I am saying is that this issue may be a hot **potato** and some may feel that we have made a bit of a **meal** of it and are getting a bit **fed** up...

Cummings (off): Enough with the food metaphors, butterball!

Boris: Look, in answer to your question,

PM can't meet Rashford, as he has a lot on his plate

Mr Snowflake, I am **not** going to eat humble pie and do **another** u-turn or rather a **chew**-turn... no, perhaps **not** the time for top-class Bojo banter. The **bottom** line is that free school meals are too **expensive** and we **can't** afford £20 million. Have you **any** idea how much we've got to **spaff** out to Crapola Management and McShittey's Consultants, not to mention the Dodge-E Mask Company, run by my old mate Hugo Sloaney-Crony who **assured** me he was very good at **making** stuff, even if it only turned out to be **money** rather than vital PPE kit? Anyway, they all cost a **fortune**, billions and billions, which leaves nothing in the kitty for pie and **chips**, or whatever it is northern children eat.

Snowflake: That's tripe!

Boris: No, for once, it's **true**. I know the **detail** on this one. Mushy peas, **faggots**, haggis, **vindaloo**...

Snowflake: What do you say then to Marcus Rashford?

Boris: I say, "Sorry, Marcus I am not **in**". And if **that** doesn't work, I say, "Now **look** here, Marcus old bean, I really think you should stick to what you're **good** at...

Snowflake: What, politics?

Boris: No, **goalkeeping**, for Melchester United! I gather he scored a hat-trick of **saves** the other night. **Big** fan! But when it comes to **complex** financial decisions, Marcus should leave it to the **experts**, ie Rishi Sunak. If the Chancellor wants to **deny** kids a bowl of **gruel** or whatever it is, then that is up to **him**. Nothing **I** can do about it, even if it makes him look very **bad** and damages his chances of becoming **Prime Minister**. That's a risk I've just **got** to take.

AT LAST – LEADERSHIP FROM NUMBER 10

Open letter supports the government

by Our School Meals Correspondent
Spotty Dick

AFTER a terrible week for the government, in which public anger boiled over because of Downing Street's refusal to extend free school meals, there was a rare glimmer of hope today, after an open letter was published, signed by a number of famous names all 100-percent backing No 10's stance.

The signatories include such household names as The Grinch, Mr Bumble, The Grand Old Witch, The Child Catcher from *Chitty Chitty Bang Bang*, Aunt Sponge and Aunt Spiker from *James and the Giant Peach*, Count Olaf, Ebenezer Scrooge, Mrs Coulter and Miss Trunchbull, and reads as follows:

"We all agree that denying food to poor children will do the little ankle biters the world of good, and that if those little brats don't stop bellyaching for more food, they will feel the swish of the cane."

14

Keir Starmer
WRITES

Hello! It's a terrible day for the Labour party. It's with a heavy heart that I have been forced to suspend Jeremy Corbyn from the Labour party.

This is obviously terrible news – terrible, terrible news.

So I'm TERRIBLY sad about Jeremy. I have tears in my eyes while I'm writing this. I might never stop laughing.

Terribly sincerely,
Keir.

POETRY CORNER

Lines written to celebrate the 40th Birthday of Ms Kim Kardashian, Reality TV star and internet celebrity

So. Happy Birthday
Then Kim Kardashian.

For your birthday treat
On your sun-kissed,
Private island,
You danced,
You kayaked
You swam with whales.

You humbly flaunted
Your wealth and
Privilege on
Social media.

And sensitively
Told your millions
Of followers that your
Life had returned
To "normal".

Oh dear.

Not for the first time,
Ms Kardashian,
People are saying,
"What an enormous arse".

E.J. Thribb
(17½ followers)

MONDAY

SPONGING ILLEGAL IMMIGRANTS FLOOD INTO BRITAIN

WEDNESDAY

TRAGIC FAMILY DROWNED IN SEARCH FOR BETTER LIFE

Queen's Gambit sets new trend

THE hit Netflix sensation, featuring the female chess wizard, has started a craze amongst Britons which is sweeping the nation during lockdown.

Yes, now everybody realises they want to fill their time more usefully and are watching television.

Said one *Queen's Gambit* addict, "It had never occurred to me to watch television until I watched *The Queen's Gambit*, but now I find telly-watching a stimulating and thought-provoking pastime."

Said another, "There are so many different moves you can make on your remote: fast forward, backwards, pause – the possibilities are limitless. No wonder everybody's gone telly-watching mad."

One Grandmaster added, "So absorbing is this telly-watching that I've given up chess completely, in order to devote my life to staring at a screen."

He continued, "The programme has also opened me up to the wonders of heavy drinking and anti-depressants. I've never been so happy."

(Rotters)

Why is chess so sexist?

THE new Netflix smash hit *The Queen's Gambit* has shown that the world of chess truly is nightmarishly sexist.

From the bad old days of the 1960s up to the bad new days of the modern game, women are consistently belittled, told they are not as good as men, and otherwise demeaned and humiliated. The game clearly has a long struggle ahead of it before the world of *The Queen's Gambit* is consigned to history.

On other pages

■ Phwoar, look at this bird playing chess, wouldn't mind a knight with her! ■ She can seize my bishop any day! ■ Special 16-page photoshoot of the Castle Cutie.

News in brief

Concerns over dangerous mutation

■ Scientists are desperately worried by research suggesting a new strain of toxic virulence is threatening Britain. The research claims that the lethal ERG (European Research Group) has mutated into the even more infectious CRG (Covid Recovery Group). The two contagious organisms share many of the same characteristics, ie Steve Baker, and look very similar to the naked eye.

The mutated CRG attacks indiscriminately, provided the victim is a Conservative prime minister and, after attaching itself to the host, attempts to kill it off.

The prime minister is reportedly "very concerned" about the R number, the number of rebels who will vote with the CRG, but is confident he can keep the figure below 30 or so by agreeing with everything that the CRG says, thereby preventing his entire government from being killed off.

Said one scientific expert, "The only thing we know for sure is that the CRG, like the ERG, is revolting."

School news

St Cakes

An announcement: There have been some minor staffing changes for the rest of Paedo Term, of which we felt parents should be appraised. Mr Grope-Trouser is no longer Head of Games (Nocturnal), as he is taking a sabbatical at Her Majesty's Pleasure and will be teaching "letter writing" to fellow offenders. His position will be taken by new teacher Mr Nonce, whom we carefully vetted and who comes highly recommended from his previous job at St Biscuit's Preparatory School, which he unfortunately had to leave in a hurry, due to disagreements with the Headmaster about pastoral care after lights out. We are delighted to welcome Mr Nonce to the staff, and the boys will be seeing an awful lot of him in future.

"I was hoping you'd wipe the board with me in a defiant and sexually provocative way"

BOYCE

 HUSBAND

POETRY CORNER

In Memoriam Frank Bough

Lines written (not snorted) in tribute to the legendary broadcaster

So. Farewell
Then Frank Bough.

Grandstand,
Nationwide,
Breakfast Time,
You were a
Familiar face in
Britain's living rooms,
Not to mention
One or two houses
Of ill repute.

You will always
Be remembered
For your iconic outfits:
The Pringle sweaters,
The sports jacket,
The ladies' underwear.

Unfortunately,
Even the most generous
Obituarist can't avoid
The tabloid scandal
For which you are
Most famous.

But if it's any consolation,
At least you outlived
The *News of the World*.

      E.J. Thribb (17½ spankings)

PS So. Farewell also Nobby Stiles.

Keith's Mum says
You lost your
Front teeth, but won
The World Cup
And famously
Danced round the
Wembley pitch.

She says you should
Have been on *Strictly*.
Keith agreed and said
I should write a few
Lines on your passing.
And tackling.

      E.J.Thribb (19 then, 66 now)

In Memoriam
Ian St John

So. Farewell
Then Ian St John,
Scottish footballer
And popular broadcaster.

Now you will meet
Some other Saints
While Jimmy
Grieves ye.

      E.J. Thribb (17½)

LOVE IN THE TIME OF CORONA
A Short Story Special

by Dame Sylvie Krin, author of *100 Years of Solitude, Heir of Sorrows, Duchess of Hearts* & *You're Never Too Old*

THE STORY SO FAR: Charles is back in second lockdown at Claret House with his loving consort, the Duchess of KeepoutofCornwall, as the Grockle Royale was now officially known in the county. Now read on...

CHARLES sighed, as he attempted to fit a small piece into the vast 2,020-piece jigsaw laid out on the royal drawing room table.

"That's a bit of cloud, Chazza," said Camilla, unhelpfully. "You are trying to force it into the middle of the stream!"

The jigsaw, a thoughtful present from his son and daughter-in-law, Wills and Kate, was created from one of his own famous watercolours "Loch Doon by moonlight in the shadow of craggy Ben Macintyre", but even Charles was wearying of the complexity of assembling the assorted hues of black and brown that were so prevalent in his masterpiece.

He worried that perhaps his son and heir was trying to keep him otherwise engaged whilst he and the Duchess of St Andrews took the limelight during the second wave of this beastly pandemic lurgy chappie... Only last week he had had to read about how fruity and yet respectful "Kompassionate Kate" had looked as she sang a hymn dressed in fetchingly chic black at the Cenotaph. I mean, no one had remarked on his smart RAF greatcoat with brass buttons and matching cap, had they? This trivialisation of the monarchy was... what was the word for it? He just couldn't find it... like the antlers of the stag standing nobly in the McCartney Heather in the corner of the jigsaw – or the Tescovid shopping trolley abandoned on the shore of the Loch...

"FOR God's sake, Chaz, let's pack it in, give it a rest and watch something mindless on the gogglebox," Camilla interrupted tetchily from behind a cloud of AsterixtheGauloises extra-strength fumeurs. Like many couples during lockdown, their relationship had been tested – unlike so many of those in the country who did not have the benefit of a Palace physician to check their viral status.

"Sir Alan, put something amusing on the televisual device," Charles commanded.

"I'm not bloody Alexa, you know," replied Sir Alan, the Remote Controller Poursuivant, and last of the Fitztightlys, under his breath but loud enough for it to be heard.

Camilla guffawed, nearly spilling her Gin and It ("it" being gin) and said, "Oh, go on, Sir Alan, just press the button and bring us some relief!"

Sir Alan needed no prompting to take his

cue and leapt in: "Just as backstairs Billy used to say to the under-under footman in the glory days of your dear old nan, the Queen Mother..."

"Yes, thank you, Sir Alan – can you just put on whatever is most popular with my subjects at the moment. I want to partake in the zeitgeisty thingy... I want to enjoy whatever the common man and indeed the common woman on the Clapham Omnishambles are watching."

A mischievous glint appeared in Sir Alan's twinkly eye and his white begloved hand turned on the vast Poshiba high-class-definition plasma smart television. "Whatever you say, my liege."

Suddenly the flatscreen exploded into life. "You bitch, Diana! I never loved you!"... "Shut it, Charles! You were shagging Camilla all along! I hate your guts, you jug-eared bastard..." "Oi! You two muppets! Leave it out! You are upsetting ER indoors!"

Charles was flummoxed. "Who are these ghastly people? What is this dreadful programme?"

Sir Alan feigned innocence and replied politely, "I understand it is called *The Crown*, sire. And I believe the characters in this scene who are throwing food at each other are intended to be yourself, the late Princess Of Hearts and your father, the nearly late Duke of Edinburgh."

There was a deafening silence broken only by the sound of Diana throwing herself out of the window and Prince Philip attempting to run her over in a coach and four, shouting "Die Di!"

"Is there to be no escape for me?" bemoaned Charles. "Will this never end?"

"I'm afraid not, sire," replied Fitztightly. "This is but episode one of season 94..."

Charles groaned inwardly and not for the first time found himself lost for words.

"It really is..."

Before he could complete his sentence, the actor on the TV screen playing the future king could be heard uttering the word "...appalling".

(To be continued...)

ME AND MY SPOON

THIS WEEK

MARINA WHEELER

Do you have a favourite spoon?

Yes, my mother brought a spoon back from India when she came to...

Does Boris have a favourite spoon?

Boris' spoons are my least favourite subject.

Fair enough.

My mother's spoons on the other hand, which survived Partition, and which she...

So when Boris left you, did he take the spoons with him?

I'd rather not talk about Boris' spoons, that's not my main interest. My new book looks into my family's history from a spoon perspective.

Will your next book be about Boris' spoons?

I'm talking about my current book, which is also about my father, Charles Wheeler, who was a journalist.

Like Boris, then?

He was a distinguished correspondent, whom everyone admired.

Not like Boris, then...

I'd rather not...

Come on, love, why do you think we booked you for "Me and My Spoon"? We're not interested in your parents' cutlery, we want the dirt on Boris' spoons. Did you throw them out the window and put a lock on the cutlery drawer?

The new book is called *The Lost Homestead: My Mother, Partition and the Punjab.*

Fascinating... What do you think about Carrie's spoons? Bit new? Bit tacky? Bit fresh-out-the-box?

As a lawyer, I would remind you about the detailed cutlery disclosure agreement (CDA) we signed before I consented to do this interview. Including the penalty clauses 94B, C, not to mention D, referring to any mention of my ex-husband, his spoons, his mistresses' spoons, or any of his spooning history.

We loved the book. Tell us more about the separatist movement that led to the formation of modern Pakistan. Because I'm sure that's what our readers are interested in.

Well, the fascinating thing about the Punjab in the 1940s is...

Who's Boris forking now?!

See you in court.

Thank you very much.

NEXT WEEK: *Sir Patrick Vallance, Me and My Valance.*

Boris Johnson MP
● Live

People's Prime Minister's Press Briefing – Live on Fakebook

385,000,000 Views

👍 Like   💬 Comment

0 people **like this**

▶ THE PEOPLE'S PMQs

Greetings, folks!

And for once this isn't a **de-press** briefing! No, it's **good** news from the boffins in Belgium! **Proper** good news, **amazing** news! We've found the **miracle** vaccine that's going to save **lives**. And even **better**, it's going to save **political lives**, ie **mine**. So rejoice, rejoice, Bozza **saves** the country! Christmas is **back** on! Life is back to **normal**…

Dominic Cummings: FUCKING HELL! What the fuck's going on?

Boris: What ho, Dom! I was just telling the good folks about the **stupendous** news.

Cummings: What, that you can't even appoint your own Chief of Staff?

Boris: Steady on, Dom. I **know** you wanted your **chicken-suited** friend Lee to get the job, but I'm **afraid**…

Cummings: You're the chicken, fat boy! You can't even stand up to Carrie!

Boris: Now **hang** on, you leave my **mistress** out of this.

Cummings: She's your fiancée, fuckwit. Can't you remember any detail of anything? I told you to appoint Lee.

Boris: Look, Dom, I'm **not** going to be pushed around by **you**.

Cummings: No, you're going to be pushed around by Carrie! Talk about hen-pecked!

Boris: Let's leave chummy Cain out of it.

Lee has always been a strong advocate of **Leaving** and now he's had to **Leave**! And **I've** taken back control. And **given** it to Carrie and Allegra and Munira.

Cummings: Forget unelected Bureaucrats in Brussels, you've surrendered to Unelected Fruitocrats in Downing Street! You're pathetic!

Boris: I've got a **feeling** we might be getting things the **wrong** way round here on the communications front. **Normally**, we use a **major** event to bury **bad** news, but we seem to be creating our own **bad** news to bury the **good** news of the vaccine.

Cummings: Are you fucking criticising me and my friend Lee?

Boris: No, it's just that when you said you were "**disrupters**", I didn't realise you were going to disrupt **me**. And what I **really** want to talk about is this **vaccine**, which is a **major** breakthrough, giving hope to **millions** and offering **light** at the end of the tunnel…

Cummings: Fuck that! What about loyalty?

Boris: I have no idea **what** you mean.

Cummings: Are you going to reinstate fucking Lee or not?

Boris: **No**, absolutely **not,** won't happen.

Cummings: I'll take that as a "yes".

Boris: I am sorry Dom but I **do** think people will expect me, in this week of global medical **triumph** and the **miraculous** salvation of humanity, not to spend **too** much time on internal staffing matters. Haven't we got a jolly **graph** we can put up?

(SLIDE APPEARS – SHOWING STEEP UPWARD CURVE)

Boris: Ah! **Here** we are! **Good** to see the Stock Market bouncing back! To a record **high** of 50,000 points!

Cummings: That's Covid deaths, you prat.

Boris: See, we're **world-beating** at something! Another **cheery** graph, please.

(ANOTHER SLIDE APPEARS – SHOWING ANOTHER STEEP UPWARD CURVE)

Boris: Ah, this is the number of tests **per** day, **rocketing** upwards into the millions!

Cummings: No, it's the number of text

messages from Princess Nut Nuts per day telling you what to do…

Boris: **Steady on** Dom, you're going **too** far. It's only **25** messages a day. And most of **them** are about **important** national issues - like pictures of her in a **toga** in the Mail… now **calm** down. I'm sure we can reach a **compromise** and agree on someone **else** as Chief of Staff.

Cummings: Who did you have in mind? Carrie? Carrie's mate? Carrie's mum? Carrie's dog?

Boris: Well, actually that's **not** a bad idea. **Dilyn** is a very **obedient** little chap and **faithful** – both of which Carrie is very keen on.

Cummings: Watch it! I could just follow Lee and fuck off, you know?

Boris: You mean "**cluck off**"? Like an **oven-ready** chicken – or a **chlorinated** chicken? **Top** poultry-themed banter. Proving **Bojo** hasn't lost his **mojo**.

Cummings: Get stuffed!

Boris: Not as good as **mine**, Dom. Time to get back to the **good** news, which is about the **vaccine**. Which incidentally explains one of the **great** mysteries about my behaviour. **Why** do I like disappearing into **fridges** when things get awkward? It's **nothing** to do with **hiding** from difficult questions – it's about **looking** for places to store the vaccine when it rolls out across the **nation** in December. Or possibly January/February/March.

Cummings: Fuck the vaccine, when are you going to sort out this fiasco and show people who is in charge.

Boris: Who **is** in charge ?

Cummings: You just agree with the last person you spoke to.

Boris: I **agree**. But Dom you are putting me in an **impossible** position – forcing me to choose between **you** and the dearest person to me in the **world**… well, **I** choose the love of my life… **ME**!!!

Cummings: I give up. That's it – I'm fucking well fucking off…

Boris: No, you **can't** go until I **say** so… hello… hello… oh, he's **gone**… and what's in that box? Not the **dog**?!! Or is it the **baby**? Dom… **come back**!!!

Getting exit done

"The chief medical officer will say today that there will have to be more restrictions"

"There will have to be more restrictions"

"The chief medical officer said today that there will have to be more restrictions"

KEIR STARMER INJURES CYCLIST

LEFTY LAWYER STARMER TRIES TO DRUM UP PERSONAL INJURY TRADE BY DINGING BIKER

The Daily Telegraph

Did Starmer Think He Was Hitting Boris Johnson?

THE TIMES

Ineffective Starmer fails to properly kill bastard cyclist

theguardian

Did Starmer think he was hitting Jeremy Corbyn?

Daily Mail

SOCIALIST STARMER TRYING TO DESTROY CAR INDUSTRY BY PRETENDING VEHICLES ARE DANGEROUS

DAILY EXPRESS

STARMER CAR ACCIDENT BRINGS BACK TERRIBLE MEMORIES OF PRINCESS DIANA

EveningStandard

IF ONLY THE CYCLIST HAD BEEN IN AN UBER, NONE OF THIS WOULD HAVE HAPPENED

Exclusive to all left-wing papers
AN APOLOGY

IN recent months and years we may have given the impression that monolithic multi-national drugs giants such as Pfizer were an example of everything that was wrong with capitalism: companies driven only by profit, bringing drugs to the market at inflated prices that left those much-needed, life-saving drugs out of the reach of the sickest in society, while these grubby vultures sought to maximise their profits with barely a thought about the misery that they inflicted on the world.

We now realise, in the light of Pfizer being the first company to announce that their vaccine works against Covid-19, that nothing could be further from the truth, that multi-national drugs companies are in fact run by superheroes who work selflessly round the clock in search of new drugs which can transform our world and bring health and prosperity to all.

We apologise for any confusion, and any confusion in the future when there are problems with the pricing and distribution of the vaccine and we condemn Pfizer as grubby vultures seeking only to maximise their *(cont. p94)*

LEE CAIN 'YES, I WAS EMBARRASSED'

by Our Downing Street Correspondent **Colonel Sanders**

AS he left Downing Street for the last time, dressed casually in a loose-fitting chicken costume, Lee Cain spoke of his embarrassment at having to spend the last year dressed up as Director of Communications inside Number 10.

"It was frankly humiliating having to climb into that Moss Bros suit every day and run around after Boris Johnson and Dominic Cummings, pretending that I had the slightest idea how to formulate a comms strategy for

dealing with a global pandemic," the utterly forgettable bloke told reporters.

"I knew that all my fellow journalists were laughing behind my back about my silly get-up, but I just consoled myself by saying dressing up in a suit and tie and wearing a lanyard that said 'Director of Communications' is a rite of passage all junior journalists have to endure before Allegra Stratton arrives and they can wander off to get themselves a proper job at KFC."

NEW AMENDED SLOGANS

"Oh – it's just that when you told me you earned a living as an influencer, I thought..."

GOVE FURY OVER COVID BACKBENCH REBELS

We must listen to the experts...

...what's so funny?

HOW THE COVID MONEY SPREADS

by Our Virus Staff
Phil Boots

GOVERNMENT scientists have revealed that they have discovered the mechanism by which the money allocated to fighting Covid has spread so rapidly in Britain.

The vast amounts of cash have been passed on through personal contact, usually via universities or schools, but particularly by those living in the same house.

Lack of social distancing is the key to the transfer of Covid cash from one bank account to another and there are specific physical activities which make the transmission more effective, ie greasing palms, back scratching and arse kissing.

A number of super-spreaders in the Cabinet has meant that the amount of cash has risen exponentially, with billions of pounds appearing in pockets throughout the country.

A government spokesman said, "The key to ending this crisis is to stop people cosying up to each other and to isolate the Prime Minister, to prevent him from directly passing the money on to those closest to him".

He continued, "The only way to stop this cashdemic is to bring in some consultants, such as Chumocracy Plc, and give them billions of pounds to examine why this is happening."

Yes Minister

Unseen episode discovered

(Scene: the interior of the Home Office)

Priti Patel: Now let's get this straight. I've been completely exonerated by this report of any bullying whatsoever.

Sir Humphrey: Well, I'm afraid that's not exactly what the report said...

Priti Patel: SHUT THE FUCK UP! Before I shove your head down the toilet!

Bernard: He does have a point, Minister.

Priti Patel: You too, you public school wanker!

Sir Humphrey: I'm afraid Bernard only went to a minor public school.

Bernard: Not what one would call a top-wanking public school.

(Audience laugh uncontrollably at self-deprecating private education humour)

Priti Patel: You make me sick! You two are utterly useless. If you were any good, you would have got rid of me by now. But you haven't. Tossers! I've got the Prime Minister's full backing.

Sir Humphrey: Well, bully for you.

Bernard: Bully, Bully, Bully, as we used to say...

(Audience confused at this arcane reference to the cry "Buller, Buller, Buller" traditionally shouted by members of Oxford's elite and controversial Bullyingdon Club, of which the Prime Minister is a former member)

Priti Patel: The PM reckons I can't have bullied you because I'm too small.

Sir Humphrey: Yes, it's not only your temper that's short.

Priti Patel: I'm only five foot.

Sir Humphrey: Is that wide? Or tall?

Bernard: Awfully good, Sir Humphrey.

(Audience collapse laughing at more familiar territory of good-natured male mandarin misogyny)

Priti Patel: Whenever I bullied you it was unintentional and if I screamed and swore at you, it was only because I am passionate about my job, and I am doing the best I can to improve conditions for my country, in the teeth of opposition from *(raises voice to 94 decibels)* STUPID FUCKING SHIT-FOR-BRAIN LIBTARD SNOWFLAKES LIKE YOU TWO!!

Sir Humphrey: Message received loud and clear.

Priti Patel: Boris said, and I quote *(waves mobile phone with WhatsCrapp message from the Prime Minister)*, "Everyone must form a square around the Prittster". And that includes you two. So form a square!

(Sir Humphrey and Bernard exchange weary looks at this vulgar metaphor taken from the Prime Minister's viewing of Zulu the night before on Sky Classics Plus One Video Streaming Prime Channel)

Sir Humphrey: What the minister is saying, Bernard, is that notwithstanding our natural instincts to stand shoulder to shoulder with our colleague who has understandably resigned as a consequence of behaviour by an Executive in contravention of the Ministerial Code, it is the duty of the impartial civil servant to defend the actions of any Minister under whose jurisdiction they may happen to fall, and...

(Audience can't wait for punch line to trademark long, tortuous monologue by Sir Humphrey and are already in hysterics)

Bernard: So, in a nutshell...

Priti Patel: You're fucked!

Sir Humphrey: Yes, Prittster.

TIME TO GO?

You've got to know when your time is up and then hand over power gracefully

Ha ha ha ha ha ha

Twitter rumour 'not true'

by Our Social Media Reporter
DEE PLATFORM

THERE was widespread shock today when it turned out that a Twitter rumour was total bollocks.

"That was the 15,678th rumour this week that has proved not to be true," spluttered one Twitter user.

"Like any normal Twitter user, I completely believed in Keir Starmer's resignation, Matt Hancock being eaten by starving beavers at London Zoo, Priti Patel threatening to deport Sandi Toksvig and Chris Whitty becoming the next Doctor Who, but if this keeps up I might treat the next rumour with a smidgen of scepticism.

"It's almost as if Twitter is just people making up spurious rubbish and then other people giving that spurious rubbish credence by sharing it, without stopping to check if this nonsense has any basis in fact.

"Oh hang on... just seen that a rumour Gavin Williamson has punched a headteacher in Hartlepool is trending. I'd better share that with all my followers immediately."

Experts say the new variant of online Covid rumours spreads bullshit on social media up to 70% faster.

I've lost my job, I can't pay my rent, and I'm not allowed outside...

Do you snowflakes ever stop whining?

DIARY

DAVID BAILEY'S SWINGING SIXTIES

AMIN, General Idi: You hear a lot of rubbish about him killing innocent people, but it was just business. Fair's fair. He mainly killed people who got on the wrong side of him. When I took his photograph in the Sixties he couldn't have been more helpful. I got along great with him. One of the nicest men I ever met.

BARDOT, Brigitte: No looker. I could never abide a bird who pouts. I'd go, "Stop poutin'!" But she couldn't stop, it was like a nervous twitch.

CHAPLIN, Charlie: Always toddling around the East End when I was a kid, with his little hat and his cane, fucking boring attention-seeker.

DIXON OF DOCK GREEN: I knew PC George Dixon in the Sixties. Used to hang out on street corners looking like the cat's whiskers. Everyone said he was this lovable bobby. But he wasn't. He was a cunt.

ELIZABETH II, HRH Queen: I told her to stand still for her photo, but she wouldn't stop waving. A bit short – five foot four, max – and a bit on the fat side for me. I said to her one day, what you need is a national anthem. Then next day, they're all singing God Save the Queen at the top of their voices. Not a word of thanks. Nice bird though, good jugs.

FIELDS, Gracie: Always going on about how she had the biggest aspidistra in the world. As if I gave a fuck. I told her to shut the fuck up about it. That took the smile off her face.

GANDALF: I used to hang out with Gandalf at the Indigo. Michael Caine, Terence Stamp, Andy Warhol, me and Gandalf. He was going out with Catherine Deneuve at the time. Wizard this, wizard that. Very full of himself. But he wasn't as wise as he liked to think because all I had to do was wait till he went out to the toilet and then I asked Catherine if she wanted to fuck. We married a week later. Big mistake. Turned out she was French.

HAILE SELASSIE: We were down the Troubadour one night, and I said to him, you know, what you should do is become an emperor. That way, you could become a global icon. Next thing I know, he's tartin' around in his robes and his crown, all Jack the Lad, and worshipped as a God. All my idea. But did he ever thank me for it? Did he fuck.

IRON, Any Old: Any old iron? Any old iron? Any, any, any old iron? They'd always be dancing up to you and clickin' their heels and asking you that question when I was a kid. Why would I want any old iron? So I'd say, just fuck the fuck off.

KRAY, Ronnie: One of the nicest men I ever met.

McCARTNEY, Paul: Whenever I took his photograph, he'd keep badgering me for new song titles. Finally, I lost it. "This is from me to you," I said. "It's getting better, but it's so yesterday, you've either got to get back or let it be." I should have guessed what was happening when he took out his notebook. Never paid me a penny, fuckin' skinflint.

QUEEN MOTHER: Met her at Cecil Beaton's gaff in '61, '62. Rudolf Nureyev was there and Dirk Bogarde and Max Bygraves. She said, "And what do you do?" I could tell she was tryin' to get off with me, so I said, "Do you want a fuck?" But she just pretended not to hear, snooty cow.

ROLLING STONES: We'd often hang out in the Ad Lib club in Leicester Square. One time, Mick comes up and says to me, how you doin', and I say, you know what, Mick, I can't get no satisfaction with these honky tonk women but, then again, you can't always get what you want. Typical Mick, I give him three hits, straight off, and he never pays me a fuckin' penny.

SAVILE, Sir Jimmy: One of the nicest men I ever met.

SHRIMPTON, Jean: We all used to call her The Shrimp, fuck knows why. How the fuck should I know? Can't remember where I first made love to The Shrimp. Maybe in the countryside in Buckinghamshire or in Italy or under Brighton Pier, or it might of been Wimbledon Common. Nah – Wimbledon Common was someone else, I know that because it's where I used to hang out with my mates the Wombles when they were famous. It wouldn't have been Orinoco 'cos I'm not fuckin' queer. Probably Madame Cholet, not bad lookin', I suppose, as Wombles go, but I prefer a bird without a thick mane of hair all over her body, so we kissed but we didn't do it.

TERESA, Mother: She didn't like dancing at the Ad Lib. She just wasn't any good at it. Not that I ever asked her. You could tell she had rotten legs. Why else wear those long robes? I took her photograph once. Wasted my time. Asked her to show some cleavage and she just said no, she had her reputation to consider. Nasty woman: all me, me, me.

VICTORIA, Queen: One of my first commissions was to photograph her at Windsor. When I suggested she slip out of her heavy clothes and pose in a bath tub with her hair all wild and her legs stretched out, she wouldn't fucking play ball, even when I said, OK, you can keep your undies on. Snooty, stuck-up bitch.

WEST, Fred: One of the nicest men I ever met.

ZEBEDEE: I was mates with most of the stars of the Magic Roundabout. We'd hang out most nights in The Flamingo – Dougal and Mr Rusty and Ermintrude and me. But Zebedee got on my tits. My golden rule is never to make friends with a bloke on a spring. He'd come back from the bar with the drinks sloshed all over the floor. "What's with all that bouncing?" I'd say. Then I'd tell him to fuck the fuck off. He still alive?

As told to
CRAIG BROWN

THAT GOVERNMENT PROCUREMENT QUESTIONNAIRE DOCUMENT IN FULL

Please delete as inappropriate:

My connection is with:

The Prime Minister/Priti Patel/Dominic Raab/ Matt Hancock/Rishi Sunak

My relationship with them, not that it's relevant at all, is as follows:

A short-lived but passionate love affair/I was their pub landlord/We once shared a late-night Uber and cheesy chips after a Take That gig/they spent four weeks in my luxury villa in Mustique over Christmas/We used to play big-money poker at Mr Wong's Neasden Laundry and Casino Emporium

I have no relevant business experience but:

I am keen to learn/I'm sure we'd work it out, how hard can sourcing PPE be/I don't care/You lot owe me and if not I'll tell everyone about the baby

Do you have any other interests to declare?

No, the money will be fine/Yes, I quite fancy a knighthood, actually

Torpoint Nude Swimming Club

"Well, well... a new member!"

Xmas cheer! Festive relaxation of rules welcomed

by Our Christmas Correspondent
Sir Lent-Night

THE NEWS that everyone can mix freely between three households over the Christmas week, with all UK travel restrictions lifted, was warmly welcomed today by the Grim Reaper.

"I have to say, the second lockdown has been tough, really tough, as I was prevented from seeing so many people that I'd been looking forward to reaping, such as granny and grandad, whom I feared I wouldn't see until after they'd been vaccinated in February," said the scythe-wielding angel of death.

"So this news of a super-spreader festive break in the middle of a deadly pandemic is the best Christmas present any Grim Reaper could have ho-ho-hoped for.

"I cannot tell you how much I'm looking forward to a big family Christmas this year, with the whole extended family gathered round the table for turkey with all the trimmings, teens kissing under the mistletoe, some epic drunk dad dancing, carol singing, laughter, joy, happiness and burying Granny and Grandad via a Zoom funeral in the last week in January.

"This is the season to be jolly… jolly sure you have the public to blame when everything goes tits up in January."

"At least this artist has managed to sum up her legacy"

JUST GO TO THE LIBRARY AND READ HER BOOK

MARY WOLLSTONECRAFT MEMORIAL

RGJ

OXFORD SCIENTIST IN BREAKTHROUGH

Yes! I'm 90% useless!

HEADLINE OF THE WEEK

NO RETURN TO AUSTERITY APART FROM THE AUSTERITY, PROMISES CHANCELLOR

FURIOUS MAN FURIOUS ABOUT CHRISTMAS

A FURIOUS man today warned Boris Johnson that he wouldn't be told by the government how he can spend Christmas, which he'll be spending alone, as usual, wondering why for the past three years his son hasn't invited him to Christmas lunch.

"Christmas is a time for being with all your family and nothing is going to stop me from doing that, apart from the fact they've stopped inviting me," yelled the furious maskless man at a confused till assistant in Tesco.

"Me not being invited has nothing to do with me making my daughter-in-law cry, by having a blazing row about climate change being fake or screaming at her teenage sons that they were the 'snowflake generation'.

"No, it's all because this government wants to control and ban Christmas."

When it was pointed out to him that the government was encouraging families to see each other at Christmas, the furious man insisted that was the last straw and he'd be spending Christmas Day alone on the computer, rather than seeing his family as the Stasi government is ordering him to. *(Rotters)*

CHRISTMAS PRESENT SHOCK

I bring gold

I bring frankincense

I bring *The Thursday Murder Club* by Richard Osman

FOOTBALL WELCOMES BACK MORONS

by Our Football Correspondent **Ray Cist**

THERE was widespread joy in the footballing world as, for the first time since March, clubs were able to welcome back fans to disgrace the game.

"For too long, the games have been played behind closed doors, with not even recorded sounds of fans making monkey noises or shouting sickening racist abuse to replace the actual abuse we get from our supporters," said all players.

"It just hasn't been the same, and it doesn't give you that authentic sickening feeling in the pit of your stomach that you get in the physical presence of proper died-in-the-wool scumbags.

"To see a few thousand Millwall fans booing players who were taking the knee to support Black Lives Matter reminded us just how much football has missed having a live crowd."

IT'S GREAT TO BE BACK PLAYING IN FRONT OF THE FANS.

WANKER

Place with embarrassing name decides to change it

by Our Man in the Austrian Town of Fucking **Paul Dacre**

FOR years, the place name has prompted derision, meaning people have their photos taken by its signs while laughing.

Yes, the people of "The United Kingdom of Great Britain And Northern Ireland", a small island off the north-west coast of Europe, have for years been mortified when people see the name and think it's a big joke.

To the rest of the world, "Britain" of course refers to a complete catastrophe, or a nightmarish situation of incompetence and stupidity.

"For too long we've had this name which makes us a laughing-stock", said one local. "So we've taken a vote and we're going to change it to something much less embarrassing, like 'Fucking', instead."

Daily Telegraph Friday 18 Dec. 2020

Letters to the Editor

Time To Stop Foreign Water From Entering British Waters

SIR – This country has made magnificent strides in regaining its once-proud sovereignty. From Lands' End to John o' Groats, we see that Britons are ready to seize their destiny and make the country truly great once more.

But there is one area where nothing has been done. Every day, we see from our shores the spectacle of foreign waters sloshing their way into waters which are quite clearly British.

My good lady wife and I regularly visit the coast and observe with dismay that foreign water – cholera-laden, grey, malodorous slop – is freely and easily making its way across the proud, thin line that demarcates British territory, miscegenating its way into the clean, blue, bracing water that we have wisely allowed to lap at the Very White Cliffs of Dover. When will the madness stop?

I await the news of a dispatch of Britain's finest gunboats or the erection of a semi-permeable membrane to allow us to keep our waters once again to ourselves.

Sir Herbert Gussett
The Old Loonery, Somerset

Notes&queries

'I'm confused. Who or what is the 'Meecro Wah Vay' that Nigella Lawson is going on about on her television cookery programme?'

asks Lady Maximilla Hastings of Hastings.

● Where have you been? The Nissan Meecro Wahvay is one of the best-selling small hatchbacks on the market, and has just been developed as a hybrid Covid-safe bubble car. It was tested most amusingly in South Yemen by the *Grand Tour* team, as we now have to call them, as they drove it through a herd of goats which turned out to be grazing on a minefield. The Meecro Wahvay going from nought to ninety miles an hour straight up in the air was one of the highlights of a very entertaining series.
*Jeremilla Clarkson,
Norton Chipping Farm.*

● Ms Clarkson is a classic female driver who probably knows nothing about football, like most of the ladies. Meecro "Wah" Vey was the famous Brazilian striker who put two past Maradona's Argentina in the 1987 World Cup, as part of the legendary front three of: Meecro, Ribeanio, and Plato. He is most famous for his "Elbow of the Devil" incident, in which he elbowed the Argentinian captain in the face. Meecro was sent off, and shouted "Wah" at the referee ("Wah" being Portuguese Favela slang for "I disagree most vehemently with this decision"). This gave birth to his soubriquet, which stuck during his subsequent career as the controversial high-living maverick Mayor of Cokacabana.
*John 'Blokey' Bloke,
former Sky Sports Presenter.*

● Mr 'Blokey' Bloke clearly does not have the benefit of a classical education if he is linking this term to the World Cup of MCMLXXXVII. Those of us who went to a decent school know perfectly well that the "Meecro Wah Vay" (new Cambridge pronunciation) is in fact a corruption of the Latin greeting "Micro Ave", a very small salutation akin to a nod of the Centurion's helmet. Figures giving each other the "Micro Ave" have been discovered in mosaics on the wall's of Pompeii's finest buildings, including the Villa Aston, the Palace of Crystal, and the Arsenal. If you'll excuse me, I now have to put my ready meal for one in what I call the "Dee Shwah Sher".
Professor Salmonella Rushbridger, Lady Margaret Thatcher Hall, Oxbridge.

*Answers please:
Should the word "granular" only be used on an annular basis by your grandmother?*

"It looks amazing, Granny – but you have no social media presence, so what's the point?"

Numéro 94

Getting le French passport

Stanley Johnson *(Pour c'est him)*: Bonjour, Monsieur le Froggie, je suis Stanley Johnson, le father célèbre du Prime Minister de Britain. Je voudrais un passport français tout immédiatement!

Le Bureaucrat: Ah, c'est très amusing et ironique dans le light de Brexit, n'est-ce pas? Sûrement this will embarrasser votre son?

Stanley Johnson: Ça c'est le whole point et aussi it will getter moi dans les papiers!!

Le Bureaucrat: Ha! Ha! Ha! Vous êtes vraiment un card! Ça ne shouldn't be pas de problem, mais je dois checker le computer.

Stanley Johnson: Vitement, Froggie! Je suis sur le television de petit déjeuner very à bientôt…

Le Bureacrat: Sacré bleu! Le computer dit NON… Apparently, vous êtes un wife-beater…

Stanley Johnson: Non, c'était untrue et, in any case, un long temps ago!!

Le Bureaucrat: Le computer also dit que vous êtes très arrogant et irresponsible et vous cassez tous les Covid regulations whenever possible.

Stanley Johnson: Pourquoi dit-il such nonsense?

Le Bureaucrat: Parce-que c'est vrai! Vous ne portez pas a mask même now!

Stanley Johnson: How darez-vous! Je suis très famous et important! Connaissez-vous who je suis?

Le Bureaucrat: Oui. Et le answer est NON. Finalement il y a un positive pour Brexit. Nous pouvons snubber another member de la famille Johnson. Now clearez-vous off, Rosbif!!

© The late Miles Kilomètres 2021

OUTBREAK OF JOURNALISM IN CHINA 'UNDER CONTROL'

by Our Chinese Correspondent
Bru Tal Lee

THE People's Daily is reporting that an outbreak of journalism in Wuhan has finally been brought under control and ended with the sentencing of a citizen journalist, Zhang Zhan, to four years in jail after she was found guilty of multiple counts of journalism.

"The outbreak of citizen journalism, which it's feared could be deadly to Communist Party propaganda, was first detected in Wuhan in January 2019 when local doctors attempted to use social media to alert the world to the deadly outbreak of coronavirus ravaging their city," a Beijing official confirmed.

"These rogue doctors spouting rubbish about T cells were moved to jail cells for re-education and it was hoped that would be the end of the outbreak, but pockets of free speech worryingly continued to spread through contact with foreign journalists wanting to know why everyone was dying in the city.

"Decisive and rapid action by the local Communist party in rounding up anyone infected with the journalism bug meant the citizens in Wuhan were protected from this online pandemic which spreads the truth at an horrific rate.

"With the jailing of Zhang Zhan, a notorious superspreader of news, the Chinese people can go about their daily lives no longer in fear of contracting the free speech virus."

Do you have one of the new strains of coronavirus?
That checklist of symptoms in full…

Kronavirus Repetitive urge to win debates on the pandemic by saying "Look what happened in Sweden".

Postponavirus Sense of lethargy and inertia, leading to all decisions being made way too late. (**Vulnerable group**: The Cabinet.)

Homealonavirus Feverish suspicion that while you obeyed the rules, everyone else had a massive family Christmas.

Partydonorvirus Breathless astonishment at being bumped off the New Year Honours list, due to PR campaign to praise frontline workers.

Remoanavirus Unhealthy desire to see massive queues at Britain's ports from New Year's Day so you can say "I told you so".

Twogentlemenofveronavirus Craving to see absolutely anything at the theatre. *(That's enough new strains. Ed).*

Great Holy Men of the World **Number 94**

Martin the Fakir *(surely Bashir?)*

There once was a very godly teacher called Martin who became famous throughout the world for his revealing spiritual encounters with other saintly figures, like the former Princess, St Diana of Kensington, and the philanthropist, St Michael of Jackson.

Indeed, so revered in his own land did he become that the benevolent and all-knowing Lord Hall, the Director General of the BBC, appointed him to be the corporation's religious leader and commissioned him to inspire all faiths with his conspicuous holiness.

But, regrettably, Martin became the target of envious scribblers and was subject to cruel attacks from godless critics. The poor holy man was accused of multifarious offences, such as fraud and forgery, and all his previous good works were decried. And this all happened at a time when he was lying on his sickbed, a victim of the Covid plague, and thus unable to defend himself or refute his enemies' abominable charges.

Yet, despite his near fatal illness and the fact that he was lying, fighting for his life on a bed of nails, Fakir appeared at least twice to his followers, once buying a humble takeaway curry and then again at a service station recharging his humble Mercedes limo.

These well-attested and miraculous manifestations were proof, said his followers, that in common with many holy men, he had the ability of being in two places at the same time, which was enough to confound his opponents and confirm his undoubted saintliness to all his supporters in the BBC who *(cont. p94)*

Extract taken from the Bhashirgavad Gita

"You and your dick pics, Maureen!"

Boris Johnson MP
● Live

People's Prime Minister's Question Time – Live on Fakebook

385,000,000 Views

👍 Like   💬 Comment

0 people **like this**

Happy New Deal!

They said it was **impossible**, that I couldn't pull off a good deal for Britain. And yet, against **all** the odds, I've proved them 100% **right**. Yes, folks, it's a **fabulous** deal for everyone – not just the EU but also for every man, woman and **fish** in the United Kingdom. And to all those **fishermen** who say they've been **sold** down the river, I say at least it's **our** river now, leading to **our** sea, and you've been sold down it **without** tariffs!

Prime Minister's Special Adviser: What's this book by your ex-wife doing in this house? If you've got time to sit around reading, why don't you read that 1,246-page treaty instead?

Boris: What's the point? I've **signed** it now.

Prime Minister's Special Adviser: You are in so much trouble. You're in the doghouse. And while you're there, you can take Dilyn for a walk. And take that bloody photographer who's been sitting in the corner all day for those totally staged spontaneous snapshots.

Photographer: Could you say that again, please, Carrie? And Boris, can you put your feet on the desk to look relaxed yet statesmanlike?

Boris: **Sure**, will do!

Prime Minister's Special Adviser: Take your feet off the furniture, you great slob!

(THE PRIME MINISTER EXITS TO WALK DOG AND IS REPLACED BY MICHAEL GOVE, ON A TEMPORARY BASIS, EVEN THOUGH GOVE STILL HOPES ONE DAY IT WILL BE FOR LONGER)

Gove: I want to reassure British business that from now on trading will be frictionless and easier than ever, albeit with one or two elements of friction and difficulty. There will be bumps in the road, many of them 100 feet high, but nothing that you can't cope with, so long as you're well prepared for this last-minute deal which you can't possibly have known what to do about until it was agreed on Christmas Eve, when you were a bit busy trying to sell anything to anyone before Lockdown returned.

Prime Minister's Spokesperson: It's not Lockdown, Michael, it's Tier 4 with schools shut. Which I think you'll agree is very different.

Gove: You're brilliant, Allegra. You've captured Boris's voice perfectly. Utterly unconvincing.

Prime Minister's Spokesperson: Cripes!

Gove: So, as I was saying, here's my checklist for businesspeople who want to get out there and go about their business, free of red tape at last. All you'll need to sell, say, one box of British paperclips to our former partners in Europe are the following: your passport (soon to be blue!), proof of residency in the form of at least two utilities bills, one of which must not be owned by a European conglomerate, your cycling proficiency test, completed form A45, 46 and 47 (green copies only) through to form A94 which must be signed within the box by a responsible person, which includes your doctor, lawyer, dentist, librarian or member of the ERG (proof of their ID and residency will be required). A signature by your pet will be acceptable, so long as it is not a German shepherd or French poodle.

Labradoodles will be acceptable, if accompanied by a British bulldog.

Prime Minister's Spokesperson: Cripes! Double cripes!

Gove: I now move onto the equally simple question of Northern Irish meat 'n' mackerel products...

(HE CONTINUES FOR SEVERAL HOURS UNTIL PRIME MINISTER RETURNS FROM HISTORIC WALK WITH MUCH-LOVED PET DOG. SEE PHOTOS ON FRONT PAGE OF DAILY TELEGRAPH)

Boris: Ah **Govester**! Have you done the **bad** news about the virus thingy yet?

Gove: No, I was still on gateau tariffs, explaining from now on there's no more red tape, just a small amount of hardly noticeable red, white and blue tape.

Boris: **Damn**! I was hoping **you'd** have covered the miserable **Covid** stuff. And then **I'd** come in with the up-tempo, crowd-pleasing **rolling out** of the Oxford jab. The **second** best thing to **ever** roll out of Oxford! OK, OK, I'll do it. **Cometh** the hour, etc...

(THE PRIME MINISTER REMOVES SILLY BEANIE HAT AND SWIMMING TRUNKS, PUTS ON LONG TROUSERS AND SERIOUS FACE)

Boris: I'll be **honest**, folks, no **seriously**, it's my New Year's Resolution. No more lying. Apart from **that** one. This is a **critical** moment. In spite of the **amazing** deal and the **incredibly** bright future dawning for Britain, there is a slight **hiccup** in the form of the **resurgence** of the global pandemic and the fact that 97% of the United Kingdom has had to be closed down until further notice. You might consider this a bit of a **downer**, but rest assured we're doing everything we can to look on the **bright** side... What **was** my point, Allegra?

Prime Minister's Spokesperson: Last hurdle before sunlit uplands. All over by Easter. Don't specify the year. Final push.

Boris: Right-ho! And what if people ask me if I always act **too late**, **over**-promise and **under**-deliver?

Prime Minister's Spokesperson: You tell them that you'll get back to them tomorrow with a world-beating answer and then you disappear.

Schools demand closure

by our Education Staff **Will Shut**

SCHOOLS across the country are demanding the immediate closure of the Prime Minister's mouth.

"It's just too dangerous to allow it to stay open," said one primary school headteacher. "Every time he makes a statement urging parents to send their children to school things immediately get worse, leading to a clumsy last-minute U-turn. It's not worth the risk."

Others said the Prime Minister should be reconciled to tough new measures restricting his verbal freedom.

"As soon as I saw Boris on the Andrew Marr Show saying schools should remain open, it was inevitable they would shut," said a Year 3 pupil.

"His words are clearly out of control, and the only way to stop the spread of the new variant of misinformation is to shut his mouth down until February, at the very least."

JOHN SADLER

WHAT EXACTLY IS IN THE HISTORIC EU TRADE DEAL?

THE DAILY GNOME's forensic examination of the 2,000-page document that will determine the UK's future for the next millennium.

● We don't know
● We don't care
● We are just really glad it's over.

Han-z-z-zard

The first, second and third readings of the Bill to ratify the 'Not Theresa' EU Treaty, Wednesday 30 December

Speaker: All Honourable Members have now had a full five minutes to forensically examine the 94,000-page document, so that this House can be fully confident that it has taken back control of the legislative process.

Tory MPs: Get on with it! *The Sound of Music*'s started.

Speaker: I call upon the Right Honourable Mrs May.

Theresa May *(Iron Maydenhead South, Con)*: Could I just say, that this treaty is even worse than the one I came up with all those years ago.

Tory MPs: It's Mayja Vu! Ha! Ha! Ha!

Theresa: Okay, I'll vote for it, because I'm loyal, not like some people I could mention.

Tory MPs: Suck it up, loser!

Speaker: Order! Order!

Tory MPs: Order a takeaway – it's all you're allowed nowadays!

(When the MPs have finished laughing at their own Parliamentary wit, the Speaker calls on the Leader of the Opposition.)

Keir Starmer *(Dither-on-the-Fence, Lab)*: Having voted against Theresa May's better deal, I've decided that we should all vote for this deal. It's terrible, and I'm all for it.

Anyone disagrees with me and they're fired!

Labour MPs *(sung to the tune of "Oh, Jeremy Corbyn")*: Oooh, Keiry Starmer!

Mr Bill Cash *(Stuck-in-the-Past, Con)*: As a leading Brexiteer and Member of the highly important ERG group, may I say firstly, how important I am.

Labour and SNP MPs: Boo!

(Lib Dem MPs think about it but abstain from booing.)

Mr Bill Cash: And may I also point out that now this brilliant deal has been done, I really am still very important. And it's time for the Remoaners to look to the future, and not hark back to a nostalgic version of the past. Let's move on and rebuild the British Empire!

Lib Dem MPs *(changing minds)*: Boo!

Mr Bill Cash: And may I end by comparing the Prime Minister to Pericles, Alexander the Great, and other great Greek heroes like Zorba and Demis Roussos, not to mention Nana Mouskouri.

Speaker: That's all we've got time for. Do you want this bill or not, because there's a mince pie with my name on it...

MPs socially distancing in chamber: Hear! Hear!

100s of MPs on Zoom: We can't Hear! Hear! – You're on mute. Let's vote anyway.

Speaker: Ayes to the right. Noes to the trough.

(MPs having considered the important issues involved, weigh up the detailed ramifications of the treaty, conclude that the turkey leftovers aren't going to eat themselves, and cast their votes accordingly.)

Speaker: The "Anything but Theresa" bill is duly passed by 521 votes to 73. A majority of... Lots. Time to go home. Order! Order me a taxi!

The Eye's Controversial New Columnist

This week I am very angry with people criticising Matt Hancock crying on GMTV. There have been unkind people saying that his crying didn't look genuine or spontaneous. I take exception to that. I have been coaching Mr Hancock for this moment, and I can tell you now that we have been working tirelessly for him to be genuine and spontaneous for months. Naturally, I would have been better at doing the crying!

And I told Mr Hancock many times that I should be sent to do these interviews instead of him, on account of the fact that I do look slightly less like a pouting little baby, but I'm afraid he insisted. My advice to him was to think about these old, frail people getting their vaccine and burst into tears. I'm thinking about it now, and tears are running down my face. Tears of rage, of course! Why are we wasting these expensive vaccines on these incredibly old people? I have said time and time again via this column that anyone over the age of three should be left to *(cont. p94)*

WINNER OF PRIVATE EYE'S PHOTO OF THE YEAR

The moment when the fate of the nation hinged on whether Mark Francois would approve of the most important deal in Britain's history

Fat, boring and verbose

Don't be so hard on yourself!

Brexit deal 'delivers red tape'

■ Downing Street says the historic Brexit deal agreed by the UK and Brussels will be a massive boost for the UK red tape industry.

"Those firms which manufacture red tape are going to be cheering from the rafters come Jan 1st," said a jubilant Prime Minister. "Many have cancelled all leave and put on double shifts to cope with the demand.

"We're hoping many of the businesses driven out of business because of the extra paperwork generated by doing business with the EU post Brexit will convert themselves into manufacturing red tape because we're going to need so much of it in the months and years to come, it will be the number one growth industry in the UK."

EU-phemisms

"The deal will define EU-British relations into the future"

HOPE OF A BREXIT DEAL

E.U. DEMANDS COMPROMISE AGAIN

RGJ

Permanent mutual resentment

Health experts warn of sharp rise in Eton disorders

NHS ENGLAND has warned of a record increase during the pandemic in those suffering from Eton disorders, where members of the public gradually become "sick and tired" of the number of Old Etonians running the country.

The NHS said that, in recent months, GP surgeries have been inundated with patients who are registering symptoms including "fatigue, depression and nausea", as they succumb to the realisation that the alumni of the country's most elite public school, including Boris Johnson, Jacob Rees-Mogg and David Cameron, may not have been the ideal figures to lead Britain in the 21st century and may in fact have proved uniquely toxic and life-threatening, as they inflicted a disastrous *(cont. p94)*

GOVERNMENT IS A DISGRACE

say all the people who broke the rules at Christmas

AS thousands of people enter hospital, all the middle-class people who broke the rules about social distancing over Christmas have agreed with each other that the government have really messed things up this time.

One set of parents, who hosted all four of their children in the countryside, explained, "We made sure to buy tests and that's absolutely fine, of course. It's not like there have ever been any mistakes with tests, so it must be other people socialising over Christmas who have caused this atrocious surge. It's definitely the government's fault, either way."

Another group of young people who all went to each other's houses over Christmas said, "This is typical of Boris. A responsible government would have stationed soldiers on every street corner to shoot us as we broke the rules. Is it our fault those soldiers weren't there? No."

On other pages

■ We had a lovely Christmas, actually, explain rule-breakers to people who now feel a bit stupid for even bothering to try

'Die January' big success

THE organisers of Die January, which sees people giving up alcohol, food and life itself in January by dying from Covid-19, say they have been overwhelmed by how popular it's been in 2021.

RAILCAR TO BE POWERED BY HUMAN WASTE

A shit train service – what's new?

VACCINE LATEST

Dismay as Tony Blair seems to be right

by Our Political Staff **Juan Dose**

THERE was widespread dismay across the political spectrum today after Tony Blair was discovered talking sense.

"It is pure agony to hear Tony Blair articulating the case for a one-shot policy in the kind of clear, measured and articulate way that government ministers like Matt Hancock seem incapable of," said all Tory supporters through their off-white gritted teeth.

"How dare that murderous warmonger be right and be showing the kind of calm, clear-headed leadership that's been sorely lacking right through this pandemic," said all Corbynites, openly weeping into their badly printed t-shirts.

All sides of the political spectrum were agreed that the one thing what will always unite them is that feeling of utter revulsion about Tony Blair being even vaguely right about anything *(continued forever…)*

HEIR OF SORROWS
A Short Story Special

by Dame Sylvie Krin, author of
Duchess of Hearts & You're Never Too Old

SIR ALAN FITZTIGHTLY and his partner, the Air Vice Marshal, were enjoying a cup of English Breakdance tea in their delightful Camper Van parked near the south coast at St Leonard-Henry-on-Sea for the Christmas holidays.

There, on the portable MajorFerguson TV, they were watching the BBC Breakfast news presented by Naga Munchatty and Dan Talker – which had suspended normal broadcasting and was now playing solemn music – the theme from *East Enders* and *Carry on Camping*…

"Do you remember the fuss when she retired?" said Sir Alan, rolling his eyes. "Now she has actually passed on, I don't think Charles is going to be able to cope…"

The Air Vice Marshal grinned mischievously as he arranged his eggy airmen into a Red Arrows "V for Vaccine" formation before flying them triumphantly into his large free-range breakfast treat.

He enquired innocently of the Senior Equerry-as-Folk: "How are you going to break it to him, Fitz?"

Sir Alan pondered for a second.

"I will say something along the lines of 'A great loss of a National Treasure… tragedy in the Windsor Household… the much-loved matriarch of the nation…'"

The Air Vice Marshal joined in enthusiastically, as though it were a game of charades of the type which they had enjoyed

playing in the long lockdown evenings in their motorised bio-bubble: "You could add 'Despite her great age, she ruled her troublesome family with an iron fist inside a velvet glove, and she became a figure almost synonymous with Queen Victoria…'"

"Yes," grinned Sir Alan, naughtily. "That should definitely stop any confusion…"

"And when will you tell him?"

Sir Alan checked his GetCartier wristwatch. "Well, this would be the precise time he would be having his morning bath in his precious Kay Burlington Bateau Baignoire…"

"Well," said the Air Vice Marshal, "you had better call him now…"

Sir Alan lifted the receiver of his hotline to the heir to the throne, and dialled Claret 123…

Disclaimer as advised by the Secretary of State for Culture

■ *The public should be warned that the events they have just read may seem fictional, but are in fact more accurate than those portrayed in The Crown.*

"This next number is a little ditty I used to perform with my old band 'Skullbuggery and the Headfucks'"

DIARY

PETER HITCHENS: AT THE PANTO

Is this what we really want – the UK population in a state of superstitious terror, forced to sit in row upon row and gawp unquestioningly at Marxist propaganda?

Yes, this week I went to see a production of Cinderella. To my horror, children as young as six or seven were being forced to attend by their officious, self-righteous parents.

For the next three hours they were subjected to a barrage of hard left "woke" propaganda, no doubt sanctioned and enforced by Whitehall's secret commissars, designed to reduce our once-great nation to the level of a back-street public convenience in Erich Honecker's East Berlin.

My suspicions were aroused in the opening scene, when two obese characters – sisters, or so we were falsely told – arrived onstage in grotesque frocks.

The rest of the audience dutifully laughed in the craven manner of medieval serfs. But I refused to smile or cheer. Instead, my eyes were drawn to the sisters' hands.

Those hands told their own story. They were not the hands of ladies.

No: they were the hands of men.

A cold shudder went down my back.

Children as young as five or six were being subjected to rampant transgenderism, trained by jackbooted political correctness into believing that men are women and women are men.

These two flagrant transvestites were then joined by a third, even more unpleasant.

His name? Twankey. "Widow" Twankey.

What had become of his late partner, Mr Twankey? We were not told.

And there was no time to find out. In a scene of mass destruction, designed to undermine any remaining vestiges of respect the young of this country may have for morality, this "Widow Twankey" proceeded to throw cakes and cream pies around.

Such is the behaviour of the tyrant. Nobody is safe. Children as young as four or five are being taught that it is perfectly acceptable – perhaps even desirable – to wreck ordinary, decent households.

Chairman Mao would be proud of us.

Later, "Prince Charming" took to the stage, bent on seducing the heroine.

But this Prince was not what he seemed.

No self-respecting Prince wears heavy make-up and fishnet tights and sports an ample bust.

Yes, I have had my arguments with Prince Charles in the past. But even he has not descended into this revolting behaviour.

To my horror, I realised that Prince Charming was in fact a woman. Furthermore, children as young as three or four were being forced to watch a lesbian seduction scene as if it were normal.

At the show's end, children as young as two or three were forced to chant socialist slogans – "Love Makes The World Go Round", "It's a Lovely Day for a Party" – from incendiary placards descending with ruthless efficiency from the ceiling.

I refused to join in this travesty. And I also refused to consume a tub of pink "ice-cream" at the interval. Nobody is safe from the pink, frozen sedatives of the state.

Why can I find no hard evidence for this systemic poisoning of our ice-cream?

The answer is staring us in the face.

The powers-that-be know what they are doing. They have rounded up all the evidence and incinerated it at an unknown location, possibly in the North East.

For holding out so brazenly against the forces of this iniquitous government, I must now expect the late-night knock on my door, the hood, the handcuffs, and the trip to the windowless cell in the Black Mariah.

As told to
CRAIG BROWN

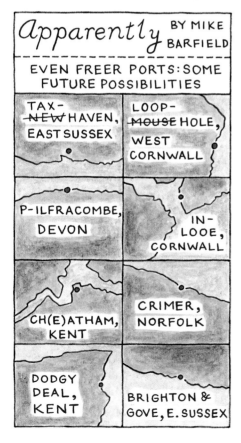

Apparently BY MIKE BARFIELD

EVEN FREER PORTS: SOME FUTURE POSSIBILITIES

TAX-~~NEW~~HAVEN, EAST SUSSEX

LOOP-~~MOUSE~~HOLE, WEST CORNWALL

P-ILFRACOMBE, DEVON

IN-LOOE, CORNWALL

CH(E)ATHAM, KENT

CRIMER, NORFOLK

DODGY DEAL, KENT

BRIGHTON & GOVE, E. SUSSEX

UK GOVT TO SHUT STABLE DOOR

by Our Border Control Staff **Noah Entry**

THE British government has confirmed today that after a long period of review it has decided to shut the stable door some ten months after the horse has bolted.

"We have thought long and hard about this and decided that now is the time to spring into action and get that stable door shut," an excitable Matt Hancock told reporters.

"Nothing is going to make more sure that the horse that escaped ten months ago doesn't get out than us slamming the stable door securely shut now."

GHISLAINE MAXWELL FACES JAIL SENTENCE

What are you hoping for?

Something under 16 years

ME AND MY SPOON

THIS WEEK

LORD SUMPTION

Do you have a favourite spoon?

The only spoons that matter are new spoons. The old spoons are less valuable. They have had their time.

Isn't that a bit harsh on older spoons who have done their bit in the cutlery draw and may not deserve to be cast aside in the twilight of their spoon years?

That's not what I said. I am so clever that you can't understand the point I am making regarding aged spoons.

Well, what point is that?

Younger spoons have their entire cutlerial lives in front of them and so are intrinsically worth more than old, tarnished has-been spoons that have done their share of stirring and ladling...

But haven't they been literally serving the community and are thus worthy of the same respect as the newer arrivals to the cutlery drawer?

No. What I am saying, but you are too stupid to comprehend, is that antique spoons must be considered in an...

You mean they are washed up ?

Aren't you going to ask me whether anything amusing has ever happened to me regarding a spoon ?

No. You're too old. I am not interested.

NEXT WEEK: *Millie Mackintosh: Me and My Mackintosh*

Billionaire financiers in share-dealing fury

by Our Wall Street Correspondent
Gordon Geeko

Billionaire Wall Street hedge fund owners facing bankruptcy after the manipulation of GameStop's stock price have accused the poorer people involved of "gambling".

"The financial regulators need to step in to stop small-time amateur investors profiting in this way simply by gambling on stocks to make themselves rich," said one billionaire hedge fund manager.

"This is nothing whatsoever like the shrewd investments we professional investors make on a daily basis to manipulate company share prices to maximise returns."

Wall Street observers advise that, as more and more billionaire hedge fund managers are ruined, people should invest in the manufacturers of the world's smallest violins, whose stocks are bound to start to soar *(cont. $94)*

"He gets me out of the house every day"

Twitter user horrified at people in park while walking in park

by Our Covid Correspondent
Ian Former

Twitter user @sarahwearamask has described her horror at seeing how many people were out in her local park as she power-walked to the coffee shop for her afternoon latte treat.

"Why are these people out, do they want to destroy the NHS?" she tweeted furiously.

"I'm sure they all think they have a valid reason for being outdoors, but the rules say stay at home, guys – is that so difficult to understand? Why do you hate the NHS so much, you absolute bastards?"

@sarahwearamask added it was exactly the same when she was in the park at lunchtime jogging with two mates she'd bumped into and even busier when she power-walked through it on the way to get her morning frappuccino.

"There are just too many people out and about!

"I am sick of hearing excuses, they are all lawbreakers and they just don't give a crap about anyone else – the selfish arseholes!"

BREXITEER RATCLIFFE MOVES PRODUCTION OF GRENADIER TO FRANCE

I think I'll rename it the Deserter

Fish incredibly surprised

▪ Fish the world over have described their huge shock after realising how short the memories of British fishermen are.

"Obviously, you hear urban legends about their complete lack of memory," gurgled one guppy. "You hear nonsense about their memories lasting only thirty seconds. But all the recent news articles show that they've completely forgotten how the fishing industry works, what it means to be outside the single market, how tariffs work and, above all, how untrustworthy the Conservative party has been for decades."

Despite this, many fish are relaxed about the distress the fishermen are currently experiencing over the collapse of their industry.

"Let's not worry too much about them. They're only fishermen. They don't feel pain the same way that other creatures do."

POETRY CORNER

**In Memoriam
One of the
Barclay Brothers**

So. Farewell
Then one of the
Barclay twins.

You owned
The Ritz and the
Daily Telegraph.

But which one are you?
Are you the weird one
Who lived with the
Other one on the
Channel island of
Brecqhou?

Or are you the
Other one?

And were you the
One spying on
The other one
At the Ritz?

Or vice versa?

Either way,
You have made
The Telegraph what
It is today.

Two pounds
Fifty.

E.J. Thribb
(17½ readers)

Excitement at tunnel that will never be built

by Our Construction Correspondent
Brie Gadoon

THERE was growing excitement today regarding "Boris's Burrow" – a 25-mile tunnel connecting mainland Britain to Northern Ireland – which will never be built.

"There is palpable excitement, almost on a par with Boris's Garden Bridge, which was never made, and Boris's Airport in the Thames Estuary, which was never constructed," said a No10 spokesman.

"With the lack of EU red tape, we expect this nonsensical vanity project to be forgotten about far quicker than those other projects. They languished for years on the drawing board before being quietly flushed down the toilet."

Downing Street also brushed aside the logistical difficulties of building a tunnel through Beaufort's Dyke, a 30-mile trench up to 300m deep, into which the MoD offloaded a million tons of munitions after WW2.

"Don't worry – this idea will blow up in Boris's face long before then."

DUMB BRITAIN

Real contestants, real quiz shows, real answers, real dumb!

The Chase, ITV

Bradley Walsh: The 2019 film *Fisherman's Friends* was set in which English county?
Contestant: Scotland.

Walsh: The "No Popery" riots of 1780 have what alternative name?
Contestant: The Magna Carta.

Walsh: Which monarch took a helicopter to visit her grandchildren?
Contestant: Queen Elizabeth the first.

Walsh: Competing with your neighbours is said to be "keeping up with"… which surname?
Contestant: The Kardashians.

Walsh: In 1797 which of the armed forces took part in the Nore Mutiny?
Contestant: The air force.

Walsh: A famous advertising slogan was "Go to work on…" what?
Contestant: An empty stomach.

Walsh: What word can mean a group of three, or a dangerous Chinese gang?
Contestant: Ku Klux Klan.

Walsh: In the second century BC, troops from which city state destroyed Carthage?
Contestant: Dunstable.

Walsh: Who is the only American First Lady to have posed nude for a magazine?
Contestant: Hillary Clinton.

Walsh: The play Golda's Balcony was about the life of which Israeli prime minister?
Contestant: Benjamin Disraeli.

Walsh: Which former Labour MP is a double Oscar winner?
Contestant: Tony Blair.

Bradley Walsh: Which underwater tunnel links Cheriton to Sangatte?
Contestant: The Suez Canal.

Walsh: What animal's height is measured in hands?
Contestant: Birds.

Walsh: In 1841, Henry Mayhew became editor of what famous satirical magazine?
Contestant: *Private Eye.*

The Chase Celebrity Special, ITV

Walsh: In the Christmas carol "I saw three ships", on what day did the ships come sailing in?
Colin Jackson: Wednesday.

Lightning, BBC2

Zoe Lyons: What is the name of the American fashion designer known for his Polo brand and polo player motif?
Contestant: Marco Polo.

Lyons: The murder victim of which classic board game was Dr Black?
Contestant: Monopoly.

Lyons: Which former vice-president secured the Democratic nomination in the 2020 race to become US president?
Contestant: Boris Trump.

Impossible, BBC1

Rick Edwards: Who succeeded Nicolas Sarkozy as president of France?
Contestant: Vladimir Putin.

Mastermind, BBC2

John Humphrys: What land is separated from Africa by the Mozambique Channel?
Contestant: The United Kingdom.

Humphrys: Budapest is the capital city of which central European country?
Contestant: Italy.

Humphrys: One of the Wonders of the Ancient World, in the country now known as Iraq, was the Hanging Gardens of… what?
Contestant: Fruit.

Humphrys: Which London art gallery has the website npg.org.uk?
Contestant: The Louvre.

Times Radio

Presenter: A bird in the hand is worth two in the…?
Caller: Pocket.

Winning Combination, ITV

Omid Djalili: Which character from *The Simpsons* shares his name with a Greek poet?
Contestant: Ned Flanders.

Djalili: What item of furniture can be gateleg or dropleaf?
Contestant: Trousers.

Djalili: Monday's child is said to be fair of what?
Contestant: Egypt.

Tipping Point, ITV

Ben Shephard: The sacred Islamic city of Mecca is located in which modern-day country?
Contestant: Israel.

Shephard: Before decimalisation in 1971, how many pennies were there in one UK pound?
Contestant: I think it was six.
Opponent: No, I think it was larger than that. I'm thinking maybe 12.

Shephard: How many of Henry VIII's wives were called Anne?
Contestant: Seven.

Shephard: Which Elizabethan playwright had children called Judith and Hamnet?
Contestant: Cinderella.

Shephard: Which former Conservative leader is often known by the initials IDS?
Contestant: Margaret Thatcher.

Shephard: In 2006, which member of the Royal Family won Sports Personality of the Year, 35 years after her mother?
Contestant: Princess Margaret.

Shephard: There are five main English baronial male titles. Which of them falls between an earl and a duke?
Contestant: Corporal.

Shephard: Regent's Canal and the Slough Arm are branches of what canal system that links London to Birmingham?
Contestant: The Suez Canal.

Shephard: Which is the only celestial body apart from Earth upon which man has set foot?
Contestant: The Sun.

Shephard: Which British artist painted a famous warship known as "The Fighting Temeraire"?
Contestant: Picasso.

Shephard: Dick who was executed for being a highwayman?
Contestant: Dick van Whittington.

Shephard: Who said, "Romeo, Romeo, wherefore art thou Romeo?"
Contestant: Romeo?

Shephard: *Meles meles* is the Latin name for which nocturnal mammal with a black and white striped face?
Contestant: The whale.

Shephard: The Suffolk Punch is a type of which equine animal?
Contestant: Tiger.

Shephard: The European principality of Andorra lies in which mountain range?
Contestant: The Himalayas.

Shephard: In 1855, which nurse established the "British Hotel" for sick and convalescent troops during the Crimean War?
Contestant: Marie Antoinette.

Shephard: Which blind and deaf female American author and educator was the subject of Oscar-winning film *The Miracle Worker*?
Contestant: J.K. Rowling.

Shephard: On which ship did the seaman Fletcher Christian famously lead a mutiny in 1789?
Contestant: The Titanic.

Shephard: What flying insect has the French name *papillon*?
Contestant: Dog.

Shephard: Which biblical character did the Dance of the Seven Veils before Herod II?
Contestant: Jesus.

Couch Potatoes Quiz, Radio 2

Rylan Clark-Neal: Fill in the blank. In *Apocalypse Now*, the Vietnam war movie, the great award-winning actor Robert Duvall said, "I love the smell of BLANK in the morning…"
Caller: Ooh, I don't know this one. I'll have to guess. Toast?

Radio 1

Greg James: People born yesterday have an Aries star sign. Name any other horoscope star sign.
Caller: Aries.
James: Any other one.
Caller: Triangle.

University Challenge, BBC2

Jeremy Paxman: King Ghidorah, Megalon and Mothra are among creatures to have fought which enduring film character in films made between 1964 and 1992?
Contestant: Lassie.

Richard Osman's House of Games, BBC2

Richard Osman: In which year did Marco Polo arrive back in Venice, having spent 17 years in China?
Contestant: 1992.

Daily Dozen Quiz, Lincs FM

Host: What was the name of the famous colonel who invented Kentucky Fried Chicken?
Caller: Was it Colonel Mustard?

Counterpoint, Radio 4

Paul Gambaccini: According to the song title by America, what didn't the horse have?
Contestant: Legs.

NATION IN SHOCK

THERE is a sense of deep and profound shock across the nation today as, despite the involvement of the government, the coronavirus vaccine rollout is going well.

"Why haven't thousands of pensioners in Colchester been accidentally injected with horse tranquilliser?" asked one deeply shocked woman.

"Why hasn't a vaccine centre exploded so Piers Morgan could get angry whilst berating Matt Hancock?" said another deeply shocked man.

"I'd have thought that by now someone would have accidentally dumped the entire supply of the Pfizer vaccine into the North Sea," said another shocked lady.

Outsourcers and PR advisors have blamed the lack of chaos and disarray, which has characterised every other aspect of the government's coronavirus strategy, on a foolish decision to allow the NHS to run the vaccination programme.

IT'S WORLD WAR FLU!

Bloody British, coming over here and stealing our jabs!

THE ✦ TIMES

1 February 2021

Yes – it's VVE Day!

V FOR VACCINE

PRIME Minister Winston Johnson today hailed Victory of the Vaccine in Europe day, as he led national celebrations throughout Britain.

There was no dancing in the street and no one jumped in the fountains in Trafalgar Square, as Johnson didn't join the Royal Family on the balcony at Buckingham Palace.

Said Johnson, "Now is not the time for Vaccine Nationalism just because we beat the frogs and the krauts and they're furious about it."

He continued, "We are not going to give them our vaccine because we need it all, due to the fact that we've got a lot more people dying than they have!"

As the crowds didn't cheer and the bands didn't play, he added, "We have won the war on the Care Home Front, partly because there aren't many old people in Homes left alive. I salute the few."

Winnie Johnson then concluded, "I hope that the voters remember this terrific victory on VVE day and don't vote me out at the first available opportunity!"

THE UNFORTUNATE FAILURE OF THE EU VACCINE ROLLOUT

Hahahahahahahahahahahahahahahahahahahahahaha hahahahahahahahahahahahahahahahahahahahahahaha hahahahahahahahahahahahahahahahahahahahahahaha hahahahahahahahahahahaha no time for gloating hahaha hahahahahahahahahahahahahahahahahahahahahahaha hahaha and furthermore hahahahahahahahahahahahaha hahahahahahahahahahahahhahahahahahahahahhahaha hahahahahahahahahahahahahahahahahahahahahahaha hahahahaha yet on the other hand hahahahahahahaha hahahahahahahahahahahahahhahahahahahahahhahahaha hahahhahahahahahahahahhahahahahahahahhahahahahaha hahahahahahahahaha our European friends hahahahaha hahahahahahahahahahahahahahahahahahahahahhahaha hahahahahahahahahahaha so in conclusion hahahahhaha hahahahahahahahahahahahahahahahahahhahahahahaha hahahahahhahahahahahahahhahahahahahahahhahahahaha

---

TRUSS ON EUROPE

It's time there was a British word for Schadenfreude

EU-phemisms

"Britain did nothing clever, they only got vaccines because they paid more and ordered them sooner"

NOD NOD

EU TRIES TO BRUSH OFF VACCINE INEQUALITY

RSJ

We are shocked to discover that's how trade works

EU IN CLIMBDOWN AFTER THREAT TO TRIGGER ARTICLE 16

■ WHERE did the EU get the idea that threatening to break international law using Northern Ireland as a bargaining chip was a good strategy?

Great Speeches from the American Civil War *Number 94*
The Getmeadoublecheesewhopperburg Address

FOUR score and seven tweets ago, I, Abraham Donald Trump, called on the American people to peacefully riot and to fight for an end to the division in our country.

As you know, nobody condoned the resulting disgraceful violence more than I did when I said I didn't, and nobody could have mistaken my pleas for you to storm the Capitol and lynch Mike Pence as anything but a respectful and appropriate call for a democratic solution to the stealing of the election. I am not going to say that the fraud was perpetrated by satanic paedophiles in a pizza parlour who vote democrat and worship the Kenyan-born crooked Hillary Clinton.

That is for respectable republican patriots like the QAnon Shaman and Yogi, also known as Jellystone Bear, to do, not forgetting Fat Betty from the Arizona Rib 'n' Donut shack (no masks here!) and Lt Colonel 'Red' Neck also known as Obergruppenführer Valknsut of the Mother's Pride Boys.

I love these people, but they are a disgrace, and I hate them. They are not Americans, and do not represent me or our movement, and are probably Antifa activists, pretending to be patriots, when they are actually left-wing Black Lives Matter supporters FAKE COUPS! And remember, guys, wear your masks at all times – it makes it harder for the FBI to identify you.

But enough of this, it is time for healing to begin, and for an orderly transfer of power to begin from the outgoing President, me, to the incoming democratically elected president, myself! There should be no violence unless anyone disagrees with me, in which case I cannot be held accountable for the actions of those who, quite rightly, fight like hell to stop me being impeached for a record second time. Pretty good, huh? Most in history. FACT!

So my message to you, the God-fearing 75 million who supported me and share my beliefs – namely that I should still be President – is to stop the witchhunt now! Burn the witchhunters, run them out of town with pitch forks, drown them on ducking stools, until they confess that they are blood-drinking cannibals in league with the devil, ie Nancy Pelosi.

I would like to end by quoting another former President of this great country of ours: President George Washington DC, who was caught cutting down a cherry tree by his father and you know what he said to this father? "Father, I cannot tell a lie, it was Antreefa, a group dedicated to the cutting down of cherry trees, thus undermining the American Constitution. But never mind, I hereby pardon myself for the crime of cutting down the tree which I didn't do." Isn't that an inspiring story?

So let me finish by saying that I believe passionately in the same things that American Presidents have always believed in: "Government of my people, by my family, for myself, shall not perish from the earth". God bless QAnonica!

This speech received a 994% approval rating from all North American horn-bearing mammals, though the President has demanded a recount in Alaska.

Exclusive to all Tory papers
An Apology

IN THE LAST four years we, like many other newspapers, may have given the impression that we thought that President Trump was in some way fit to hold the office of President of the United States and was, in the words of one of our leading writers, "an outstanding democratic leader and a genuine populist politician of extraordinary talents". We may have reinforced readers' misapprehension by running weekly editorials saying, "Ignore the boring Trump bashers – they are just a bunch of moaning libtards, wet feminazis and disgruntled race warriors."

In the last four days we have now realised that there was not a jot or scintilla of truth in the above and that, on the contrary, Donald Trump is actually, as our leading writer put it so well, "a dangerous fascist, sexist, xenophobic narcissist who has tried to mount a disgraceful coup against democracy itself". Our editorial today: "Ignore the Trump defenders – they are just a bunch of far-right lunatics, conspiracy nutters and armed criminals" makes the point very clearly.

We would like to apologise to our readers for any confusion that our earlier coverage may inadvertently have caused and to assure them that this will certainly not happen again when Trump or one of his family attempt to run for president in 2024 and we decide to back them all on the grounds that *(cont. p94)*

CONSPIRACY UPDATE
RIOT SPECIAL

Well we've all seen the mob invading the American Capitol building, waving their confederate flags, wearing their MAGA hats and their neo-Nazi t-shirts – so the big question for us is: who was REALLY behind the riots?

QANON fan MAGA435 had a theory. Live tweeting from inside the senate chamber where he was laying explosives he said:

"It is all a plot to undermine Prezident Trump! From were I am standing holding my pipe bomb I can see lots of libberals hiding under there desks. What are they doing here in the bilding? Why are they hiding? This is too suspishus to ignor!"

Another contributor 'KillAllDemocrats' somehow found access to a laptop just before being cuffed at the airport and has pointed out something very interesting on his frightening website:

"Does anyone think it's odd that after me and my friends stormed the capitol to try and kill Mike Pence and Nancy Pelosi, we ALL got arrested for 'breaking' the law?"

"Coincident? I think not!"

TRUTH-IS-OUT-THERE4356, as usual, thinks it's aliens. His scary Facebook page says:

"It's obvious aliens have taken over the brains of the rioters to discredit President Trump. It's all a plot so President Biden (who is also an alien) can safely disband 'Space Force' and leave the planet open to alien invasion."

He goes on to say that 'brain being taken over by aliens' is also his defense plea when he comes up against the federal judge next week.

Who should lead Britain's conspiracy loonies? You decide...

Toby Young | **Julia Hartley-Brewer** | **Laurence Fox** | **Allison Pearson** | **Peter Hitchens** | **Nigel Farage** | **Piers Corbyn** | **Eamonn Holmes**

🔍 Boris Johnson

Home   Create

Boris Johnson MP
● Live   385,000,000 Views

Prime Minister's Question Time Live on Fakebook

👍 Like   💬 Comment

0 people **like** this

Prime Minister hails Special Relationship – with his personal photographer

Hi folks, hi photographer!

(ANDY LENSCAPP [PHOTOGRAPHER] IN CORNER OF ROOM TAKES PHOTO OF PRIME MINISTER SPONTANEOUSLY SAYING HELLO)

Boris: This is a **sobering** moment and the figure of 100,000 is **not** one I take lightly. It means I have to put on my most **serious** face yet.

(ANDY TAKES 100,000TH PHOTO OF PRIME MINISTER ATTEMPTING TO LOOK SERIOUS)

Boris: 100,000 people is enough to **fill** Wembley Stadium. Though not at the moment. **Obviously**. That would be **irresponsible**. And I am **responsible**. **Not** for all the deaths, clearly, as we did **everything** we could.

(ANDY TAKES PICTURE OF PRIME MINISTER TRYING TO APPEAR AS IF HE ACTUALLY BELIEVES THIS)

Boris: People are saying it's **poor** decisions that are behind the UK's high death rate. And I'm **sorry** to say that they're **right**. You, the public, have made **several** poor decisions. You **eat** too much, you **live** too long, you **voted** for us, **whoops!**

Prime Minister's Spokesperson: You idiot!

(PHONE RINGS)

Boris: **Saved** by the bell! **Hurrah**! With one bound, the Bozzster's **free!**

(PHONE KEEPS RINGING)

Boris: Yikes! It could be the President of the United States of America. Andy! Get ready to take a **historic** picture (PICKS UP PHONE). **Yo**, Sleepy Joe!

Voice of Joe Biden: Is that Mrs Merkel?

Boris: No, actually...

Biden: Goddam Trump! Messed up all the phones. The hotline was for McDonald's. And you've sure got a nerve calling me "Sleepy", I hear it's you who's napping every afternoon.

Boris: Er, that's **Fake Snooze**. It's the **baby** who keeps snoring.

Biden: Yeah, sure, whatever. Gotta go... important people to talk to.

Boris: **Wow**! Did you get that, Andy? The **first** person that the new President spoke to was **yours truly**. **King** of the world! **Top** of the morning!

Andy Lenscapp: Can you do the big spur-of-the-moment triumphant thumbs up thing again? It wasn't quite working.

Boris: Can do. How's the **hair**?

Andy: A bit tidy to be honest.

(ONE HOUR LATER)

Boris: I think we've **nailed** it. Now **quick**, Andy, get your skates on and get round to the Daily Telegraph before they put a picture of Kate Middleton on the front page, looking **fruity**.

Prime Minister's Special Advisor: Watch it!

(PRIME MINISTER EXITS)

GLENDA SLAGG

She's Fleet Street's top influenza!???! Geddit!!???

■ **LIZ HURLEY??!!!** Hats and clothes off to lovely Liz as she warms up winter with a cheering photo of herself in the snow in a fur coat and knickers – and nothing else!??!! And why not??!! Just 'cos a gal is getting on a bit doesn't mean she can't get 'em out and flaunt 'em!!! You've got your knockers (Geddit, Liz??!!!?) But I'm not one of them!?!! Talk about a *snow*-stopper??!!! (Like show-stopper – you see what I did there?!!!?) Ice work if you can get it!!?!!

LIZ HURLEY??!!!! Put 'em away darling!??!! We've all seen 'em now and we don't need reminding!?!! Aren't you a bit cold – or do I mean old!!??!! No offence!!?! Love your work!!??! Just feel that a friend needs to tell you that it's *snow* time to freeze your assets off??!! Not an ice look at your age!!! Just sayin'!??!!

SUSANNA REID!?!! Who do you think you are, wearing a low-cut dress on breakfast telly??!?! Liz Hurley??!! Put 'em away, love, it's too early in the morning to be gawpin' at your embonpoint over the Rice Krispies!!!! There's a pair of tits on the screen already, darling – that's you and Piers!!??! Just sayin'!!?!! Love your work, really, holding government ministers to account!!??!!

DAVINA McCALL!!?! Who do you think you are, wearing a skimpy dress on the Masked Singer!?!! Susanna Reid!!?? Come off it, Davina, and put 'em away!!!! Or else I'll have to start wearing a mask – over my eyes!!!!! Geddit???!! Just sayin'!!?!! Love your work, really brave at your age!??!! Wearing that little you'll be growing c-old disgracefully!??!!!

HOLLY WILLOUGHBY!!!?? Who do you think you are, wearing those revealing numbers on Dancing on Ice??!? Davina McCall!!?? *(Haven't you done this? Ed.)* Take a tip or two from Aunty Glenda, Holly love, and put 'em away before people start comparing you to lovely Liz Hurley in the snow!!?! It's a slippery slope for the Holly and the Icy (Geddit??!!) and snow business can easily turn into NO business!!!! *(You're fired, Ed.)*

Byeee!!

GLASTONBURY 2021 CANCELLED

Moo-sic to my ears

ZOO GRAND REOPENING

BANANA BREAD £3

SITUATION VACANT
The post of Speechwriter to the Home Secretary has become available as of February 1st 2021

SO CAN YOU FUCKIN' WRITE OR NOT, YOU WANKER?! I'm not goin' to ask again. Either you can capture my inimimimititable style or you fuckin' can't. Are you useless or what?! You're fired and I haven't even hired you yet. I'll pay you the goin' rate for this kind of work, namely: 12, 38 thousand hundred pounds, 27 hundred. Holidays? Are you kiddin'? Unless you want to be fuckin' deported somewhere sunny! Right – all you have to do is get the fuckin' tone right, which can't be that hard! Now fuck off!

Home Office

The Home Office is an equal opportunities employer and would like to remind the successful candidate that they will have to sign up to a HMG-approved course on Bullying in the Workplace and How to Do It.

Lines on the Invocation of the Poet Rabbie Burns by Scotland's First Minister

'Twas Nicola Sturgeon in the year of twenty twenty one

Who quoted Scotland's second most favourite poetical son.

The first, of course, as all readers will no doubt recall,

Is a bard by the name of William McGonagall.

But I digress from the point which fair Nicola would ne'er do,

For the only thing she ever talks about is Indyref Two!

And so on the TV show presented by fellow scot, Andy Marr,

She cannily got in a Rabbie Burns quote using a crowbar.

"Boris Johnson," she said, is a "wee sleekit timorous beastie",

On the very eve of the traditional Burns night feastie,

Thus hoping to appeal to every true-born Caledonian,

Whilst cocking a snook at the sassenach Old Etonian.

By this she meant Boris was a mouse, timid and sly,

Who from the will o' the Scottish people would fearfully shy.

This emotive poetic appeal to all celts, whether short or lanky,

Was a typical political ploy by the wee lookalike Krankie.

You'd hae thought, mid-Covid, there were more pressing concerns

Than co-opting for her campaign the great Rabbie Burns.

Particularly when his keen-eyed biographers have noted

That it is not entirely clear whether for Indyref he'd have voted.

So the next time yon Nicola wishes the Prime Minister to goad,

Perhaps it would be wiser not to quote this particular ode.

For all she achieved by selecting this all too familiar verse

Was to make the split in Scotland appear even worse.

And trying to force through a hasty and emotional exit

Did not go so well in the recent case of Brexit.

For risking a fifty-fifty vote in a toxic referendum

Could lead to rancour and bitterness that would never ever endum.

© *William McGonagall 1867*

POETRY CORNER

**In Memoriam
Michael Apted,
Director of the
historic TV series
'Seven Up!'**

So. Farewell
Then Michael Apted.

You interviewed a
Number of 7 year-olds
In 1964 and then
Interviewed them again
Every 7 years.

All the way to
63 Up! In 2019.

It is, says Keith,
An amazing and
Moving chronicle of
A changing and yet
Unchanging Britain.

Now we are all
Feeling a bit
Down.

But let's hope
You are going
Up!

E.J. Thribb
(17½ Up)

Boohoo acquires Debenhams

The fast-fashion retailer Boohoo has confirmed that it has bought Debenhams on the cheap.

"Yes, we're very excited with our purchase," said a Boohoo spokesperson.

"We are certain there's no chance that we'll just try it on for size, realise it's a bad fit for us, and then return it in a couple of weeks."

Despite confirming that it would be shutting all remaining Debenhams shops with the loss of 12,000 jobs, a Boohoo spokesman said all staff would be offered work in the expanding fashion retailer's Birmingham sweatshops.

"We're always on the lookout for employees who have lost decent, well-paying jobs on the High Street and, faced with the prospect of losing everything, are desperate enough to come and work for us."

(*Rotters*)

News in brief
Myanmar coup latest

■ Myanmar's military has seized power after detaining civilian leader Aung San Suu Kyi, accusing her of using her period in charge to ruthlessly **not** undermine them.

"During her time in office, Aung San Suu Kyi used up every bit of goodwill she'd built up as a Nobel peace prize winner defending our genocide of the Muslim Rohingya minority, turning herself into an international pariah," said one senior General.

"We want to send out a clear message to those politicians who dare to agree with us and do our bidding in office: do so at your own peril."

Countries around the world have condemned the coup, saying that having written off Aung San Suu Kyi as a puppet of the military, they really can't be bothered to turn her back into a saintly Nelson Mandela-style freedom-loving hero again.

America horrified

■ America has expressed its horror at the military coup in Myanmar that unseated the democratically elected government, saying it's shameful just how well organised it was.

"You've made us look total amateurs at staging a coup," said tens of millions of disgruntled MAGA supporters.

"Where were the dumb rednecks live-streaming their storming of the Capitol building? Where were the frat boys stealing lecturns and where was the shaman in a bear costume?

"Who would have thought that to actually stage a successful coup, all you need is heavily armed military personnel and a few tanks?

"We sure do feel pretty stupid now. Yup."

MASSIVE SALE NOW ON!

All jobs must go!

DIARY
GREGG WALLACE WATCHES PAINT DRY

I'm Gregg Wallace – and tonight I'm planning to WATCH PAINT DRY!!

We Brits just LOVE a pot of paint! In fact, we buy enough pots of paint to fill 500 MILLION Olympic-size swimming pools EVERY YEAR!

I've come to the Pickford Paint Factory in Prestwich to find out exactly WHY we Brits have a love affair with PAINT!!!

Here's Bernice, the production manager of Pickford Paints!

So, Bernice, what EXACTLY do you do here?

BERNICE: I'm the production manager, Gregg.

GREGG: Whoo! Sounds pretty darned important to me! And what EXACTLY does that involve, Bernice?

BERNICE: Well, Gregg, it basically means I manage production.

GREGG: You're kiddin' me? Fan-TASTIC! And that just goes to show it's true what I always say – we Brits just LOVE a pot of paint!!! In fact, we love it so much – we even hire a PRODUCTION MANAGER!

So, tell me this, Bernice. Something I've always wondered. What EXACTLY is BEHIND the love affair we Brits have with paint?!!

BERNICE: Well, Gregg, I suppose we like to paint things – houses and walls and that – and to paint things you need, well, paint.

GREGG: And that's where you come in – am I right?!!

BERNICE: That's right, Gregg.

GREGG: Because to paint anything you need your paint which means you gotta buy it – and you're not gonna be able to buy your paint until... SOMEONE HAS MADE IT!!! Brilliant!

@greggwallace: Tune into ITV2 tonight to watch yours truly zipping down the aisles on Celebrity Supermarket Sweep and then switch over to BBC1 for The Underwater World of Gregg Wallace, though that'll mean you'll have to miss half of my appearance on Celebrity Sun Dials on Sky One...

@greggwallace: ...but at least that means you'll be in plenty of time for Celebrity Masterchef: The Great British Shepherd's Pie. And I'll be talking about my smashing new series Gregg's Great Celebrity Mushroom Hunt earlier in the evening on The One Show. See you there!

GREGG: Love it or loathe it, paint never ceases to AMAZE ME! Just think about it. You dip your brush in it, you spread it all over something – and – splish, splash, splosh! – your wall or whatever becomes a TOTALLY DIFFERENT colour! That's what I call AMAZING!!!

So what EXACTLY is it about paint that makes it so PERFECT FOR PAINTING WITH? That's the question I plan to put to paint factory supremo, Pete.

Pete, you make literally HUNDREDS of pots of paint here every day! It must be literally COMING OUT YOUR EARS! HA! HA! HA!

So tell me this, Pete. How exactly do you get the paint from the factory onto that all-important paint-shop shelf? You must have to put it in a container of some kind or it'll just spill all over the place!

PETE: That's exactly right, Gregg. We put it in a pot. A paint pot.

GREGG: And correct me if I'm wrong but that's must be where we get the expression A POT OF PAINT?

PETE: That's correct, Gregg.

GREGG: You're kiddin' me! Who'der thought it! IN-CREDIBLE! Knock me down with a feather! Now I'm getting the hang of this paint lark! Blimey, you learn something new every day!

@greggwallace: Watch me getting to grips with a lobster, a rack of lamb, banoffee pie and a Dover sole, plus other all-time classic moments of Masterchef: The First 20 Years (BBC2) then switch over to see me eating a great big beautiful doughnut with Ann Widdecombe at the Doughnut Factory in Crediton on Celebrity Antiques Road Trip.

GREGG: So, we've been round the paint factory and learned how they make LITERALLY MILLIONS of pots of paint a year! And now we come to the all-important part of the show where we paint a wall – AND WATCH PAINT DRY!

I've got Annette here to help me. But before we get goin', what's that you got for me, Annette?

ANNETTE: It's a sausage roll, Gregg.

GREGG: Talk about SCRUMPTIOUS! I can never resist a sausage roll! In fact, sausage rolls NEVER CEASE TO AMAZE ME! Mmmm!! You get the great sausagey taste of the sausage, you get the ever-so-slightly rolly taste of the roll, and then, when it comes down to it, you get the full-flavoured sausage roll effect from the combination of the two. Now that's what I call a SAUSAGE ROLL!!!

So, Annette, we're planning to paint this wall all over?

ANNETTE: That's right, Gregg.

GREGG: And presumably we won't be using our bare hands?!!!

ANNETTE: No, Gregg. I've brought some paintbrushes along!

GREGG: Cor! You had me worried there for a second, Annette!!! HAHAHA! HAHAHA! Okay, so we now have our wall and we have our paint. What colour would you call this, Annette?

ANNETTE: Red, Gregg.

GREGG: Red! A truly ICONIC colour! Apply red to a wall, and what do you get? Yes – a red wall. So – LET'S PAINT!

@greggwallace: Join me for sticky buns, pork scratchings and chocolate pud tonight on GREGG's GREAT BRITISH PIG-OUT (C4, 9pm). It's never too late to enjoy yourself! And don't forget to tune into BBC2 tomorrow at 8pm for a brilliant new series of diets and home work-outs in GREGG'S SHOW ME FIT. It's never too late to lose weight!

GREGG: All done and dusted! We've painted our wall red – so now let's sit back and – WATCH IT DRY!

Oh, it don't get much better than this! Once you've painted your wall – and we've painted it red, but, believe me, it's totally up to you, it really is, you can paint it any colour you want – green, blue, yellow, orange, whatever, any colour at all, and you know what – the SHEER VARIETY of colours NEVER CEASES TO AMAZE ME – so once you've painted your wall, as I was saying, you can afford to SIT BACK AND WATCH IT DRY! And that's what I call a truly ICONIC MOMENT!

As told to
CRAIG BROWN

"You've got a crocapoo? Surely you mean cockapoo?"

I once had a ship that put
  to sea
And the name of that ship
  was 'Tariff Free'
Then Brexit came,
  land-bound were we,
Blow my profits, blow
  (huh)

Soon may the Fishermen
  come
From France and Holland
  and Bel-gi-um
One day, when the
  paperwork's done,
We'll curse Vote Leave
  and go, huh!

And now our fish is rotting
  on shore
And filling in forms is
  such a bore
The captain called all
  hands and swore
At BBC Radio (huh)

Soon may the Fishermen
  come
From Spain and Iceland
  and Bel-gi-um
One day, when the
  paperwork's done
We'll curse Vote Leave
  and Gove. Huh!

*(Continues for
94 verses)*

Nursery Times

Friday, Once-upon-a-time

POSTMAN McPAT SEA SHANTY GOES VIRAL

by Our Nautical Staff **Captain Musical-Hook**

MUCH-LOVED local Postman McPat has become an internet sensation after his sea shanty went viral on HikoryTikoryTok and racked up over a squillion hits.

Postman McPat was amazed at the reaction across Greendale, saying, "It was just something I did to amuse Mrs Goggins. I had no idea it would have a wider appeal."

The shanty harks back to a bygone age when the Post Office used to deliver mail on a regular basis, before postmen became too busy singing sea shanties and getting lucrative recording

contracts. For those who've been living on another planet (the Clangers, etc), we're delighted to print the lyrics of the sea shanty in full:

*"Postman McPat, Postman
  McPat,
Postman McPat and his black
  and white video,
Early in the morning, he will
  start recording
And picks up all the contracts in
  his van.
All the birds are singing, his
  career is just beginning,
  McPat knows he's a
  really lucky man."*

Postman McPat's video has broken all online Greendale records formerly set by his cat, Jess, doing something vaguely amusing.

LATE NEWS

■ French fishermen complain Britain has unfair monopoly on sea shanties. EU demands Britain hands over shanties now. Britain claims EU tried to harmonise shanties, leading to long shanty delays. New shanty 'We'll Praise Vote Leave and Go' goes viral, as UK fishermen all become postmen.

Next week

Notes and Queries: What is a Wellerman?

■ Is it 18th century Scottish slang for a record producer, named after the famous Georgian record producers Stock, Aitken and Wellermen?

■ Are Wellermen the workers employed by Lucky Wishing

Wells in Ireland, who dredge through the murky water to retrieve all the pennies thrown in by hapless tourists?

■ Were the Wellermen the terrifying monsters in 1970s' *Doctor Who*, that even the Cybermen were afraid of, due to their excellent health and glowing complexions?

(That's enough shanty-based material, Ed – huh!)

Worrying results from new lockdown survey

by **Polly Time-Filla**

A NEW report reveals that, despite this having been going on for nearly a year now, the task you meant to complete around the home has still not been finished.

Studies throughout the year have shown that "it'll only take twenty minutes tops" and that "it's so bloody easy – why can't you just do it, you lazy swine?"

Sadly, on the other hand, counter-studies have also shown that "you'll do it tomorrow" and that, when tomorrow comes, "you can't do it without a special tool which you'll order right away, or possibly in half an hour, or possibly tomorrow".

The anonymised respondents to the survey (your spouse, your children and the dog) have revealed a very pessimistic outlook over both the project management outlines and the approximate deadlines set for the completion of the task.

Feasibility studies conducted at the very highest level have concluded that "it'll never happen" and "nothing ever gets done around here".

Other reports recently published have shown: a) that jogger definitely could have given you a wider berth if he wasn't such a selfish bastard, b) the people behind you in the supermarket queue are definitely standing 20 percent too close, and c) there's no way it's your turn to take out the bins already.

School news

Public School Headmaster Comes Out

The headmaster of St Cakes, the prestigious Midlands independent boys boarding school (motto: *Quis paget entrat*) has shocked parents by publicly admitting on a virtual Zoom Assembly that he is "straight".

Mr Kipling admitted that he was worried about traditional parents expecting the headmaster

at such a school to be homosexual, but felt that times had moved on and the school was now ready to accept a heterosexual headmaster.

Mr Kipling revealed in the Assembly that he was actually married to a woman, Mrs Kipling, and that he hoped parents, staff and pupils would welcome Mrs Kipling into "the Cakes family".

"Mrs Kipling is an exceedingly good Cakeian," he quipped, as parents withdrew their children in outrage at the *(cont. p94)*

*"And how have
you been
coping during
lockdown?"*

WHO dismisses Chinese coronavirus lab theory

by Our China Correspondent
Wu Gojing Tojaill

A team of international experts from the World Health Organization, in China to investigate the origins of Covid-19, have dismissed a theory that the virus came from a laboratory in Wuhan.

"The Chinese government representatives escorting us around Wuhan's jails gave us unfettered access to the cells which held the whistleblowing doctors who tried to warn the world about coronavirus last January," said the scientists.

"We also got to see all the torture chambers where the citizen journalists who video-blogged the early days of the pandemic in February and March ended up.

"Based on these detailed observations about what happens to troublemakers in China, we've come to the conclusion that the Beijing authorities have been telling the whole truth about the emergence of Covid-19 – which clearly came from frozen sandwiches imported from the USA. Please can we get on the first plane home now, as we're scared and just want to see our families again..."

THOSE CHINESE-FUNDED OXFORD COLLEGES IN FULL

★ Maogdalen College

★ Christ Xiurch

★ Beijingliol College

★ Exieter College

★ Huaworcester College

★ Xisus College

★ Lady Margaret Wall

★ St Hughawei's College

★ Teddy Cotta Hall

★ Corpus Xisti College

★ Mingsfield College

(That's enough colleges. Ed.)

Five reasons Biden will love Britain

by Our Desperate Correspondent
Christopher Hope-We-Get-A-State-Visit

SOME people are worried that Biden is going to be hostile to a Brexit Britain whose PM insulted his former boss, Barack Obama.

It's very clear that Biden will actually love the UK. Here are the reasons why:

1 Joe Biden is Irish, and the Irish are noted for their love of Britain. In the 1970s, some Irish people were so devoted in their love of the British state that they would attempt to detonate parts of it just so the British would pay them the attention they craved.

2 Both "Biden" and "Britain" begin and end with the letters "B" and "N". This will create a powerful subconscious urge in the new President's mind to befriend our nation. The countries of Bahrain, Benin and Bhutan will also be relying on this effect.

3 Biden's dogs are called "Champ" and "Major". This is clearly a tribute not only to Britain's fourth-most-recent Conservative PM, John Major, but also to the "Champ-agne" which is drunk at all Conservative dinners.

4 Biden had a stutter as a child. Our own Prime Minister's habit of starting sentences with "I, I, I, I, I..." or "Well, er, um, er, um..." will seem charmingly familiar to him, as a result.

5 Biden is a Catholic. Catholics have lots of children. Boris Johnson has lots of children. Therefore, Boris Johnson is essentially a Catholic, and when Biden visits the UK this summer the two of them will have a wonderful time kissing the Blarney Stone in the Confessional and dancing a Four Leaf Clover jig to the sounds of the Lucky Potato band, while *(That's enough insanity. Ed.)*

THE TOUGH BUDGET DECISIONS THAT MUST BE MADE

THE British economy has recorded its worst set of figures for over three centuries.

The Chancellor has borrowed more money than any other administration since the Wars of the Roses and Rishi Sunak is now faced with some difficult and painful choices. How can he fill the enormous £400bn black hole in the nation's coffers?

One thing is for sure. Raising taxes is not the answer. Oh no. Definitely not. That would be irresponsible and wrong and counter-productive and extremely unpopular with myself.

Another solution must urgently be found to the widening deficit that threatens to overwhelm Britain.

But it must not involve me paying anything extra because I am perfectly happy with the money I have, thank you very much, and I would rather keep it all for myself, if that's alright with you, rather than waste it all paying for some stupid pandemic that wasn't my fault and which *(cont. p94)*

Daily Telegraph

Why isn't the BBC making more comedy?

by **B.B.C. Basher**

IT IS a crying shame that the BBC is so toothless when it comes to making fresh, original sitcoms and sketch shows.

For too long this newspaper has been willing the BBC to make some brilliant, exciting new comedies which not only shock and delight but also reflect our changing nation.

And yet they haven't been making them or broadcasting. Not for the first time we are asking: why can this be? Is there something which has made the BBC timid in its comedy output or made it reluctant to broadcast controversial material? We may never know.

ON OTHER PAGES

● Why are all these BBC comedies so terrible?

● All BBC so-called "comedies" are bloody useless, the corporation should be quaking in its boots, let's take away all their money

● We put the boot into all recent BBC comedies that are not Morecambe and Wise

What are we all doing in lockdown this time round?

by **Phil Space** and **Des Pratt**

FIRST it was baking. Then it was knitting. Then it was doing jigsaws. Then it was wild swimming. But now in lockdown three there's a new hobby on the block that's got everyone talking.

Yes, it's stabbing! In London alone the figures are at a record high, as young people flock to the new pastime that is easy to pick up and fun to do when you've had enough of bingeing on box sets and *(This is too bad taste even for me. You're both fired. Ed.)*

HOME ??? SCHOOLING QUIZ

IF MUMMY has to do three Zoom work meetings today, plus home school Katie in fractions, Simon in geography and Toby in biology, how many glasses of wine will Mummy drink tonight?

A Two glasses

B Two bottles

C Two cases

D All of the above

BABY JOY FOR MEGHAN AND HARRY

Any thoughts on names?

Sue if it's a girl or Rich if it's a boy

I can feel it giving the Press a kicking!

You won't believe what this Danish court jester looks like now...

ROB MURRAY

From The Message Boards

Members of the online community respond to the major issues of the day...

Snowman assaulted

Please, please join my Facebook group #SACK THE SNOWMAN KILLER 😃 A binman in Hereford was filmed kicking a snowman's head off and he was rightly let go by his employers. Amazingly, people petitioned for his reinstatement, saying that he worked through Covid and has children to support. They even claim the snowman would have melted anyway! Let's be clear. The snowman was built by a THREE-YEAR-OLD. The implications for his mental health are obvious and will probably affect his exam results in the future. If one child is spared it will be worthwhile. – *Supermum*

+100000 HOWARD THESE PEOPLE FEEL IF THEY KICKED THERE KIDS HEAD OFF – *proudmum*

maybe the snowman offended his beliefs and he just had to behead it? maybe his ancestors were slave traders and he had to be toppled? – *just sayin*

The child built a snowman in a public space during lock-down. That is an illegal act. The council worker was correct to destroy it. The parents must be prosecuted and the boy placed in care. – *Public Spirited Citizen*

peple learn some sience god make's snow melt all the time with the sun and counsel's put salt on roads and kill snow evry day and nobody complanes but o no its a WHITE snow MAN so evryones upset – *godsiensesence*

hereford is the home of the SAS and this has all the haulmarks of a top secret deployment. if you watch the video closely you will see SERTAIN SIGNALS i will say no more out of respect for my personel friend's SAS HERO'S andy mcnab and chris ryan – *Bravo 2 Zero*

I worked on the dust for years and believe me this is nothing. Body parts, explosives, poisonous chemicals, you took your life in your hands every day. My memoir No Hot Ashes is available on Audible. – *Bin there done that*

Reminds me of when kids built a snowman in our street and it looked a bit like Jimmy Savile. They weren't to know that of course but some blokes from the local pub kicked it down just to be on the safe side. Pub is closed now but that sort of community spirit makes me proud. – *Del*

del thats quality! when they done the snowman for the school play my boy joined in the song but he sung I'M WANKING IN THE AIR 😃 even the headmaster laughed as it goes but theres no way the baldy cunt aint a nonce – *Sidcup Lion*

bring your snowman to stoke and we will kick his fuckin head in – *stokie steve*

Nursery Times

···················· Friday, Once-upon-a-time ····················

PRINCE CHARMLESS GIVES INTERVIEW TO JESTER

by Our Royal Staff

THE Nurseryland Broadcasting Service (NBS) last night screened a revelatory interview with the former Prince Charming who is now living in Lalaland with his fairy wife, Meghan Le Fay.

The renowned jester, Mr James Corblimey, delighted viewers of his "Mate, Mate" show by taking the Prince on an omnibus ride around Lollywood whilst drinking cups of British-style tea.

Prince Charmless was quizzed by the jolly jester about how passionately he wanted to protect his private life and then answered lots of cheeky questions about his new baby, his wife, the queen, the Duke of Edinburgh and everything else he passionately doesn't want to talk about.

He then called up the intensely private sorceress, Meghan Le Fee, for a very private and personal phone call, broadcast to millions, in which the joke was that the couple were buying another hugely expensive palace.

"It would be perfect for you," chuckled Corblimey, as he waved his pig's bladder and jingled the bells on his jester's cap. "It was the former home of the Prince of Bel End."

Charmless continued with a withering attack on the Fairy Tales published about him by the Brother Grimm and said he much preferred the Disney film version of Royal Life where everyone lives happily ever after.

The two mates then did an assault course where Corblimey was assaulted by the public for being so sycophantic. Corblimey however did end the interview with a probing question for the prince. "What does the future hold for you next, sire?" to which the Prince answered, "Why, lots more interviews telling all and demanding to be left alone."

Anger over Fatberg shaming

THERE was fury in London last week when a huge lump of undissolved waste was labelled "a Fatberg" by engineers trying to unblock the system.

Said one angry local council official, "The Berg may be on the chunky side, but to call it fat is completely unnecessary and insulting." Even if it is the size of a bungalow, it helps no one to use pejorative language about the unfortunate Lardberg." (Surely "Largeberg"? Ed.)

NEW EU SEAFOOD POLICY

We're going to start flexing our mussels

They're being incredibly shellfish

THE ALTERNATIVE VOICE

THE REV J.C. SPART

A Sermon by the Church of England's controversial new media curate on the theme of the life of Captain Sir Tom.

I am sorry but I am just not going to join in this cult of worshipping a white male figure, however iconic he may seem to be and, yes, he went around doing good and trying to heal people, but I think this is missing the point and that the adulation of this man as a sort of "saviour" is just not helpful or credible in today's world and, yes, all right, Jesus was a perfectly nice person who was taken from us at quite an early age and that's very sad and of course he deserves some respect for all that walking up and down on water etc, but let's not get carried away here and start putting up statues and having special holidays to commemorate his birth and death and generally thinking of him as some sort of supernatural hero or Captain Tom figure *(Is this right? Ed.)*

GLENDA SLAGG

She's Fleet Street's same old variant

■ Aren'tcha sick of those influencers??!!! It's all right for some, swanning off to sunny shores over Christmas to top up their tans and have a holiday!!?!! And then having the nerve to come back and no doubt spread the disease to all of us mugs who stayed at home, shivering in our kitchens under lockdown!!?! How dare you!!?! It's you I'm talking about, Captain Sir Tom!!?! Okay, so the Caribbean's lovely, and you had the chance to take a freebie holiday. Who wouldn't?!!?! On second thoughts, hats off to Captain Sir Tom. Good for you!!?! Hope you had a great holiday, Sir!!!?! We love you!!!! *(You're fired! Ed. And you can answer all the letters of complaint.)*

Byeee!!

ONE DAY, NONE OF THIS WILL BE YOURS

Keir Starmer WRITES

HELLO!

Well, I'm afraid the honeymoon is well and truly over. I'm down in the polls, and I'm getting criticism from friendly newspapers and my own shadow cabinet!

I don't understand. This is only supposed to happen to Labour leaders who wear duffle coats, eat sandwiches weirdly and make their own chutney, not a nice well-turned out chap like me!

But fear not, because I have the solution to my decline in popularity. Peter Mandelson! Because if there's one person whose name is synonymous with the word "popular", it's good old Peter Mandelson!

I made the pilgrimage to see him and he got his huge dusty book of winning elections down from the top shelf. Thank goodness! It turns out I have been doing everything right thus far: I'm a wealthy, centre-right lawyer who looks good in a suit, and who has devoted himself to not being his predecessor and not saying anything of substance to anybody.

Just one small snag, he's told me; my hair is a bit too lustrous – it doesn't have that indefinable look that winning Labour leaders have. He's sent me away with a bottle of Blair Restorer, which is guaranteed to make me look like a cross between Julius Caesar and a mad vampire, but until then, he wants me to use a filter on all my Zoom calls.

Will do, Peter!

Sincerely, Keir.

POETRY CORNER

In Memoriam Christopher Plummer, legendary actor

So. So long
Farewell
Auf Wiedersehen
Goodbye
Adieu to yieu,
Christopher Plummer.

Yes, I know you
Were sick of the
Sound of Music
And felt your career
Had been overshadowed
By the role of
Captain von Trapp.
So I won't go on
About it.

The hills are alive,
Even though, sadly,
You are not.

Like brown paper packages
Tied up with string,
You were one of my
Favourite things.

Altogether now:
"Edelweiss, edelweiss",
Okay, so you didn't
Actually sing it,
But we don't
Actually care.

"Edelweiss, edelweiss,
Every morning
You greet me
Dum deed dum
Dum dee dee
You look happy to
Something."

E.J. Thribb
(17½ going on 17)

FEARS AS RADICAL SOCIALISM REARS HEAD IN UK

by Our Dangerous Leftie Correspondent **Des Kapital**

THERE was outrage from prominent Tory backbenchers as Chancellor Rishi Sunak finally made his move and hinted at some form of tax rise in the distant future.

"This is exactly what we've been warning about – a socialist chancellor like Rishi was bound to try and pull this nonsense off sooner or later," said a furious, overweight businessman in an angry bow tie.

"I didn't fight for Brexit and pay £15,000 for a seat at a Tory party fundraiser so that some left-wing British government could unilaterally make decisions like this.

"I fought for Brexit and endured Robert Jenrick's aftershave so that a right-wing British government could unilaterally make decisions that I specifically approved of.

"Thank heavens we have sensible right-wing politicians like Keir Starmer who can fight against this Marxist madness."

39

DIARY

HRH THE PRINCESS ROYAL'S A-Z OF THE HOME

ARRANGING FLOWERS: Perfect waste of time.

BAKING: Why go to all the bother when there's perfectly decent sponge bases at your local cash-and-carry, often with ten or even fifteen percent discounts for a bulk-buy. For a special occasion, one can always spoon a bit of raspberry jam over them.

CANS: Canned veg is infinitely preferable to fresh because it lasts longer. And once you've scraped every last scrap off the bottom, you can string all the cans together to make a highly effective bird-scarer. Another good use for old cans is as candle-holders. We have solid silver candlesticks like everyone else, but they're a nuisance to polish.

DOGS: You'll never find a more loyal and affectionate dog than a Bull Terrier. We've had quite a number over the years. I particularly remember Fang, a splendid girl who we were sadly forced to have put down after a neighbour insisted on inserting his leg into her mouth. Then there was darling Dotty, who had a killing sense of humour and loved chasing children. I told them not to run away, but would they listen? And – can you beat it? – the second they ended up in A&E their wretched parents blamed it all on Dotty!

ELEPHANT IN THE ROOM: Why this incessant talk of elephants in the room? In all my years, I have never seen an elephant in a room, so why go on about it?

FUSS: I loathe, loathe, LOATHE any sort of fuss. In my day, we just got on with it. Quite why people can't treat one as a perfectly normal human being, I have no idea. If I'm going to an official function, I always instruct my ladies-in-waiting to tell whichever Lord Lieutenant is dancing attendance that I don't want any fuss. Of course, that's something one's chauffeur already knows.

GARDEN: Like most people, I find that flowers simply get in the way. A garden is above all a place for dogs and children to let off steam. I'm told the Prince of Wales thinks differently. They say he's stuffed his garden full of all sorts of organic Buddhist shrines and what not. Each to his own, but honestly!

HOSTING: Not a word I am happy with. I'm sorry, but I don't go in for all that "double-kissing" on the doorstep. Needless to say, the younger generation won't hear of shaking hands. Nowadays, they're all looking for, "Oh, let's do it a new way". But no – please don't reinvent that particular wheel. We've been there, done that, found it didn't work. A brief handshake is more than enough.

ITALIAN FOOD: Spaghetti I can just about handle. But I draw the line at mozzarella. I wouldn't put it into my mouth if you paid me, quite frankly.

KNUCKLE DOWN: Not an expression you hear these days, I'm sorry to say. I'm not sure the younger generation understands what it means! I've no wish to name names, or to give them the attention they crave, but a certain young couple who are intent on "following their dreams", and in California, of all places, might do better to Knuckle Down.

As it happens, knuckle down is by far the best way to cook a trotter.

LEFTOVERS: Waste not, want not. If the dogs don't finish what's in their bowls, just scoop it into the stew. It'll make it go that little bit further, as well as giving it what I always call "that little something extra".

LLEWELYN-BOWEN, LAURENCE: Is he that funny little man? I'm imagining he's a man. That's entirely up to him. Personally, I wouldn't let him within a hundred yards of our house. If I want my garden covered in "decking", WHICH I DON'T, then I'll do it myself, thanks awfully.

MANTELPIECE: The perfect place to place one's snaps. We have gorgeous colour photos of Fang and Dotty, of course, but, rather more unusually, we also have a few photos of our children and grandchildren. It helps us keep tabs on which is which.

MENTAL HEALTH: All the rage. Mental health this, mental health that. If I hear any more about mental health, I'll go mad.

OLD SPOT: My favourite breed of pig. Pigs make the perfect pets. And they help keep down the wildflowers, which is a blessing.

PILLOWS: I'm frankly sick and tired of overnight guests saying, "My pillows were too hard". I tell them it was probably the sand we put in them, and they look shocked. When I ask them what on earth they're expecting them to be filled with, their answer is always the same. Feathers!!! Do they think money grows on trees?

QUEEN'S CHRISTMAS MESSAGE: If it were left to me, I'd just say "Hello. Happy Whatever. Cheerio," and be done with it. No need for all the extra verbiage.

RYVITA: A piece of Ryvita makes a perfectly acceptable starter. If you prefer something more fancy, you're welcome to a bit of marge.

SOAP: If the Wright's Coal Tar in the guest bathroom is getting small just mould it into the remnants of the Coal Tar you used for the dog's de-worming and then return it to its perch. It's not to be sniffed at. No one will notice, and all it takes is a bit of elbow grease.

TOASTER: There's no need for a toaster. If you really must have your bread browned, simply hold it over a cigarette lighter. I'm reliably informed that the electrical toasters you see in shop windows cost anything up to £20. No, thank you! Anyone would think we were the Beckhams!

WPB: For heaven's sake, no one wants to go through all that dreadful rigmarole of saying "Waste Paper Basket". Life's too short. Just say WPB and be done with it.

XMAS: Always Xmas rather than Christmas. Five letters less to deal with. These things mount up, you know.

YO-YO: What on earth's the point? Why toss something away if you know it's going to come bouncing back? An easy way to deal with them is to cut the piece of string off. That way, they stay put.

ZOOM: Hello? Hello? Can you hear me? No, I jolly well can't and nor do I want to, so go away.

As told to
CRAIG BROWN

"Ah, yes – I should have mentioned – it is under a flight path"

Facebook hoax goes viral

THE internet was in hysterics yesterday at a wonderfully funny new meme which showed Nick Clegg defending Facebook's policy on paying for news.

Said internet sensation, Jackie Weaver, "It's a blast. The funniest thing I've seen online for years."

Hundreds of amusing cats agreed, saying, "It's barely worth us trying to do anything humorous when the former Leader of the LibDems goes public with something as laughable as this."

In the video, Nick Clegg compares Facebook paying for news content to carmakers having to pay radio stations for the music playing in the car.

He then adds, "It's like students having to pay for their own tuition fees. Or large multi-nationals paying greedy, washed-up politicians to offer pisspoor defences for their aggressive and amoral behaviour."

In the funniest final section of the meme that's set to break the internet, Mark Zuckerberg concludes, "At least this isn't the most humiliating job Nick Clegg's ever taken." To which Clegg replies, "I agree with Mark." *(Rotters)*

WHY HAS BRITAIN GOT THE TOUGHEST LOCKDOWN IN THE WORLD?

Probably because it has the highest death rate.

New Lockdown Report reaches conclusion:
'THIS IS DRAGGING ON A BIT NOW'

A NEW report commissioned by this paper can reveal that people's tempers are fraying like never before due to a combination of WILL YOU PLEASE TURN THAT DOWN I AM TRYING TO WRITE AN ARTICLE the ongoing lockdown, the extremely cold weather, and the complete economic armageddon soon to envelop the entire country.

A revolutionary new surveying technique designed to gauge the public's mood and sensitivity to perceived slights has confirmed that, in their own households, 94 percent of people have I DON'T KNOW WHERE THE BLOODY OREGANO IS LOOK FOR YOURSELF I'M NOT YOUR SLAVE started to lose their tempers at the slightest pretext.

At any given moment, 78 percent of adults have become completely furious within the last ten minutes, and it's all because NO I WILL NOT WALK THE DOG AGAIN I DID IT THIS MORNING AND HE SHAT ON MY BOOT of this unprecedented combination of circumstances.

Some 53 percent of people reading this article right now would describe themselves as "apoplectic", 17 percent as "volcanic" and a further 14 percent as "simmering with rage". It is uncertain whether the easing of lockdown will help matters, or if things are now so far gone that WHO LEFT THIS SMALL PIECE OF PAPER ON THE CARPET RIGHT THAT'S IT I'M MOVING TO NEW ZEALAND.

IRA man in shameful confession

by Our Political Staff
Shameless O'Letterbomb

ONE of the IRA's most respected members, Professor Roy Greenslade, last night admitted that he had been leading a secret life as an undercover editor of a national newspaper.

"Yes, I worked for Robert Maxwell as his chief henchman on the Daily Mirror," he said in a statement, "and I don't regret it for a minute."

Greenslade also confessed to a long history of "supporting journalism", which included working for Rupert Murdoch on the Sun and even for Andrew Neil on the Sunday Times.

"So what?" he said, unapologetically. "Making lots of money is something that I happen to believe in," before adding that he didn't care how many lives he ruined in Fleet Street while

maintaining a respectable front as a member of the Irish Republican Army.

The news has come as a shock to the IRA, who were appalled at his double life.

"All the time we were out kneecapping and murdering people, there he was rigging the Mirror readers' competitions, running stories about hamsters and printing pictures of page three girls."

Greedslade denied that the two roles in his life were incompatible, saying, "There is no conflict of interest in these two roles in my life. My work as a journalist has been entirely dedicated to undermining British life as we know it, and my IRA colleagues should be proud of me."

Billions offered in cladding settlement

by Our Housing Correspondent
Glenn Fell

IN YET another massive U-turn, the housing minister Robert Jenrick has announced the government will commit an extra £3.5 billion to give themselves "a protective shield" when accused of doing nothing about removing dangerous cladding from tower blocks around the UK.

"This move is intended to give a thin cladding of respectability to the shameful manner in which we've treated the residents stuck in these potential death traps since the 2017 Grenfell fire," the minister told reporters.

"But the grants will not stand up to inspection or scrutiny and the whole scheme is quite likely to fail badly."

There was fresh anger when it was revealed that these billions-

worth of grants would only apply to buildings over 18 metres, with residents in buildings under that height still only having access to loans.

"We needed a ceiling," insisted Jenrick, "unlike those residents who won't have a ceiling or anything else if their flat goes up in flames."

"Hopelessly inadequate," was the response of many MPs watching the housing secretary's announcement, "and these cobbled together proposals aren't much better."

Brushing aside the criticism, Robert Jenrick insisted this could all have been sorted out years ago, if the residents facing bankruptcy had simply booked a table to sit next to him at a £12,000-a-head Tory Party fundraising dinner and he would have sorted everything out with a few phone calls the next morning.

The Eye's Controversial New Columnist

This week I am announcing that I am setting up my own television station. I have noticed that, apart from CBeebies, Cartoon Network, LittleBe, CBBC, Boomerang, Pop, Tiny Pop, Ketchup TV, YAAAS! The Disney Channel, CITV, Milkshake, Nickelodeon, Nicktoons and Nicktoonster, there is very little content aimed at the selfish and easily fractious toddler. The subjects discussed will be wide-ranging, and will be a break from the "herd mentality" of other shows (unless it comes to herd immunity, then I'm all for it!). Here is an example of my first day's schedule:

9.00am Why do leftist snowflakes tell us that throwing breakfast at the wall is "bad"?

11.00am The Woke brigade frowns on swallowing bits of Lego. Do not let them have the final word.

12.00pm Broccoli is a weapon invented by the Rothschilds to keep your mouth full so you can't scream the place down.

1.00pm Napping is a construct the mainstream media invented to keep us docile.

3.00pm Naptime.

5.00pm Why it's the Elite's fault that you feel compelled to throw your toys out of your pram.

6.00pm Close down. Bedtime stories read by Julia Hartley-Brewer. Why *The Very Hungry Caterpillar* is the embodiment of the spoilt cry-baby leftist Twitterati *(cont. p94)*

Lookalikes

Patel **Neferata**

Sir,
I was reading through the rule book of an old role-playing game, and saw this illustration of "Neferata, Queen of Vampires". I'm not a superstitious man, but I would be very greatly comforted if trusted sources could confirm that they have seen our esteemed Home Secretary in the daylight.
KIT FINN.

Steve Bannon **Tim Martin**

Sir,
I cannot help but notice the similarity between Steve Bannon, one-time key advisor to Donald Trump, and Tim Martin, one-time key adviser to Boris Johnson. Are they possibly related?
Regards from Germany,
RICHARD SALTER.

Taylor-Greene **Neanderthal woman**

Sir,
Have any of your readers noticed the extraordinary resemblance between this model of a prehistoric Neanderthal woman in a museum in Lyon and QAnon-supporting Republican Congresswoman, Marjorie Taylor-Greene?
ENA B. TAYLOR.

Wicker Man **Carrie and Boris**

Sir,
I couldn't help but notice the similarity of a certain hush-hush ceremony to another in 1973's Wicker Man. In one, the leader of a crazed, cut-off-from-the-real-world, megalomaniacal cult is making what he likely considers the ultimate sacrifice. In the other, the main character is played by Christopher Lee.
N.J. McGARRIGLE.

Munch **Hitchens**

Sir,
I wonder if other readers have noted the similarity between your recently-rebearded regular correspondent Peter "Hitch-Cov2" Hitchens and Edvard Munch's Self-Portrait with the Spanish Flu (1919)? Of course, one uses just a few deft strokes to represent himself as an isolated but heroic cultural force of his century, grappling with the profound existential effects of a major pandemic; the other is apparently a decadent old Norwegian dauber.
ENA B. GOMBRICH

Faithfull **Archbishop**

Sir,
Has anyone else noticed a likeness between between "Sister Morphine" songstress Marianne Faithfull, and Tudor martyr Archbishop Thomas Cranmer? Do they share a tailor?
ALASTAIR PRICE.

Edward **Harry**

Sir,
I wonder if any other readers have noticed the likeness between the Plantagenet king Edward II of England, and Harry Kane, the England football captain? The similarities now extend to both having missed a few chances with southern Europe.
CAROLINE SOMMERVILLE.

Dark Glasses **Dark Ages**

Sir,
Anna Wintour and the Sutton Hoo helmet?
JUDITH WRIGHT.

Fester **Javid**

Sir,
One is a completely hairless, hunched and barrel-shaped man with dark, sunken eyes and often a deranged smile, the other is Uncle Fester.
KEVIN FARROW.

Shrek & Fiona **Salmond & Sturgeon**

Sir,
I happened to come across a couple of Fairytale Partnerships.
RICHARD SHEPPARD.

Drooper **Hamilton**

Sir,
Could it be that Lewis Hamilton actually began his career on those dune buggies on The Banana Splits?
C. DEWICK.

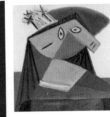

Rev Vennells **Wally**

Sir,
Might this explain the difficulty in locating the Rev. Vennells for interviews in relation to her leadership of the Post Office?
DR JIM NIXON.

Peppa Pig **Picasso painting**

Sir,
Anyone else see a similarity between Picasso's "Femme Assise Dans Un Fauteuil" and popular cartoon character Peppa Pig?
ANDREW RYAN.

Perkins   **Burnham**

Sir,
    Have any readers noticed the striking similarity in appearance between Labour's saviour-in-waiting Andy Burnham and the ubiquitous television personality, Sue Perkins? Could they be related? I think we should be told.

CATHY BURCH.

Jolson

Trump

Sir,
    One is a racially insensitive, face-painted relic of a bygone era, the other one has funny hands...

ENA B. ELLEM.

Rembrandt   **Nicky Morgan**

Sir,
    Nicky Morgan and Rembrandt (Self Portrait)?

SIMON MADDISON.

Munster   **Elliott**

Sir,
    Has anyone else noted the similarity between Tory party co-chairman Ben Elliott and 1960s sit-com freak Herman Munster? I believe both have rather frightful relatives and friends, though only one comes across as genuinely creepy.

ENA B. ARFIELD.

The Kiss   **The Grope**

Sir,
    I am sure readers will have been amused to see Health Secretary Matt Hancock and his "advisor", Gina Coladangelo, seeking to emulate Rodin's statue, The Kiss, in the hallowed corridors of Whitehall.
    The Kiss was based on two characters borrowed from Dante's Divine Comedy who were slain by a betrayed husband who surprised them as they exchanged their first kiss. The two lovers were condemned to wander eternally through the Gates of Hell or, maybe in this case, No 10 Downing Street.

LYNNE BOOTH.

Chesney Hawkes   **Ursula von der Leyen**

Sir,
    Are European Commission President Ursula von der Leyen and one-hit wonder Chesney Hawkes perhaps related? Chesney gave the world a brilliant song, whereas Ursula finally granted what could be the UK's One And Only chance to re-gain control of our laws, money and borders.

PETER CARDWELL.

Kryten   **Biden**

Sir,
    Have any of your readers noticed the similarity between genial, bumbling, avuncular android Kryten from TV sitcom Red Dwarf and incoming US president "Uncle: Joe Biden?

MICHAEL PANTELI.

Meerkat   **Sheikh Mohammed**

Sir,
    Observe the meerkats.
PETE DAVIES.

Giuliani   **Von Aschenbach**

Sir,
    Have any of your readers noticed the remarkable resemblance between Gustav Von Aschenbach, tragic hero of Death in Venice (played by Dirk Bogarde), and Rudy Giuliani, modern-day tragic anti-hero? Perhaps they are related? I think we should be told.

JOHN WHITFIELD.

Pickles   **Blobby**

Sir,
    Just wondered what the connection was between Eric "Mr Lobby" Pickles and Mr Blobby?

MIKE FOSTER.

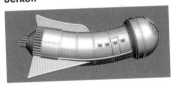

Jerkoff

Besos

Sir,
    I couldn't help but notice the striking similarity between Jeff Bezos' New Shepard spacecraft, and that designed by Professor Flexi Jerkoff in the classic Flesh Gordon.
    Did he design both? I think we should be told.

JOHN DAVEY.

Wallis   **Meghan**

Sir,
    Has anyone noticed, as I have, the extraordinary similarity between the Duchess of Sussex and the former Duchess of Windsor?
    Perhaps they are related?

ENA B. HARRIS.

Boris Johnson MP
● Live   385,000,000 Views

People's Prime Minister's Question Time – Live on Fakebook

👍 Like   💬 Comment

0 people **like this**

(ENTERS TO 'THINGS CAN ONLY GET BETTER' BY D.REAM... WHICH IS RAPIDLY TAKEN OFF, WHEN SOMEONE REALISES IT'S BEEN USED BEFORE. REPLACED BY 'HIT THE ROAD, MAP' BY THE LATE RAY CHARLES)

Boris: Today's the **big** day, the day you've **all** been waiting for. The **day** when I reveal when the **other** big days are going to be. Yes, folks, the important thing is the **data** not the **dates**. So put **these** dates in your diary: March 8th, March 29th, April 12th, May 17th and June 21st. That's the **data** you need. **Quick** summary, March 8th **schools** going back, provided Year 7 wear **two** masks in the corridor or Year 2 wear **seven** masks, one of the two, **either** way parents can rest assured that from March 29th they can have a drink with **six** members of another household in the garden of their **hairdresser**, allowing them on April 12th to play **tennis** with their pub landlord,

providing they are both working at home, which means that on May 17th non-essential **gyms** can reopen with up to a **thousand** ticket holders so long as it's **outside**, leading the way to June 21st which is when **essential** key-worker **druids** can meet on the solstice of their choice for **weddings**, funerals and human **sacrifices**, if they so wish.

PM's Press Secretary: Oh God. What are you talking about?

Boris: Sorry, Allegra, Dilyn **ate** my notes.

PM's Press Secretary: Get on with the blustering boterism!

Boris: Yes, folks, **spring** has sprung and we can see in the **sunshine** the **crocus** of hope poking through the **frost** of despair. Or is it the **Crockus** of shit, poking through the **Lord Frost** of Brexit?

PM's Press Secretary: No, it isn't, just read the script.

Boris: It's **all** very well for you to say, Allegra, but Carrie's handwriting's pretty **hard** to decipher. Ah, this bit's in **caps**: 'THINGS TO DO: MAKE IT CLEAR THAT **YOU'RE** IN CHARGE AND **I'M** NOT TELLING YOU WHAT TO DO.' Will do, boss.

PM's Press Secretary: This is going terribly, let's have some questions.

Boris: Laura Koronaberg from the BBC... or, as **we** call it, the **Bye Bye** Corporation.

Laura Koronaberg: Prime Minister, this is all very cautious. Have you learned your lesson about overpromising and underdelivering?

Boris: Yes, from now on I'm **underpromising** and **overdelivering**. It's going to be **amazing**. I'm going to do it **so** well, I'll be the most **popular** underpromiser and overdeliverer the country has **ever** seen. **Next** question?

Robert Pestilence: Robert Pestilence, ITNNNNNNNNNNNN. Is a roadmap a good ideeeeeeaaa – given your government's habit of UUUUUUUUU-turns, hitting bumps in the road and swerrrrrrrrrving into a ditch, etceteraaaaaaa?

Boris: Absolutely **not.** I'm in the driving seat, **opening** up the map, turning it upside down, **obliterating** the view through the windscreen, **foot** on the gas, hands off the wheel, **nothing** could be safer!

Assembled journalists: Aaaaaaaaagh! We're all going to die! Time to reverse!

Boris: There's only **one** answer to that, and that's '**Next question**'. Let's have a European angle, from the **German** editor of Paris Thatch.

Herr Dressing: Guten tag, I would like to ask you a qvestion about the recent disaster, by vich I mean your haircut. Who committed zis outrage?

Boris: It was Carrie. She came at me with a pair of **scissors** and naturally I assumed the **worst**, but then she went for my **hair** instead.

PM's Press Secretary: Enough, Prime Minister, tell them your off-the-cuff joke about Keir Starmer. It's written in green.

Boris: Right, ha, **yes.** Now the thing about my honourable friend is that he **vacillates** – and wait for it, here it comes – we **vaccinate**! See what I did there? I'm **glad** you liked it, because we were going to introduce it **earlier**, but we weren't sure it would work and the Cabinet couldn't agree, so we **delayed** a bit. But now we're **rolling out** the joke and it's **96%** effective – and not much **more** effective when told **twice**! **Hoorah**!!!

(PRIME MINISTER EXITS TO SOUND OF KOOL AND THE FRIDGE'S CLASSIC DISCO HIT 'VACCINATE, GOOD TIMES, COME ON!')

Biden administration releases Khashoggi intelligence

by Our Diplomatic Staff **Jo Standing-Biden**

President Biden says his decision to release a 2018 US intelligence report showing that Saudi Crown Prince Mohammed bin Salman ordered the killing of journalist Jamal Khashoggi demonstrates how different his administration will be from that of Donald Trump's.

"Whereas Trump turned a blind eye to the killing and refused to sanction the Crown Prince, for fear it would damage the billions of dollars' worth of deals America does with the oil-rich kingdom," the President told reporters, "I will not shy away from hard truths. And one of those truths is that I will do exactly the same."

Faced with accusations that its response to Khashoggi's murder was as feeble as the Trump administration's, the White House furiously pointed out that, as a direct result of the release of this report, it had imposed sanctions on Saudi Prince BoxWhalla, a junior aide in the finance ministry, who once met Prince Salman briefly at a party in 2013.

Crown Prince Salman welcomed the lack of US sanctions being imposed on him, saying it would be stupid for President Biden to cut off his nose to spite his face, as that's the sort of thing that happens to Saudi dissidents.

"We're the Saudi Arabia of wind!"

MY YEAR IN LOCKDOWN HELL

Top columnist **Phil Space** writes

WHO'D HAVE thought a year has passed since my first lockdown article, and since then millions of words have been dedicated to the lockdown phenomenon? Here's my diary of Lockdown Fill. I mean Hell.

MARCH 2020 Lockdown begins. Write first piece about lockdown beginning.

APRIL Lockdown continues. Write a piece about my first month in lockdown.

MAY Discover Zoom and write first piece about not wearing trousers whilst not wearing trousers!

JUNE Lockdown disaster! Editor won't take another piece about sourdough bread.

JULY Lockdown triumph! Write first 'Top 100 Must-See Lockdown Box Sets' feature.

AUGUST Lockdown lifted! Write article about adjusting to life post-lockdown.

SEPTEMBER Lockdown returns! Write article about adjusting to lockdown life post post-lockdown.

OCTOBER Lockdown depression! Editor won't take another piece about lockdown podcasts on lockdown hair.

NOVEMBER Lockdown insomnia! Stay awake all night worrying how I'm going to get another piece out of lockdown insomnia.

DECEMBER Advance lockdown Christmas piece turns out to be entirely inaccurate. Never mind – they run it anyway.

JANUARY Lockdown non-lockdown Christmas, eh? How did we all get it so wrong?

FEBRUARY To beard or not to beard? that is the question I ask the editor. He says, "Great – grow a beard, take a photo, write a piece – by lunchtime!"

MARCH 2021 It's one whole year since lockdown began. Commence anniversary piece: "My Lockdown Hell", as editor says don't mention Zoom, sourdough, box sets, hair, beards, insomnia, yoga classes, buying a dog, Joe Wicks, home schooling, home deliveries, working from home, or the problems of writing filler articles about lockdown. HELP!

Why this disastrous roadmap is a disaster for my industry which should be allowed to open up

by Industry Spokesperson
Ann Exception

OF COURSE I realise that the entire country has been affected by the pandemic and of course I welcome the government's cautious approach to easing lockdown for businesses, but whatever the wider public health considerations, the fact remains that my industry has been uniquely affected and remains a unique case for unique consideration.

So, whilst it is entirely appropriate for other sectors of the economy to remain closed, there can be no doubt that the situation is very different for our industry and that the balance of risk is entirely different.

This means that the only sensible course for this government is to let us start trading immediately, with no further restrictions, so that we can make up some of the vast amount of money we have thrown down the bloody toilet in the last year before *(cont. p94)*

Lady Macbeth

Writes exclusively for the **Daily Chain Mail**

'Why do men always call powerful women Lady Macbeth?' asks Lady Macbeth

IT'S THE same old boring story. As soon as men are confronted with a powerful, independent woman, with her own voice and opinions, she is immediately labelled as some sort of Lady Macbeth figure. How pathetic is that?

Take it from me, if a woman merely voices an innocent opinion to her husband, such as "Why don't you stab your colleague in the back and claim the mantle of power that is yours by right?", she is suddenly caricatured as a scheming psychopath.

The latest unfortunate victim of this rampant misogyny is Carrie, the partner of the current Thane of Westminister and World King, who, through no fault of her own, has managed to have all her husband's previous lieutenants assassinated and replaced by her own friends.

And, of course, the lazy male pundits are reaching for their Shakespeare and saying she is the ruthless power behind the throne and that she is the one with blood on her hands that no amount of washing will cleanse. Honestly!

And worst of all, they misquote her, claiming she said "Out! Out! Damned Spot!", when the dog's name, as everyone knows, is Dilyn. No, the whole thing is a tragic misrepresentation of historical events and the stuff of overwrought theatricals, rather than political journalism!

My advice to Carrie, as someone who has unjustly been given the title "Lady MacGove", is to find out who the jealous men briefing against her are and then to kill them all!! Just saying. No offence!!

© *Sarah Vile*

MARS PERSEVERANCE ROVER UPDATE

SENSATIONAL data comes back from the Red Planet, which changes our view of Mars forever. Now we know for sure that the following incredible facts are true:

■ Mars is quite boring

■ It makes the moon look quite interesting

■ $800 billion is a lot to spend for some pictures of red dust

■ Did we mention that it's quite dull?

"The rewildeing's going well"

Public approve higher tax

■ A survey has found that the public is prepared for higher taxes to pay for the government's unprecedented pandemic spending, provided someone else is paying them.

"Of course we have to balance the books and that has to mean higher taxes," agreed all voters.

"We fully support tax rises happening to someone else, as we haven't got two pennies to rub together right now. Haven't you heard? We're in the middle of a pandemic. So we're right behind this increase in taxes, so long as it doesn't apply to us."

ACTRESS SAYS SHE WAS GIVEN LARGER BREASTS IN MOVIE POSTER

by Our Hot Under The Collar Correspondent **RON SLEEZE**

An actress has said she was given digitally enhanced breasts in a poster for a film which came out ten years ago.

We are now pleased to reproduce this photo in full in today's paper, to show the dangers of digitally altering already attractive actresses and making them look even more attractive than they already are.

More on this story

■ See here for more full-page photos of attractive actress who has been given larger breasts in movie poster, just so we all know the dangers of digital enhancement

■ Click here for a photo gallery of attractive women who've been digitally altered to look even hotter than they were in the first place

■ Exclusive: middle-aged picture editor needs to have a bit of a lie-down

The Daily Telegruff

Friday 5 March 2021

He's messy, smelly and annoying, but I stand by him!

by Dilyn, Downing Street's First Dog, writing exclusively for the Telegruff

THE unpleasant briefing against my owner Boris is just a calculated attempt to undermine my position as unofficial Top Dog and to sow the seeds of discord between me and my best friend.

There are people who cannot bear anyone else to be close to me and will spread malicious rumours to try and destabilise the happy relationship that we enjoy in Downing Street.

Ok, so he creates a mess wherever he goes and pours wine on sofas and laptops.

Ok, so he humps the leg of any woman who comes through the door and I have to shout "Bad Prime Minister, down boy!" at him.

Ok, so he chews the carpet and is barking most of the time. He's a human for heaven's sake. That's what they do!

It is certainly no reason for me to get rid of Boris or for him to be put down. Yes, someone did shout "Can someone please shoot the fucking PM?", but it was meant more in jest than in earnest, and he was chewing the only copy of the roadmap at the time, which makes it understandable!

So can we be a bit more understanding of our two-legged friend and accept him for what he is – a randy mongrel who was "rescued" by me because I felt sorry for him and thought he might amuse and distract the country in difficult times?

© *Dilyn 2021*

On other pages

■ **Allison Poodle** writes: Isn't Dilyn great? **p2**

■ **Charles Paw** defends the Pedigree Chumocracy **p3**

■ **Christopher Howse-Trained** on Saint Fido, the little-known 14th century canine mystic **p94**

POETRY CORNER

In Memoriam Murray Walker, motor racing commentator

So. Farewell
Then Murray Walker.

"Bang! Off come
Mansell's Wheels,"
Yes, that was
Your catchphrase.

97 years.
That's a pretty
Good time.

But now the
Chequered flag
Has been
Waved.

Your race
Is run
And it has
All gone by
Too fast.

E.J. Thribb
(17½ laps)

GRADUATE CAREERS ADVICE

"I'm afraid the middle class is full"

CHINESE PARLIAMENT VOTES TO TIGHTEN CONTROL OF HONG KONG ELECTIONS

For the motion
2895

Against the motion
0

Abstention
1
(the late Mr Hu)

GLENDA SLAGG

She's man's best friend! Geddit!!!??!!

■ Hats and trousers off to Jon Snow – for becoming a dad again at the grand old age of 97 (subs – please check)!!??!! The news anchor for Channel Phwoar (Geddit???!!!) may be getting on a bit, but he can still keep it up for an hour a night, and then repeat it all again an hour later!!??!!! That's PRESENTING, I'm talking about, Mister Dirty-Minded Reader – he's on Channel Phwoar News followed by Channel Phwoar Plus One, I meant!!!?! And as for his love life – it's like his trademark socks and ties – impressive!!?!! Talk about socks appeal!?!!? (Geddit???!!! Jon certainly has it!!??!)

■ Put a sock in it, Jon Snow!??!! (See what I did there??!!?) It's YOU I'm talking to, Mister Channel Four-Letter-Word News!!??! What on EARTH were you thinking of, becoming a dad again at the grand old age of 103 (subs – please recheck)??!!? I've heard of romances that are May/December, but this is Snow joke!!??! No offence, Jon Snowflake, love your work and always impressed with the way you hold the government to account!!?! But still, you should treat your love life like one of your snazzy ties – and tie a knot in it!!??! (Geddit!!!???)

■ Hijab's off to Shamima Begum, the Jihadi Bride who's shed her burqa to show the world she's a Caliphate Cutie!!!?? Forget about I-SIS!!!?? It's I-CANDY more like!?!!! So come on, Priti Patel, show some compassion and mercy!!!??! Let Shamazing Shamima back into the country so we columnists can all have a go at you and demand La Begum, the Daesh Diva, be sent packing!!??!

■ Did you see the story about the telephone box library that's full of smutty books???!!? Talk about Fifty Shades of Red Faces!!!?!! Come on, Mr Yokel, it's HAMPshire – not HUMPshire!!??!! What were the good folk of (subs – please fill in village name) thinking of???!! A phone box is no place for raunchy reads and torrid tomes, Ms Librarian!!?? It's a place for dominatrix flyers and call-girl calling cards!!!!

Byeee!!

CENTENARY OF THE CHINESE COMMUNIST PARTY: REJECTED COMMEMORATIVE T-SHIRTS

DIARY

HENRY 'CHIPS' CHANNON: THE DIARIES 1917-38

1917: Paris. The war continues to take its toll. The Comtesse d'Hautpoul was beside herself with anxiety last night: three men short for a dinner party.

1918: News reaches us that Tommy Lawrence has been up to his old tricks, prancing about on a camel in, of all places, Arabia. If he thinks that playing the billygoat is the way to swing an invitation to the Devonshires' summer ball at Chatsworth, then I fear he is barking up the wrong tree.

1919: I have never met a human being so devoid of interest or charm as my father. Dull, dreary, selfish and bad-tempered, he deliberately drags his heels and takes up to four or five hours before cabling me the money I ask for. Does he think I've nothing better to do than sit around waiting for his cash to arrive? When it finally comes, I treat myself to a new limousine resplendent with fittings of crimson and gold. The crimson will serve to remind one of the blood shed by one's hapless contemporaries dans les tranchées. It's the least one can do.

1920: Feeling exhausted and horribly over-worked. After a frenetic morning struggling to powder my hair and match a bow-tie with my new silk pantalons, I managed to pull myself to luncheon with Princesse Violette Murat. In the afternoon, I attempted to relax, but the vulgar shade of the curtains – wisteria! – proved impossibly distracting.

1921: Forty-three people have tried to make love to me this past week. Forty-four, if one includes oneself.

1922: Was there ever anyone quite so common as Lord Curzon?

1924: Joseph Conrad has died. A common Pole of negligible talent who made no effort to hide his foreign accent, he must have imagined that penning wordy books about getting soaking wet at sea might provide him with an entrée into the aristocracy, but in that he was mistaken.

1929: Cliveden. A squat little hut of a place. On my first visit, I mistook it for a gatehouse, and demanded to be directed to the main building. I said nothing to poor Nancy Astor, of course, preferring to congratulate her on its cosiness, easiness of heating, and so forth. But Blenheim is so much more roomy.

1933: My wedding day arrives. By wonderful chance, my bride is the eldest daughter of the Earl of Iveagh, heiress to the Guinness brewing fortune, and as attractive as a woman can be. Thoughtful friends keep reminding me of her Christian name. In conversation with her, I take special care to mention it every now and then: a thoughtful touch that will surely stand me in good stead should I wish to consolidate our marriage in the future.

1935: I am elected to parliament. A kindly little man at the House of Commons takes the trouble to inform me that my constituency is in Essex, which comes as quite a shock. But if one is keen to establish a parliamentary presence, it is as well to come armed with these funny little details.

July: To Emerald Cunard's for luncheon. Lady Troutmore introduces me to a mousey little thing called Wallis Simpson, horribly plain, common, dull, unashamedly American and exhibiting nothing of interest beyond a prominent mole. Why must one be bothered with these femmes ordinaires?

August: I am reliably informed that the Prince of Wales is quite smitten with Mrs Simpson. When I encountered her over luncheon last month, we struck up an immediate rapport, and we vowed to see each other again. She is a remarkable woman, a brilliant conversationalist, yes, but also strangely alluring, refreshingly American, and with the most delicate hint of a mole.

1936: Hermann Goring is a poppet. A large, jovial figure, perhaps a little on the plump side, but dressed in a most becoming crisp white uniform with shiny gold medals, clinking away. Why do none of our own politicians exude such bonhomie?

With customary largesse, Hermann hosted un déjeuner intime for 650. One found oneself placed next to Frau Goebbels, who is never easy. In an effort to break the ice, I asked her if she had heard what Emerald Cunard had said about Lavinia, Duchess of Abercrombie, but drew a blank. Thankfully, she livened up considerably when filling me in on Germany's marvellous strides towards international peace.

"Fascinating!" I replied. "I must remember to tell the Duke and Duchess of Cholmondeley when I get back – do you know Frank and Clarissa, at all?" But sadly these attempts to "broaden out" our conversation proved fruitless.

After coffee, Hermann invited us to put our heads around the door of the Olympic stadium. We delighted in watching slender young men in next-to-nothing leaping about and hurling little sticks and what-not hither and thither. One of them had the thickest auburn hair, and reminded me of the dashing young Prince Baltasar of Spain, a close friend of Duchesse de Brissac, whom I encountered in a discreet armoire at Blenheim the summer before last.

1937: Thanks to Joachim von Ribbentrop, I am given a guided tour of one of the prettiest labour camps in all of Germany. One has heard so many tales of the "hardships" in these camps, but quite the reverse! They are wonderfully tidy, spruce and even gay, and the boys, all about 18, are all fair, healthy and sun-tanned. Apparently, Adolf Hitler is the most gracious host, and makes every effort to ensure that bad hats and moaning minnies disappear, of their own accord.

1938: This morning, my wife, who, as I may have mentioned, is the eldest daughter of the Earl of Iveagh, and very much a woman, chanced upon me sorting through our bedroom cupboard with our under-butler. To ensure our clothes were not creased in the process, we had first removed them. Over luncheon, my wife remains silent. It is almost as though she would prefer to see one in creased clothing. Has she no breeding?

As told to
CRAIG BROWN

DESPERATE BUSINESS

JON & MICK / MODERN TOSS

congratulations your probation period is over

does that mean I have to work here?

Delivery

Cheers, that'll be a pair of socks, saves me going all the way upstairs to get some out of a drawer

Guys, just realised I'm going to have to wrap this meeting up, I've got a 3.15 with Columbo

INTERVIEW

how would other people describe you?

Steve?

nice dog, what breed is it?

dunno, I only got it so I don't look like a pervert when I'm down the park

VIGIL SHAME
NO ONE TO BE SACKED

Who says we don't protect women?

POLICE LOG
Neasden Central Police Station

09.34 Officers gather to hear about new project 'Operation Gentle Touch', shortly to be launched across Greater Neasden area before planned protests in Neasden Park. Officers will spread out across area, offering advice and support on a person-by-person basis, reassuring the public that their safety is paramount and gently encouraging them to return home.

17.23 With crowds refusing to politely disperse, and worrying radical elements from the Neasden Libraries Campaign showing up, officers call in support from surrounding branches to encourage protesters to return home immediately, as a matter of urgent public safety (ie theirs). The Neasden Chopper is launched to monitor the situation and 200 officers from surrounding branches slowly move protesters into a smaller and smaller area.

18.12 Crowds are now breaching Covid security guidelines and are blaming police for "moving us into a smaller and smaller area". Officers respond to increasing hostility by calmly and sensitively deploying tasers, big bright lights and SMPC (Shoulder-Mounted Peace Cannons), in the name of calming community tensions. 'Operation Gentle Touch' is re-classified as 'Operation Get On The Floor Now'.

"From now on, two's company, three's a demonstration"

KenPyne

EYE EXCLUSIVE!
LATE ROYAL NEWS

■ Friends of Meghan call for Kate to be arrested after flouting Vigil regulations. "Meghan has reached out to the police and demanded that the Duchess be put in jail, but only in a compassionate way."

Cressida Dick defends police vigil tactics

by Our Police Violence Correspondent **Ed Butts**

MET POLICE Commissioner Cressida Dick has defended the shocking scenes at the Clapham Common vigil for Sarah Everard, saying trouble there only started as night fell.

"During the day, the vigil was lovely and peaceful with Kate Middleton and other lovely women playing their respects in a lovely and dignified manner," Cressida told reporters. "But as night fell, they were joined by a group of men intent on causing trouble and provoking violence, described by one woman in attendance as 'the police'.

"Once the police arrived it was inevitable that things were going to kick off, especially given that some of the women in attendance were seen brandishing floral tributes in an aggressive manner whilst others were in possession of sharp opinions.

"You have to remember this was taking place in South London. There's no telling how many of these women were wearing backpacks, and could later have jumped the barriers at Stockwell station and turned into international terrorists who would have to be gunned down and killed."

How about some restraint?

She's right... get the handcuffs, Sarge!

World's first tweet sold for $2.9 million

THIS week, Twitter founder Jack Dorsey sold the first ever tweet in history for an extraordinary sum.

The tweet read: "Just setting up my twttr."

Top online auction house Gnomebys.com commented, "Wait till you see the second tweet ever sent. We're hoping for much more money for this digital artwork for the ages."

The second tweet reads: "Fuck off Dorsey you fascist. Hope you die of cancer. LOL."

(Rotters.com)

"I get fed up patrolling the same boring route, night after night..."

Jan.

Goldman Sachs: concerns over 95-hour week

by Our Wall Street Correspondent **Gordon Gekko**

The chief executive of Goldman Sachs, David Solomon, has expressed shock after a group of young analysts revealed they were working a 95-hour week, saying he had no idea there were such lazy slackers working at the investment firm.

"That means they're only working 14 hours a day, seven days a week. Who are these snowflakes?" asked the shouty man wearing a pinstripe suit and braces.

"When I was a junior analyst I was expected to work 36 hours in the one day, regularly putting in 200 hours' work every week."

Mr Solomon said he would also personally intervene over claims the trainees were being shouted at and humiliated, to shout at them and humiliate them some more.

"When the trainees talk about never seeing their families, you need to keep in mind that's just one of the major upsides of the job – the others being hookers on tap 24/7 and the opportunity to develop a massive drug problem.

"I agree these kids starting out in the city have to draw the line somewhere, then snort that line, do another one, and get back to their desks to go the extra mile for the client."

LORD FROST
IRONY METER CAN'T COPE AND BLOWS UP

Hardline Brexiteer argues that Britain should not be run by unelected bureaucrats

Brexiteer bureaucrat is made unelected member of the House of Lords and appointed to the Cabinet as Brexit Minister

---

Daily Telegraph Friday 5 March 2021

Letters to the Editor

The Last Test?

SIR – As a lifelong connoisseur of leather on willow, I am both shocked and appalled by the English Cricket Board's proposals for a new-fangled format of the truly Beautiful Game.

The so-called "The Hundred", in which each team is expected to play an innings of one hundred balls, is nothing short of a travesty, and a betrayal of the historic ethos of Test Cricket.

To expect eleven English batsmen to survive for that many deliveries without throwing away all of their wickets is frankly preposterous.

Might I suggest to the august powers at Lord's that the game be rebranded, if indeed it must, as "The Fifty" or, more realistically, "The Thirty", or, if we progress the way we have on the current tour of India, perhaps "The Ten".

Only then can we hope to see a satisfactory day's play. I trust you will forgive me for writing this letter, but I find myself with an unexpected three days to fill.

I remain your humble servant,

Sir Herbert Gussett,
The Old Pavilion,
Sticky Wicket-on-the-Mud,
Hurts LBW 001.

"I made biscuits – they're very Moore-ish"

BBC job shock

THERE was outrage yesterday when a BBC job was not given to Amol Rajan.

The prestigious post of Traffic Correspondent for Radio Cornwall's '*Good Morning Land's End* show became vacant last week, yet Rajan was overlooked in favour of local woman Penny Pothole.

Said a furious BBC insider, "Amol could easily have combined the role with his other jobs, presenting *The Today Programme*, *Start the Week*, *The One Show*, *The 6 O'Clock News*, *The 10 O'Clock News*, *Newsnight*, *You and Yours*, *Antiques Roadshow*, *Top Gear*, *CBeebies* and appearing in *The Archers*."

The insider continued, "There are at least 5 minutes in the day when Amol is not on telly or radio, and I see no reason why he shouldn't be telling us about a build-up of sheep behind a caravan on the B74302 outside Penzance."

Late News

■ BBC insider has now been replaced by Amol Rajan.

Covid tests positive for Assad

THE situation in Syria this week took another grim twist as it was revealed that the coronavirus had tested positive for the toxic and deadly Assad-19.

Said the coronavirus, "This is deeply worrying. Assad can cause untold damage, particularly to the weak and the vulnerable. Long Assad can last for decades and cause endless misery."

It is nearly ten years since the World Health Organization pronounced that Assad was a threat to humanity, and Assad has since forced lots of people to social distance – by following the so-called "two countries" rule of putting at least two national borders between themselves and their homeland.

Said the coronavirus, "It's been a terrible year, I thought I was over the worst when I managed to shake off Johnson and then Trump, but now I've got this new Syrian variant. I have no idea how I'm going to get rid of him."

(Rotters)

Clerihew Corner

Sheikh Mohammed Bin Rashid Al Maktoum
Keeps his daughter in a locked-up room
Unlike poor Latifa, he's often seen
Out hobnobbing with HM The Queen.

You couldn't lock up Andrew, could you?

HEIR OF SORROWS

by Dame Sylvie Krin, author of *Duchess of Hearts* & *You're Never Too Old*

THE STORY SO FAR: It is the night of the Big Interview and in Claret House, one couple in particular are nervously glued to their television set...

"ARE you going to spend the entire evening behind the sofa, Chazza?" rasped Camilla, as she lit up a nerve-soothing Nevergoingtobeking-size Marlborough College Lite.

A tremulous voice replied from behind the John Louis XVth Debenham sofa. "It's just appalling. How much longer is this going to go on for?"

"Another 87 minutes, Chazza. It's just started and she's barely put the boot in yet."

"What about Harry?"

"Oh, he's just a bit part, he's coming on at the end."

The heir to the throne crawled uneasily around and onto the chaise longueur, hiding his face behind a cushion, as on the screen the familiar face of Meghan, the Duchess of Sparkle, held back the tears. Movingly, she described how much she admired the Queen and how disappointed she was to find that the people working for the monarch had all clearly disobeyed their boss and jealously conspired against Meghan.

"The Palace couldn't cope with a strong, independent woman," complained the Duchess of Onion to her sympathetic interlocutor, the legendary Oprah Whingey. At this, Camilla burst out laughing, spraying gin and tonic all over Charles' tweed pyjamas. "What do you think the Queen is, darling?" she shouted at the television. "And who do you think gave you the chop?"

Charles lowered the William Morrissey-designed cushion only to see Meghan tenderly empathising with a group of rescue hens.

"I love rescuing things," she said compassionately, "including headless, lost chickens like Harry."

Oprah laughed conspiratorially as the two sat in the agreeable Californian sunshine, before an advert broke the spell and the former cake-show host, Scandi Toksvig, tried to sell 11 million Britons a tub of Carte d'Orful ice cream to warm them up in the cold March weather.

But the relief was temporary and it was time to move spontaneously to the agreed discussion about how ghastly the Duchess of Cambridge was.

"This is my truth," said Meghan, "even if it's different from everyone else's." Oprah nodded sagely as the Duchess continued, "I don't want to disparage Kate. Kate's a good person. But Kate made me cry. But then Kate apologised. And I forgive Kate. Because I'm an even gooder person than she is. I certainly don't want to disparage Kate for reducing me to tears and then lying about it and then letting the falsehoods go uncorrected. Kate's great."

Oprah swooped with an incisive "Wow…" An argument over bridesmaids' dresses had lit a timebomb that, with Oprah's help, would put an end to the 1200-year history of the British monarchy. Oprah knew she had a scoop – and not of Carte d'Orful ice cream!

"This was the turning point," said Meghan, as indeed it was for the whole interview, and suddenly Meghan dispensed with the pleasantries and went in for the kill, with the forensic precision of a top TV lawyer from the series *Suits You Sir*.

Charles watched on in horror, as a smiling Meghan accused an unnamed member of the Firm of being racist towards her son, Archewell Foundation Mountbatten Windsor™. Oprah's jaw dropped in a perfect cutaway that was clearly not in any way rehearsed. "Woah, woah! What are you saying here, sister? Let me get this straight. You're telling me that the whole Royal Family are members of the Ku Klux Klan, White Supremacy is openly supported by the entire British population, and one of the princes is a member of the Proud Boys?"

Meghan diplomatically batted her eyelashes, immaculately made up with Di-Panorama 95 Max Factor mascara, and answered enigmatically, "You may well come to that conclusion and in that case you would certainly be justified."

AT this point, Harry appeared on screen, happily attired in Californian leisurewear, rather than Nazi uniform. He sat down beside his beloved wife and gripped her hand firmly. "I agree with everything Meghan's just said, especially the racist bit – but I will never discuss that conversation with anyone."

The tension in the room in Claret House was suddenly broken by the antique Bakeoffalite telephone with its ancient trill. Charles picked up the receiver.

"Hello…? Of course I'm watching!" Charles recognised the voice at once, from endless family parties. But then his face fell. "What's that you say? 'Which one's Meghan and which one's Oprah?' They all look the same to you? You simply can't say that in this day and age!" He put down the receiver sharply. "That really is… what's the word?"

"Appalling," said Camilla quickly, keen to find out more. "Who on earth was that, Chazza?"

But Charles was tight-lipped. "I can't possibly say. It would be very damaging to them and I will never discuss that conversation with anyone."

As Meghan and Harry continued to swing the wrecking-ball into his mother's life's work and his entire future, a horrified Charles pondered aloud, "I mean, who started this tawdry royal interview business?"

"You did, Chazza!" replied Camilla, "When you spilt the beans about us to Dimblebum back in the day. Didn't do you any good. Or me." She looked at him

meaningfully as she filled her glass to the brim with Bryony Gordon's gin, leaving little room for the Saturday Night Fevertree Tonic.

"What I can't stand is the self-pity," he continued. "Where did Harry get that whiny, entitled attitude from? Why does he blame the rest of the world and particularly me? It's just not fair."

Camilla guffawed. She was enjoying this evening far more than she'd imagined and was now glad she had resisted Charles' attempts to take over the remote and watch Masterchef with Gregg Sausageroll.

"It certainly proves he's your son, Chazza. All that refusal to take responsibility for his own actions – that's your boy! And to think, when he was born we all gossiped about what colour the baby's hair was. Ginger! Ha!"

Charles could not help thinking of the famous dictum: History, as so often, was repeating itself – the first time as farce, and then again as farce. He turned back to the screen, where Harry was describing his brother and father as being trapped in a gilded cage with no hope of escape.

"I'm not trapped and I'm going to send a letter to the Telegraph saying so."

"They won't let you do that, Chazza," said his wise companion. "And by 'they' I mean 'she'."

On the television, Harry was saluting the aforementioned, all-powerful Queen.

"She's my grandma, I love her, I'm totally loyal to her. She's my Colonel-in-Chief."

"Not any more, mate! She stripped you of every rank," chortled Camilla.

"It's a fairy tale!" Meghan agreed with a neat, not at-all-scripted summation of their narrative of the journey they were on. "Life is about storytelling and I've told a great big one tonight. It's just like the Little Mermaid, the beautiful clever girl gets her Prince, loses her voice and then finds it again…"

"And it's all extremely fishy," shouted Camilla at the 94-inch Pandemasonic plasma screen, a gift, like Meghan's charming blood diamond earrings, from his Highness Mohammed Bin Linah of Saudi Arabia.

The most important broadcast of the 21st Century ended with Meghan reminding viewers that *The Little Mermaid* was available on the Disney Channel, she was available for cartoon voiceover work, and that Oprah and Harry's mental health show was on Apple TV. And then it was time for the adverts.

"That's it, it's all over, Chazza," laughed Camilla.

"No, it can't be! I haven't been King yet!"

"I meant the programme, cloth-ears!"

"I'm not so sure," murmured the man who was, for now, still heir to the historic throne. But as the logo for Harpie Productions faded from the screen, so too did Charles' long-held vision of his future destiny. Was it the end? Were those the final credits? Was it now time to succumb to temptation and send an equerry out to buy some Carte d'Orful ice cream?

(To be continued…?)

MEGHAN INTERVIEW ROCKS PALACE

BIGGEST ROYAL SCANDAL IN 85 YEARS*

*If you don't count a prince who was best friends with a notorious paedophile who killed himself in jail to avoid trial, and who is refusing to be questioned by the FBI about his involvement in sex-trafficking underage girls.

MR PIERS MORON
An Apology

FOR a number of years we have conducted a campaign of vilification against the above-named gentleman, a well-known journalist and television personality, invariably referred to in our pages with the controversial soubriquet of "Moron". Headlines such as "Is Moron a terrific charlatan and crook?" may well have conveyed the impression that we regarded Mr Moron as someone considerably less scrupulous than the majority of our readers.

We now realise that there was never a jot or scintilla of truth in any of our comments and, in light of his recent remarks about the Duchess of Sussex, we would like to make it clear that we wholeheartedly salute Mr Moron as a champion of free speech and a valiant crusader for the truth.

We would like to apologise to Mr Moron* for any offence occasioned by our previous references.

*We regret that, owing to the restrictions on our production processes caused by the Covid pandemic, we are unable to rectify the unfortunate typographical error that has been pre-programmed into the system.

PRINCESS SAYS 'I FEEL TRAPPED' AND BLAMES ROYAL FAMILY

by Our Court Correspondent **Ali Babarus**

The world did not pay much attention at all when Princess Latifa complained that she had spent many months in total lock-up in the Royal Palace in Dubai.

She said that she had not been allowed to go out and said that the Palace was telling lies about her and her mental health.

"We should be very concerned," said a media spokesman, "and Latifa's video where she accuses her father of abducting her against her will should send shockwaves throughout the globe."

He continued, "She has been through hell, but she's not exactly Meghan Maktoum, is she?"

EYE'S ROYAL INTERVIEW QUIZ

HOW WILL YOU SCORE IN THIS PALACE PUZZLER?

ALL YOU have to do is spot the logical fallacy in Harry and Meghan's reasoning, as featured in their historic ratings-busting Oprah interview

1. I don't read the tabloids, but they are so unpleasant I had to leave the country.

2. The racism in Britain was so bad we've come to the United States.

3. For security reasons, it's better to live in a country where everyone has a gun.

4. As a mere A-list actress on a top-rated show I was totally unprepared to enter the media spotlight.

5. We wanted our son to be a royal prince, although royalty is a gilded cage that makes people trapped and unhappy.

6. As an American actress and friend of Hollywood celebrities, I did not have the phone number of a therapist.

7. My letter to my father is deeply private, Harry's unanswered phone call to his father should be shared with the world.

8. Meghan is not to blame for me leaving the royal family. I couldn't have done it without her.

9. I'm broke, apart from the millions my mother left me.

10. I love my grandmother so much I'm completely loyal to her. Fuck you, granny.

Did you spot any logical howlers? Tell us how you scored and we'll send you a signed chicken!

JOY AS CARE HOMES REOPEN TO VISITORS

by Our Care Home Correspondent **Dee Mentia**

THERE was widespread joy across Britain that, following the succesful vaccination rollout, care homes would be reopening to visitors, meaning families across Britain will once again be allowed to dream up excuses not to visit Granny.

"We'd love to go and see my Mum, as we've all missed her so much, but the eldest has resumed school football training, so sadly this weekend is a wipeout," said 43-year-old Emily in Cirencester.

"It has been hell not being allowed to visit Granny, so we're overjoyed that this weekend we can see her... not that we will be going, as we're all exhausted from the children being back at school and we still haven't found a new cleaner to replace Maria who went home to Poland in October," said Felicity in Buckinghamshire.

"We can't wait to go visit Grandad, unless the weather is good, as we can now meet people outdoors again, can't we? Hurrah! I'm sure he'd understand us postponing, as Toby and I have been cooped up here with the kids in this tiny five-bedroom house and massive garden for months now and we'd like to go *(cont. p94)*

MACRON NOW SAYS YES TO ASTRA-ZENECA VACCINE

At least the phrase *volte-face* is French!

Boris Johnson MP
● Live

People's Prime Minister's Question Time – Live on Fakebook

385,000,000 Views

👍 Like   💬 Comment

0 people like this

(SOMBRE MUSIC)

(PRIME MINISTER APPEARS WITH LIGHTED CANDLE IN DESIGNER HOLDER BOUGHT BY PRIME MINISTER'S SPECIAL ADVISOR [SYMONDS, C] FROM 'I SAW YOU COMING' ORGANIC LIGHTING SHOP [£2,600 – CANDLE NOT INCLUDED])

Boris: **Serious** face. Hair **extra** messed **up**. Looking like **elderly** version of own **father**. So, one year **on** and it's time for us **all** to **reflect** on all those whom we've we **lost**. And let's take a **minute** to think about the **departed**, particularly Dominic **Cummings** and **more** than a minute's silence from **him** would be **very** welcome. (WIPES TEARS FROM EYE, COURTESY OF ONION FROM 'I SAW YOU COMING' ORGANIC GROCERY SHOP [£260 – NOT INCLUDING HOME DELIVERY]). Who'd have thought **Dom**, of all people, would rewrite **history** to make himself look **good**? It's also time to pay **tribute** to those who have played such a **crucial** part in our response to the pandemic. I'm thinking of those on the front **line**, like Matt Hancock, who's **selflessly** put himself forward on **breakfast** television, **exposing** himself to the very **real** danger of Susanna **Reid** and I don't think I can say often **enough** how grateful I am to Matt for taking the **blame**. And I don't know **where** I'd be without Dido **Harding**,

but then **she** doesn't know where I am either. But I can't name **everyone**, because I'd pretty **soon** end up naming **myself**. And with that **sombre** thought, I now **must** leave you.

(PRIME MINISTER EXITS INTO SIDE ROOM FOR MEETING WITH 1822 COMMITTEE OF CONSERVATIVE BACKBENCHERS. MARIACHI-STYLE MEXICAN FIESTA MUSIC PLAYS)

Boris: What ho, **chaps**! That's **enough** of Mr Sombre, now it's Mr **Sombrero**. (PUTS ON SOMBRERO AND SHAKES MARACAS) **Olé**! Well, it's all going **incredibly** well and this **vaccine** is going to save us **all**. In fact, it's a vaccine passport to **success**! For **me** in the next election. And **what's** the lesson we **learn** from the vaccine? Yes, my friends, capitalism **works**! Greed is **good**!

(SILENCE)

Boris: Oh, that bit of Bozzbantz didn't get the **roars** of laughter I was expecting. **Cheer** up, Gloomsters! And why are you **all** on your phones? **Cripes**! Don't leak the **greed** bit, obviously. We need to **contain** that quote. We **don't** want it getting out there. It could be very dangerous and **spread** like, erm, what's the **expression**...? Well, it could **go** viral anyway.

(PRIME MINISTER'S PRESS SECRETARY RACES IN, HOLDING PHONE WHICH IS PINGING REPEATEDLY)

Prime Minister's Press Secretary: What have you said now? I told you you should let me do the talking.

Boris: All I was **doing**, Allegra, was quoting that **brilliant** Michael Douglas film, where the **bunny**-boiler comes after the **innocent** adulterous chappie... No, maybe that was the other one. This was the one with the **chap** in the city, Gordon Brown, **no**, Gecko, who **explains** the profit motive and **lives** by the mantra "Greed is **good**". Also said "**Lunch** is for wimps", on which I **beg** to differ...

Prime Minister's Press Secretary: You didn't say it about the vaccine rollout, did you?

Boris: Ermmm, I might have done.

Prime Minister's Press Secretary: But that's wrong. Particularly about AstraZeneca. It's simply not true.

Boris: And your **point** is? Blimey, sometimes I **wonder** about you, Allegra. All I said was "**forget** philanthropy, it's **all** about fill-your-bootsery"! Eh, chaps?

(MORE SILENCE, AS ASSEMBLED MPS LEAK LATEST REMARKS ONTO TWITTER)

Boris: Oh, **come** on now, chums! Get off your phones! Don't you **know** the meaning of the word "loyalty"? Oh hello Carrie!

(PRIME MINISTER'S SPECIAL ADVISER ENTERS)

Boris: And before you **ask**, what I actually said was "**Green** is good", isn't it, darling? Feel **free** to leak that, fellahs!

(MORE SILENCE, AS ASSEMBLED MPS FAIL TO LEAK PITIFUL COVER-UP)

Boris: Right, that's enough of **you** lot. I'm going back into the **sombre** room, it's more **fun** there.

(BORIS RETURNS TO PM'S BRIEFING ROOM, WHERE PROFESSOR SCAREYOUWHITTYLESS AND SIR PATRICK VALIUMNEEDED ARE WARNING THE UK ABOUT THE INEVITABILITY OF A THIRD WAVE)

Whittyless: I'm afraid holidays are off for this year and probably forever.

Valiumneeded: I think that's a bit optimistic actually.

Boris: **Truly** these are **tough** times.

Whittyless: Why are you wearing a sombrero?

Boris: **Cripes**, wrong **hat**, wrong **face**, wrong **mood**! Let me **assure** you, that I will never forget this **harrowing** time and I will always be aware of how **lucky** I was to **survive**. As Prime Minister.

(BROKEN CANDLE-HOLDER SETS FIRE TO PRIME MINISTER'S TROUSERS, NECESSITATING THE END OF SOLEMN ANNIVERSARY BRIEFING)

Boris: **Yarooo**! Where are those Mexican firemen, José and Hose B?!!! I'm here all **week**, folks. **Help**, my bants **are** on fire!! See what I did there?

(PRIME MINISTER LEAVES SOLEMN BRIEFING AND RE-ENTERS ROOM OF LOYAL TORY COLLEAGUES – WHICH IS NOW EMPTY)

SOOTHSAYER IN GRIM WARNING

Beware the slides of March!

nhs.uk/coronavirus

"These Sunday afternoons really feel interminable"

"It's Tuesday"

Test and trace rejects criticism

by Our Economic Staff
Princess Dido

NHS Test and Trace has rejected criticism by the public accounts committee that it has proved ineffective despite the £37 billion the government has spent on it.

"We have been unable to find one person in the country who agrees with you on this," a furious Baroness Dido Harding told the committee. "And that was after weeks of trying.

"We spent a huge amount of money, but still could not find anyone annoyed that a system set up by the government after the first lockdown to prevent future lockdowns did absolutely nothing to prevent two further lockdowns and cost the taxpayer 37 billion quid. That's a pretty ringing endorsement of us if you ask me."

Bottomless pit insists it's good value for money

by Our NHS Staff **Tracy Test**

A bottomless pit today defended itself against accusations that it wasn't good value for money after there was criticism of the government's decision to shovel tens of billions of pounds of taxpayers' money into it.

"How dare people accuse me of being a complete waste of money?" said the bottomless pit, furiously. "The only reason I haven't delivered on my promises is that I haven't had nearly enough money shoved into me."

The government agreed that the problems with the effectiveness of the bottomless pit was entirely down to the government not shoving enough money into the bottomless pit, as it shovelled another £15 billion into it.

"You know the old saying," Health Secretary Matt Hancock told the Commons, "when you're in a hole, give the owner of the hole lots of money because they seem nice."

Lockdown joy as restrictions ease

by Our Pandemic Correspondent
Vic Scene

THERE was widespread joy across England as the easing of lockdown rules meant that people could finally do what they've already been doing for the past month.

"It'll be so wonderful that we can meet up with groups of six people in the park as we have been for the last month," agreed everyone.

"And finally we're allowed to entertain people in our garden, as we have been doing ever since the weather improved at the start of March.

"We were all saying at a dinner party with friends at the weekend just how hard this lockdown has been, not seeing anyone, and how we all can't wait for April when we'll finally be allowed to meet people indoors again."

Toby Hitchingpole-Brewer-Fox

The Contrarian Voice that tells it like it isn't

FOR the last 12 months the government has been trying to control every aspect of our lives and impose a nightmare authoritarian dictatorship on a once free people based on the evidence of so-called scientists. I TOLD YOU TO IGNORE THEM. Now this same government and the same scientists are telling us that "things are getting better" and it is time to "ease the lockdown". DO NOT BELIEVE THEM. DO NOT BELIEVE THEIR MOUTHPIECES IN THE MAINSTREAM MEDIA. THEY ARE LYING. Now is the time to be really worried and to wear two masks, lock yourself in your basement, and never come out, ever again. TRUST ME.
© *The Maily Spectatorgraph*

ON OTHER PAGES

"Has lockdown affected our mental health?" ask all our bonkers columnists

"Don't you worry, I'm still having fun"

ME AND MY SPOON

MATT HANCOCK

Do you have a favourite spoon?

Before coming to my point, could I begin by paying a heart-felt tribute to you and your colleagues for the brilliant way in which you have worked so tirelessly throughout the Covid Crisis and I would like, on behalf of all the readers of this column, to take the opportunity to say a HUGE THANK YOU to those of you whom I know have been working flat-out, 24/7, to ensure that the supply of spoon-based editorial content has been maintained, despite the many operational challenges that have stood in your way when faced with a crisis unparalleled in the long history of your magazine. I would suggest, to show our gratitude, that readers, on a date and at a time to be agreed, should stand outside our homes and bang our spoons together, as a way of showing our heartfelt appreciation for the truly magnificent work that all of those involved in the publication of *Me and My Spoon* – interviewers, designers, print-workers, distributors *(That's enough interview. Ed.)*

School news

St Cakes

Misogyny Term begins today. There are 279 alleged offenders in the school and 37 girls. R.J. Toxic-Masculinity (Predators) is Head of Harassment and Miss A. Non (Inquiries) is Head Whistleblower. Cover-ups will be held on June 23rd. The Social Media Studies course has been suspended until further notice. There will be a governors' meeting every day until the end of the term or the school, whichever is sooner. Parents' evening has been postponed until the possibly outgoing Headmaster, Mr Kipling, has finished helping the police with their *(That's enough of this. Ed.)*

Bridgerton lead actor tipped to be new Bond – the Eye reveals those new Bridgerton Bond films in full

- The Spy Who Wooed Me
- Thundermaskedball
- Swoonraker
- Live and Let Duel
- Quantum of Bodice
- On His Majesty George III's Secret Service
- Ne'er Say Ne'er Again
- The Man with the Golden Embroidered Waistcoat
- The World is not Snuff
- From Prussia with Love
- Apothecary No

All written by Phoebe Waller-Bridgerton

A Bridgerton Too Far

MR LOBBY IS BACK!

HE'S been out of the public eye since 2016 when 'Dave's House Party' was suddenly cancelled. But now, despite public demand, the pink roly-poly figure of fun is back.

Yes, it's Mr Lobby! Keeping us amused with new idiotic antics, and his inimitable catchphrase: "Lobby! Lobby! Lobby!"

His new sketch has already had millions in tears of laughter and disbelief as he loses a fortune.

He then, even more hilariously, tries to claw it back by breaking the anti-lobbying sleaze rules that he himself implemented when he lived at Number 10, Crinkley Bottom.

Okay, so the new character, Dishi Rishi, who doesn't help him out, is a bit thin and unfunny, but in every great double act you've got to have a straight man to go with a crooked man.

Dear Sir,
We represent Mr Lobby, and the suggestion that our client, Mr Lobby, was in some way trying to lobby Mr Sunak in order to further his own interests is deeply defamatory and sadly true. All the same, see you in court. Lolly! Lolly! Lolly!

UK PUBLIC VERY SAD TO HEAR CAMERON LOST MILLIONS

Returning to the office
A guide

■ Do not talk to your colleagues as if they are children or pets

■ Wear clothes, especially trousers

■ Do not talk to yourself, instead talk to other

■ Attempt light conversation, not mentioning the weather or last night's television

■ Make eye contact

"I may have to go back to the office – we're running out of stationery"

Nowadays, I'm taking it sleazy

WAYS TO HOLD A LEGAL FUNERAL IN BRITAIN

✝ Hide your loved one in a snooker table and dress as Ronnie O'Sullivan. 1,000 friends and family will be able to attend, provided snooker is played on top of the deceased at all times.

✝ Get the departed nominated for a Brit Award. They'll be able to attend the ceremony and take dozens of loved ones with them!

✝ Dress your ex-family member in a tracksuit and drop them off at the local gym. As long as they appear to be exercising, dozens of people can file past paying their respects!

The Eye's Controversial New Columnist

The columnist who stormed out of his first job before he could work

This week I am very angry about Prince William being voted sexiest bald man in the world. This is a travesty of democracy, more serious than those rigged elections in Central America and Eastern Europe. Anyone who is anyone can see who is the sexiest bald man in the world (*see photo*) and I have a number of testimonials from aunts, grandmothers and cousins that prove it. They have said (and I quote), "Oo is the cutest wickle boy in all da world? You is! You is!" And there you have it. Proof. I feel very aggrieved by Prince William doing this to me, and I feel slighted by the entire royal family for not calling out this story as "fake news". They are obviously prejudiced against babies behind the scenes, as I will say after I've set up my tearful interview with Mr Tumble on CBeebies to explain how badly I've been *(cont. p94)*

VIOLENT PROTESTS DEMANDING THE RIGHT TO PROTEST PEACEFULLY CONTINUE

by Our Crime Correspondent **John Locke-Down**

VIOLENT protests against the government's new Police, Crime and Sentencing Bill, with protestors defending the right to protest peacefully, have continued for a second night in Bristol.

"We're demanding that the right to protest peacefully be defended," said a group of protestors, overturning a police van and setting it alight.

"This legislation assumes protests are violent, thuggish events, with little or no evidence to back that up," said one protestor, hurling Molotov cocktails at the police line. "All we want is the right to protest peacefully."

"Everyone should have the right to protest peacefully," said another group of protestors.

"Where is the proof that protests need to be curbed because they attract violent, nasty, anti-social troublemakers?" they added, as they rammed the police station and began looting local shops.

MASS-SHOOTING JOY AS AMERICA RETURNS TO NORMAL

by Our Gun Correspondent **Hans Upp**

THERE was joy this week in the US as two mass shootings in less than a week indicated that the country was returning to normal.

"Our long nightmare of being trapped in our homes by Covid is almost over," said a prominent Republican senator, wearing baseball cap and bullet belt. "Let us hope we can return to our long nightmare of hiding under desks waiting to be killed by a homicidal nutter with a machine gun.

"Soon, the only thing socially distanced will be the angry, disgruntled loners, who couldn't get a date to the prom, crowding back into the nation's gun shops to make up for lost time, now that the schools have reopened.

"If this trend continues, tragic unpatriotic deaths from a foreign un-American virus will soon be outstripped by glorious patriotic deaths from American-made AR-15s."

We Must Do Nothing Faster, say Democrats

THE NEW US government has declared that the traditional approach has not been working, and that now it's time to accelerate massively the process by which nothing happens between one mass shooting and the next.

A presidential spokesman said, "For too long, we have stood by after horrific, awful events

like these, and taken years to completely fail to stop the next one. Well, no longer. Now we have control over all the branches of government, we're going to be able to do nothing almost immediately, so that when people ask what we did, we can show them exactly how fast we didn't do anything at all."

SCHOOL FACES MORE PROTEST

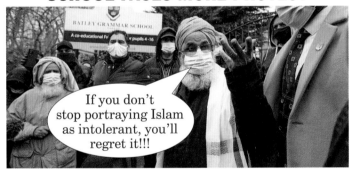

If you don't stop portraying Islam as intolerant, you'll regret it!!!

Kremlin defends Alexei Navalny treatment

by Our Medical Staff
Doctor Evidence

THE Kremlin has insisted that jailed Putin critic Alexei Navalny is receiving "'appropriate treatment' in prison after displaying possible coronavirus symptoms, including a persistent cough and a raised temperature.

According to a Kremlin spokesman, Navalny has been moved to the prison morgue *(surely "hospital"? Ed.)* where he is being treated by powerful thugs *(surely "drugs"? Ed.)* who are administering the new experimental Novichok vaccine *(surely "Sputnik" vaccine? Ed.)*

The spokesman said they had been worried that Mr Navalny would survive *(surely, "would not survive?" Ed.)* but that he was now responding well to treatment and would soon no longer have a fever, a cough or a pulse *(surely "temperature"? Ed.)*.

Russia's top independent doctor flies in to treat Navalny

ARMED FORCES TO BE REPLACED WITH DRONES

Send her victorious, happy and glorious, long… *(cont. pages 1939-45, Hanzzzzzard)*

Nursery Times

···················· Friday, Once-upon-a-time ····················

DEFENCE REVIEW SHOCKS NURSERYLAND

by Our Military Staff **Tim Soldiers**

THE people of Nurseryland were reeling last night after the announcement that the Grand Old Duke of York's army of 10,000 men was to be cut by 10,000 men.

The Grand Old Duke immediately criticised the decision, saying, "If I march 10,000 fewer men up to the top of the hill or down again, nobody's going to notice."

He added, "When troop numbers are up they are up, and when they're down they're down, and when they are only half-way up they are a lot better than they are at the moment."

Defence Minister Big Ben Wallace said, "Nurseryland will be better able to defend itself with a slimmed-down force of zero troops. I have ordered instead 10,000 drones which are all being manufactured by China Dolls Inc, and we are assured that they will not be programmed to turn on the Grand Old Duke and zap him off the top of the hill."

The Prime Minister, Mr Pinocchio, said, "This is entirely in line with what I promised. I said I wouldn't cut troop numbers and I have. If the Grand Old Duke is disappointed, he really should know me better by now."

Defence review 'identifies threat'

by Our Armed Forces Correspondent
Hugh Dares-Winns

DEFENCE Secretary Ben Wallace has told the Commons that the government's defence review has identified the country that poses the greatest threat to the UK's Armed Forces.

"It's the UK. It's pretty clear now that for over a decade our armed forces have come under sustained attack from repeated UK defence reviews."

He continued, "These attacks are launched from Westminster by the UK government, with the sole aim of demoralising the troops and crippling the army's ability to fight on the ground."

"This most recent defence review will see another ten thousand soldiers gone," said a clearly shocked general. "If we don't find a way to stop the UK, there'll be no British army left to defend."

THAT PRINCE PHILIP COVERAGE IN FULL

ROCK... strength and stay... duty... service... difficult childhood... Gordonstoun... Royal Navy... Lord Mountbatten... wartime generation... service... duty... palace outsider... royal moderniser... early environmentalist... hunting, shooting and fishing... shy and sensitive... bluff manner... so-called gaffes... great sense of humour... rock... love-match... croquet with Princess Lilibet... devotion to the Queen... service... duty... duty and service... loyalty and dedication... inspiration for young people... Duke of Edinburgh awards... building confidence... shy and sensitive... Duke waterskiing... action man... suffer fools gladly... barbecues in the garden... wartime generation... distinguished service... duty... shy and sensitive... moderniser... brought cameras into the palace... enthusiast for engineering... mother bonkers became nun... louche playboy father... sisters married Nazis... back to the duty and service... rock... strength and stay...*(continued for 94 hours on all channels and in all newspapers)*

PRINCE PHILIP ARRANGES LOW-KEY FUNERAL

I'll do anything for money

A Californian Doctor Writes

AS A doctor, I am often asked "Hey, doc, can you get me out of going to this funeral?" The simple answer is "Yes".

What happens is that the patient, let's call her "M", is pregnant, and rings me at my country club where I am playing golf and tells me her symptoms. These include severe "mourning sickness", which involves feeling very sick of all her husband's relatives mourning their ghastly grandfather. This nausea is accompanied by

irritation, spleen and weariness at the thought of not being the centre of attention.

This is clearly a case of what we Californian doctors call Markle Syndrome (or *Pregnancis Conveniensis Normalis*, to give it the full medical name).

Treatment involves not flying anywhere, staying at home, lighting an Archewellness Mental Wealth Candle ($999) and recording a heartfelt tribute to the late elderly relative, with the aid of a medicinal onion.

If you are worried about getting out of a funeral, you should seek professional medical advice or, failing that, give me a ring.

© A Californian Doctor 2021

READ HOW PRINCE PHILIP WOULDN'T HAVE WANTED PEOPLE MAKING A FUSS AND A SONG AND DANCE ABOUT HIS DEATH IN OUR HISTORIC 194-PAGE MAGICAL COMMEMORATIVE PULL-OUT SOUVENIR ROYAL BEREAVEMENT SUPPLEMENT

PRINCE PHILIP TRIBUTES POUR IN FROM AROUND THE WORLD

Kim Jong-un, North Korea "Really... all this public display of grief is a bit over the top. It's sad obviously but 8 days of mourning? Get a grip!"

President Trump, Florida "30 people at the funeral? Pathetic! Millions are still mourning the loss of myself in the stolen election! Fact! #LoserDukeofEdinburgh"

President Xi, China "I may have slitty eyes, but at least they are open. Who is the old waxwork now? Ha ha ha ha"

President Putin, Russia "Did we kill him? I can't remember... but if we did, I deny it categorically. Those two agents were just innocent tourists visiting Windsor Castle with its very famous tall turret"

Mohammed Al Fayed, Scotland "The fuggin' Duke of Edinburgh deserved to be run over by himself in a white Fiat Uno! He fuggin' murdered Diana in league with MI5, the CIA Mossad and Her Majesty the fuggin Queen!"

BACKWARDS ISLAND THAT WORSHIPPED PHILIP PLUNGED INTO GRIEF

FAR, far away from here, a small island that has spent years worshipping Prince Philip as a god has been cast into deep mourning.

The island, known in the local language as "Great Britain", has a charming and primitive culture which most of the rest of the world has long since moved on from.

The rituals of mourning have involved a) drinking lots of cups of ceremonial tea and saying "Yes, it's very sad" four times an hour, b) printing millions and millions of photos of the departed Duke then holding them up to each other and saying "Oh, look, this is a good one", and c) saying "I wonder how the Queen is feeling?"

Our photographers have been visiting the island to patronise the people living there for many years now, and we can reveal that they really do wear those awful clothes and *(cont. p94)*

"Wait – I don't think this is our Uber driver"

DIARY

FAREWELL, PRINCE PHILIP

LIZ JONES: There were two stand-out stars on the Funeral Fashion Front.

First, the Duchess of Cambridge sporting a perfect chignon and dazzlingly well-defined eyebrows above her black mask. Was it just me, or were those lovingly-trimmed, five-star, to-die-for eyebrows bowing in grief of their own accord? And was it just me or did I hear one eyebrow say to the other, "Let's keep ourselves in check 'til it's over, and then we can have a bloody good sob?"

Her Majesty's outfit was also impeccable. Not for her those beloved Highland tweeds, or the casual headscarf she loves to wear out riding. No – she chose to opt for fashionable retro black, which is always a must-have for mourners. Personally, I'd like to have seen Camilla in something just that bit more sexy and daring, maybe a busty bodycon in black lace by Roland Mouret, with a hint of thigh. That would certainly have given Princess Meghan – banished to LA, forced to watch it all on her state-of-the art telly, green-eyed in her jim-jams – something to moan about.

JAMES MORRISON-MORRISON QC: Well do I remember my grandfather, a Queen's Counsellor like myself, telling me of a Royal visit to Wiltshire when I was but a boy, and not yet a Queen's Counsellor, like my grandfather before me.

Prince Philip (obituary April 9) was received by all the local dignitaries including the mayor in all his finery. Upon being introduced to the town clerk, Prince Philip asked him, completely off the cuff, what exactly his job entailed.

As the elderly town clerk began to list his duties, at somewhat tedious length, the immortal moment came when Prince Philip shot back: "Good God, man, spare us the bloody details!"

Result? The assembled company collapsed in fits of laughter, delighted to have witnessed such a wonderful example of the Prince's ice-breaking wit. Needless to say, I've dined out on it ever since.

And now, as a Queen's Counsellor, I like to share this marvellous memory with my own grandson, who will one day, I feel quietly confident, have the honour to be appointed a Queen's Counsellor, just like myself.

OWEN JONES: I'm sorry but I've got to say it the Duke did nothing whatsoever for the LGBTQ community I mean I don't know how that family dares call itself Royal when it does not contain a single repeat a single member who is actively transgender but instead perpetrates the bigoted Aryan ideal of an all-white hetero-normative patriarchy founded on a reprehensible throwback espousal of racist imperialism in all its forms as evidenced to the bitter end by the Duke's blind refusal to let his corpse be carried to its so-called final resting place in a vehicle that was black and frankly I'm sorry but I think that's a bit sad.

SUE FLATTERY, BODY-LANGUAGE EXPERT: I noticed that Prince Charles and his family chose to walk very slowly behind the funeral hearse, rather than jogging and/or running at full speed. This tells me they didn't want to overtake it: for them, it was much, much more than a race. Also, did you notice the way none of them waved? We've got so used to the Royals waving and smiling when out in public that this came as a bit of a shock. It tells us so much more than words could ever say about what is clearly the deeply fractured relationship between the two brothers, William and Harry. Prior to the ceremony, many feared that they would use the funeral procession to start punching each other over and over again in a most unseemly manner. From the way they kept looking down at the ground, with their fists half-clenched, I could tell that this was on their minds, but thankfully the presence of Her Majesty forced them to hold back.

ROYAL EXPERT GEOFFREY GORDON-GODFREY: Over the course of a vair long and remarkable life the Duke proved himself a man of great contrasts, a keen barbecuer and sportsman who gave a lifetime of service on the one hand as well as a much loved father and grandfather who was born on a kitchen table and didn't suffer fools gladly and barbecued all sorts of things with an expert hand and over the course of a vair long and remarkable life developed a close bond with the armed forces while continuing to barbecue sausages, lamb chops, bacon, baps and so forth whenever he could – perhaps the occasional steak – though I should add that over the course of a vair long and remarkable life he didn't suffer fools gladly but took a keen interest in the environment and developed a close bond with the armed forces and never stopped barbecuing over the course of what I should add was a vair long and remarkable life.

As told to
CRAIG BROWN

THE DUKE OF EDINBURGH I NEVER MET

I WILL never forget the moment I didn't meet the Duke of Edinburgh. It will be forever etched in my memory as a historic encounter which I can recount to my children and they can pass on to theirs.

I was sitting at my desk when the editor came in and said, "I want a thousand words on Prince Philip by lunchtime."

I immediately thought back to that key moment when I never met him and how he hadn't been rude to me at all, and how he hadn't put me at my ease, and how I hadn't been charmed by his no-nonsense brusque but friendly manner.

I said to the editor, "I never met him," and his reply spoke volumes: "Who cares? Make it 2,000 words."

So I did and I think it's fair to say that never meeting "Your Royal Highness", as I didn't call him, completely changed my life and that after that day we didn't become close and I could never claim I was proud to call him my friend *(continues for another 3,000 words)*

DofE SCHEME GIVES PEOPLE SECOND CHANCE

The Duke was the nation's grandfather

And you're its creepy uncle

AN APOLOGY

IN recent months and years we may have given the impression that the BBC is an inept, out-of-date corporation that should be destroyed. This is clearly demonstrated by its lack of deference to the Crown and the appalling way it ignores our royal family, choosing to screen tacky game shows and inane cookery programmes, rather than showing the deference expected from the national broadcaster.

We now realise, in the light of the BBC clearing all the schedules after the death of Prince Philip with tributes, that nothing could be further from the truth, and that the Corporation's descent into toe-curlingly mawkish sentimentality clearly exposes the BBC as an inept, out-of-date corporation that should be destroyed and replaced by us *(That's enough Royal Exclusives. Ed.)*

TV & Radio HIGHLIGHTS

Just a Minute
(All Channels)

Hilarious panel show in which Gyles Brandreth has to talk for 60 hours non-stop on the subject of the late Duke of Edinburgh. Join Gyles as the Minute's Silence waltz fades and he effortlessly spins a web of anecdotes and memories – without deviation or hesitation, but with, let's be honest, quite a lot of repetition.

VIAGRA FALLS

Yes, Prime Minister

A hilarious lost episode of the classic sitcom, featuring David Cameron as Prime Minister Jim Hacker, Jeremy Heywood as Chief Civil Servant Sir Humphrey and Derek Fowlds as Bernard

Prime Minister: Now look here, Sir Humphrey, what am I to do with this Lex Greensill chappie?

Bernard: He seems like a bit of a wide-boy, clearly on the make.

Sir Humphrey: Not at all, Bernard, he's a highly respected entrepreneur. Just because he didn't go to a decent school...

Bernard: Neither did you.

(Audience have hysterics at public school banter between old Wykehamist civil servant and chap who went to Quaker school)

Sir Humphrey: Look, I met Lex when I was having a sabbatical at Citibank. Frightfully bright for an Australian. And could save us a great deal of money in government.

Bernard: In other words, he's a complete banker.

(Audience carried out on stretchers)

Sir Humphrey: Allow me to explain supply chain finance to you. It allows a financial institution to insert itself in the mechanisms of inter-departmental payment structures with a view to a beneficial outcome for the involved parties by facilitating loan arrangements in cases of procrastinational late payment situations.

(Audience carried back in on stretchers and call for CPR in advance of punchline after long sentence)

Prime Minister: What's that in layman's terms?

Bernard: Bollocks!

Prime Minister: Are you suggesting that Sir Humphrey's judgement on this important matter is clouded by self-interest and over-proximity to Mr Greensill?

Bernard: In a way, Prime Minister...

Prime Minister: So, no problem then – count me in! Give him a desk and a Downing Street business card! Introduce him to everyone! Access all areas!

Sir Humphrey: Yes, Prime Minister!

Prime Minister: And on the off chance I go on to make a mess of being Prime Minister, by doing something stupid like holding a referendum causing irreparable damage, perhaps he can give me a job afterwards with some share options? I can see myself making millions!

Sir Humphrey: Less, Prime Minister!

(Undertakers arrive to remove bodies of entire audience for whom the hilarity of governmental opportunism has proved sadly fatal)

■ **This episode is dedicated to the memory of the late Lord Heywood of Whitehall.**

JOY AS LIFE RETURNS TO NORMAL IN NORTHERN IRELAND

"Now, you're not going to talk all through this, are you?"

Lines on the Various Enquiries into the Conduct of the Scottish Government

'Twas in twenty twenty-one, the Covid Year,
That the Scottish Parliament was wracked by fear.
Was this the end for Sturgeon and the SNP?
Would this be revenge for Alex Salmond, he
Of the roving eye and possibly hands,
Whose role in the drama almost no one understands?
It was all about the political winners and losers
Rather than when and where Alex lost his troosers!
The whole of Holyrude with tension would explode –
Had Sturgeon broken the ministerial code?
What would the verdict of the enquiries be?
Because there was not just one enquiry, you see.
Like buses on yon country lanes in stormy weather
You wait ages and then three of them come together.
Nicola's faithful followers in a good light were determined to see her,
Like the dutiful disciples of the great leader in North Korea.
Did she have knowledge of Salmond's inappropriate behaviour?
Would the Irish barrister be Nicola's saviour?
James Hamilton QC – that was the Hibernian lawyer's name –
Would he point at Nicola the finger of blame?
'Twas on Hamilton's verdict that all would depend.
If Nicola had been in 'the room where it happened'?
(I may be a nineteenth century Caledonian bard,
But references to contemporary rap musicals are nae so hard.)
Did she mislead the committee and parliament 'knowingly'?
"Nae," said the lawyer, which was reported glowingly
By the loyal Scottish media and the BBC
Whose love of Nicola is certainly not wee!
Yes, they all agreed yon Hamilton was the man, key
To the survival of the wee lookalike Krankie.
Then came the crossparty Committee's report
Which said the opposite that, perish the thought,
Ms Sturgeon had indeed misled parliament and the committee,
And that the ruthless First Minister should be shown no pity;
And that despite her gruelling eight hours of self-defence,
They did not believe her account of these events.
The Committee insisted the process of the complaints was flawed,
But now I think puir reader you may well be bored...
And who can blame you as you begin to snooze
At yet another report by Sarah Smith on the Ten O'clock News.
And this in the end is what will save the First Minister
From any justice that righteous folk would like to administer.
So Nicola, like Alex, escaped "Scot Free"
And imagined all was clear for the road to victory.
© *William McGonagall 1867*

ARCURI REVEALS BORIS WAS GENEROUS LOVER

(particularly with public money)

We had nicknames – I called him Alexander the Great

And I called her when I wanted a quick, er…

Vaccines 90% effective at neutralising sleaze

THERE was good news for Downing Street as the latest opinion polls showed that the successful vaccine programme was 90 percent effective at protecting Boris Johnson from sleaze accusations.

It appears that as long as people can go back to the pub with their mates and the sun is shining, the successful vaccine rollout means the chances of Boris Johnson being killed off politically appears to be negligible.

ANTI-LOCKDOWN MARCH DEMANDS SOMETHING THAT IS ALREADY HAPPENING

by Our Covid Sceptic Correspondent **Aunty Vex**

TENS of thousands of anti-lockdown marchers have taken to the streets demanding an end to the lockdown, which began ending two weeks ago.

"This government wants to lock us up in our houses forever," the protestors chanted as they walked past people enjoying a pint in pub beer gardens and shopping in newly opened stores.

Many of the protestors said they refused to believe that the lockdown had been lifted, as whenever they rang their friends to suggest heading to the pub, they were always out, had changed their number or moved house without telling them.

GNOME EXCLUSIVE INTERVIEW

You think you've read about the Arcuri/Johnson affair from every angle? Think again.

THE SOFA SPEAKS

I WAS an innocent sofa from a distant land (IKEA) when I came into Boris's life.

As soon as he ripped the plastic off me, I knew immediately that Boris was interested. I wasn't surprised. I knew from the gossip from the other items of furniture in the house that he definitely had a "type" and I was definitely that type: big, squashy, well upholstered, something to grab onto!

I was flattered, of course, but as he flopped down on top of me, I knew I was being used. He used to playfully slip his hands down the back of my cushions, but then I realised he was only looking for small change to buy beer for some blonde IT specialist.

We had a short time together and then he moved on to other sofas in other flats. I'm not bitter, because now I know that I'm not the only one. He uses furniture like me and discards us when he gets bored. When I read how he dropped red wine on Carrie Symonds' sofa, I thought "yeah, babe, now you know how I feel, I was there", and so I had little choice but to sell my *(cont. p94)*

Film highlights

Carry on Camping! (2020)

Hilarious remake of the 1960s' comedy classic in which the hapless Dave Cameron (played by an in-form Jim Dale) goes on a camping holiday in the middle of Saudi Arabia with his new friend, Mohammed bin Salman (Bernard Bresslaw in questionable makeup), and old pal, Lex Greensill (Sid James with a dubious Australian accent).

The fun starts when Dave is busy sucking up to the Saudi prince and fails to ask him about anyone he has murdered recently. Highlights include the exotic belly dance when Dave crawls on his belly and asks the Prince if he can have some free money. And don't miss the infamous "topless" scene where a female driver (Barbara Windsor) protests against the regime and gets beheaded. You will laugh as Dave and Lex fail to laugh all the way to the bank!

SHEEP'S EYE RATING: *"Yes, Offendi!"*

Dave Snooty AND HIS PAY PALS

I'VE CHANGED, READERS! I'M NO LONGER DAVE SNOOTY...

I'M DAVE LOOTY!

OH NO! MY PAL LEX GREEDSILL HAS GONE BELLY UP - SO I WON'T BECOME DAVE **FILLBOOTY** AFTER ALL!

SOB!

CRASHPOINT

OOPS!

LOOK ON THE BRIGHT SIDE, DAVE - NOW I'M NOT THE GRUBBIEST OLD ETONIAN PRIME MINISTER OF ALL TIME! HOORAH FOR DAVE **SLEAZY**!

THAT'S WHAT I CALL A REBOOT, EH, READERS!?!

KICK!

BULLY BULLY BULLY!!!

THE KABUL KHRONICLE
December 1842
AFGHAN WAR OVER

THE armed forces have announced a general retreat from Afghanistan, in what is thought to be the most significant military development in the region for centuries.

"Quite simply, we think the job is done," explained an officer fleeing a mob of Afghan warriors chasing him with sharp bayonets. "We think we can say this has been a successful... arg... a successful mission which... OW... has made its point."

Another senior officer, interviewed as he lay calmly in a Kabul street ("just having a nice rest here, definitely haven't been shot"), added, "The local population have taken us to their hearts and now we see it's time to go."

He continued, "One good thing is that we've definitely learned our lesson here, and I can't see us getting involved in an unwise, protracted conflict in this part of the world any time in the near future. That's why we've decided to call this conflict The First And Definitely The Only Afghan War."

Mission accomplished

The Daily Telegraph

New 'royal yacht' to solve all Britain's problems

WITH the new proposal for a royal yacht to replace *Britannia* currently at record-breaking levels of popularity, according to the Daily Telegraph, this newspaper is proud to offer a new social charter to sort the UK out:

POOR SCHOOLING
SOLUTION: All children to undergo two weeks of compulsory training on the new royal yacht. Result: brilliant children who know the value of hard work and that if you really

try, you too can become King.
SOCIAL CARE
SOLUTION: all old people to be driven to the coast so they can watch the royal yacht pass by and temporarily forget that they're all still working at the age of 85.

MIGRATION
SOLUTION: New royal yacht to be issued with powers of arrest and small deck-mounted cannons to deter any would-be migrants from trying to reach Britain.

CLIMATE CHANGE
SOLUTION: All cars to be replaced by small models of the royal yacht, meaning commuters can sail to work using natural wind currents and avoid causing any emissions.

(That's enough awful royal yacht suggestions. Ed.)

"Hmph! We'll see what the internet says about that!"

FARAGE QUITS POLITICS FOR GOOD

My work is done

INDIAN STATE VISIT GOES AHEAD

by Our Diplomatic Staff
Covidia Naipaul

DESPITE Boris Johnson being forced to cancel his trip to India at the last minute, the state visit of the Indian double mutant Covid variant to the UK has gone ahead as planned.

The highly infectious variant took advantage of the government's failure to put India on the red list of banned countries, when it arrived in Britain last weekend for a visit, which will take it across London, into the Home Counties, then on to Wales and, finally, Scotland.

Downing Street insisted the

decision not to place India on the red list earlier was solely a matter for the scientists.

"They had to carefully weigh up both sides of the argument, with Downing Street on the one hand, insisting Boris's state visit was going ahead, to the cabinet office on the other, warning of the dire consequences of cancelling it."

Arriving in Aberdeenshire, the Indian double mutant variant said people here in the UK couldn't have been more welcoming.

"I'd go so far as to say that they've been the perfect hosts."

U.S. STUNNED AS WHITE POLICEMAN CONVICTED OF MURDER MILLIONS SAW HIM COMMIT

by Our American Correspondent **Jim Crow**

America was stunned last night when a white policeman, Derek Chauvin, was found guilty of murdering George Floyd.

"Most Americans had expected Chauvin to be acquitted, as all the prosecution had was a nine-minute video of Chauvin murdering George Floyd by kneeling on his neck, whilst Chauvin's lawyer had been able to mount a strong defence, establishing beyond reasonable doubt not just that Chauvin was white, but that George Floyd was black."

There were dramatic scenes outside the courthouse in Minnesota as the jury returned its sensational verdict in the case that has gripped the whole of the United States.

The world held its breath as the judge read out the historic conclusion of this landmark

US legal case, and pronounced that from now on "murder is illegal".

The assembled crowds were shocked by the unexpected outcome, since until that moment it had looked likely that murder would continue to be a crime one could get away with, if you are a member of the US police force.

But the ruling drew criticism from law enforcement lobby groups who saw it as a threat to the Constitution.

Said one tearful police officer, "This directly contravenes the 94th amendment, which states that it is the right of every person in uniform to murder someone whatever the colour of their skin."

Another cop added, "It's a historic moment, ushering in a new era of care and diligence in policing. From now on we'll have to modify our behaviour and check that nobody's filming before we murder someone."

'LONG COVID' FEARS AS LOCKDOWN EASES

by Our Coronavirus Correspondent **Fey Tal**

DOCTORS say they are growing increasingly concerned, as the pubs reopen, about the prevalence of long Covid anecdotes.

"We're seeing more and more people meeting up for the first time in months, or even a year, having to endure the pain of their friends' long, dull Covid stories," said one GP.

"When Jenny started telling friends about learning new hobbies over lockdown, they thought she'd shut up after a few minutes, but an hour later her long, boring Covid anecdote about learning to knit a life-size Captain Tom doll was still going on," he added.

"It was nightmarishly dreary," agreed a close friend of Jenny, who wished to remain anonymous, in case Jenny found her and told her the one about stitching her own designer masks.

The GP had more evidence for his theory, adding "Tony is a good guy, but his long Covid anecdote about how he thought he had caught the virus, even though the test he took was negative, and how he swears the best way to beat Covid is ice baths every three hours and rubbing a mixture of Vicks, almond oil and fresh rosemary on your chest, was the dullest thing any of his friends had ever heard."

In a final case study, the GP recounted how a woman called Angela had gone on for nearly 90 minutes with a long Covid anecdote about how she was so lonely in lockdown she started talking to the hat-stand, like Tom Hanks in that movie, how she muted herself on Zoom in an important meeting with clients and discovered Schitts Creek and now wants to live every minute to the full. "This is terrifying," he said, and he advised people most at risk of long, boring Covid anecdotes to shield from their friends in the pub until at least 2022, when people should have moved on to talking about something else.

I've written you a song, it's about covid, lockdown, life, love, loss and hope, would you like to hear it?

No!

LOSING UNWANTED LOCKDOWN WEIGHT

1. Take newspaper
2. Remove 94-page lockdown weight loss supplement
3. Throw it in the bin
4. Newspaper now perfect size
5. Er...
6. That's it.

School news

St Cakes to rename Houses after pupil complaints

The prestigious independent Midlands boarding school has announced a series of name changes to its Houses in order to reflect "a more modern educational agenda". From now on, the Junior Houses will no longer honour the imperialist and colonialist British naval war criminals, Drake, Raleigh and Nelson, but will instead pay tribute to contemporary role models more in keeping with the world of today. The Headmaster, Mr R.J. Kipling, told parents that in future the Houses will be called Thunberg, Waller-Bridge and Mandela, after the activist Greta, the writer Phoebe and the political leader Winnie. *(Is this right? Ed.)*

JOKE CANDIDATE 'UNDERMINES THE SERIOUSNESS OF THE MAYORAL RACE'

by Our London Politics Staff
May Oral

IN A furious outburst, the highly respected Count Binface hit out at Laurence Fox for devaluing the democratic process by standing as a Mayoral candidate for the ridiculous Reclaim Party.

Speaking from inside his bin, the Count continued, "Some of us are trying to come up with sensible policies that will appeal to Londoners, such as bringing back Ceefax, and yet we have to listen to the absurd Laurence Fox, travelling around on a bus, telling people he's going to end lockdown yesterday."

The Count continued, "I've got a sense of humour, and I know the public like a joke, but really, Fox is a disgrace and he's making London look like a laughing stock. If he's now got the backing of Nigel Farage and Richard Tice, then how can we possibly take him seriously?" Binface concluded, "I'm wheely cross!"

Experts are worried that the Fox could split the Binface vote, allowing the left-field Sadiq Khan to come from nowhere and remain in office.

Those London Mayoral candidates in full

Laurence 'Fantastic' Fox
(Reflux Party)

Piers Corbyn
(Anti-mask, Pro-Covid Alliance)

Sadiq Khan't
(Anti-Corbyn, Pro-Starmer Formerly Labour Party)

Shaun Bailey
(Conservative Anti-Winning, Pro-Losing Party)

Peter Gammons
(UKIP Nominal Determinist)

Luisa Porritt
(Liberal Democratic Deficit Party)

Count Binface
(Stop The Count Alliance)

Keir Starmer WRITES

HELLO! I'm sure you saw last week that I was ejected from a drinking establishment for my very sensible views on the lockdown. I have been told that I have made history – the first man ever to be thrown out of a pub for being too sober!

Of course I was very honoured to take part in this ancient English ritual. From my studies of working class people (I've spent literally hours watching *Eastenders* omnibuses!), being thrown out of a pub is a sacred right of passage for any citizen of this fair country and, rest assured, I will be sending my deputy, Angela Rayner, back to the pub in due course to kick over the furniture in the beer garden, in the time-honoured tradition.

Of course, I'm not worried about the effect this will have on my political career. I follow a long line of great politicians who've been thrown out of pubs and gone onto greater things.

Nigel Farage was just a humble UKIP leader when he was thrown out of an Edinburgh pub and now look at him – popping up in ads on YouTube, telling you the amazing economic benefits of storing your own urine under your bed. I can only dream of power like that!

Let's not forget, this incident was not only a thrilling piece of footage, but also a chance to unveil my double – the chap who looks exactly like me but is taller, stronger and quite handy in a fight. With any luck some people will think that that's me and my poll ratings will go up through the roof, to just a few percent behind the Tories!

Sincerely, Keir.

HOSPITALITY INDUSTRY REOPENS

Fuck off!

61

Daily Mail

125 YEARS OF THE MAIL

How we covered the major events in the life of Britain and reflected the spirit of the age in times of the nation's happiness and sorrow

Daily Mail — QUEEN VICTORIA IS DEAD — Nation mourns as house prices fall
23 JANUARY 1901

Daily Mail — KING EDWARD VIII ABDICATES — Nation in shock as house prices tumble
11 DECEMBER 1936

Daily Mail — PRINCESS ELIZABETH MARRIES PHILIP — Nation rejoices as house prices soar
21 NOVEMBER 1947

Daily Mail — PROFUMO RESIGNS — Nation uncertain as house prices don't rise or fall
6 JUNE 1963

Daily Mail — CHARLES MARRIES DIANA — Nation ecstatic at fairytale rise in house prices
30 JULY 1981

Daily Mail — NATION WEEPS AS DIANA'S CAR AND HOUSE PRICES CRASH
1 SEPTEMBER 1997

(That's enough Daily Mail. Ed.)

Huge metaphor causes global disruption

by Our Disaster Staff
Eva Green

THE international trade in political cartoons was brought to a standstill this morning, as the giant metaphor in the Suez Canal was refloated.

The metaphor, which was based on a container ship which had run aground in the canal, had provided cartoonists with an unending supply of ideas for a week.

Said one, "Cartoonists were queuing up to draw the stranded ship, with labels such as 'EU Vaccines', 'Lockdown' and 'New Suez Crisis over Britain's Role in the World'."

He continued, "But now the container vessel has been refloated, that political metaphor ship has sailed. Quite literally."

Cartoonists around the world are now counting the cost of the news that the metaphor has moved on.

"It's the worst news since the success of the vaccine roll-out. One can only hope that the Ever Given container ship now sails into an iceberg, on which we can draw the words 'Covid Variant', or is sunk by a tsunami which can be labelled 'Third Wave.'"

EVERGREEN

ME AND MY SPOON

THIS WEEK

SAMANTHA CAMERON
Designer

Does your husband, David, have a favourite spoon?

I am sorry?

Does David like any particular type of spoon? What about crooked ones?

Sam's PR: I am afraid we agreed that Samantha would not talk about any of those issues.

Of course. Samantha, would you like to tell us how tough it has been for your business in the pandemic and how you have managed to survive?

Yes, well, it's been a difficult year for retail and…

Did it help having Lord Brownlow as an investor, the one who coughed up for Boris' Number Ten refurbishment and clearly likes to keep in with prime ministers' wives and girlfriends?

I think it's all too easy to blame Carrie, in a kind of Lady Macbeth way, but I will always support the women in these cases…

What if they are actually Lady Macbeth?

Er…

How much would you pay for a new designer spoon? £58,000? More? Do you think they were ripped off?

Can we stick to the pre-approved questions please ? Otherwise I am going to have to refer this to the Spoon Editor.

I appreciate that. Samantha, you are wonderfully slim and attractive and capable and well-connected…

Yes…

And you run your own very successful business…

Yes…

And no doubt own lots of spoons…

Some, yes…

Did you get any of the spoons cheap through Lex Greensill? And are any of them bought with dirty Saudi money? And is David going to have to sell up his spoons now that he has lost all…

PR: Thanks very much. I think it's time for this interview to finish.

Can I ask if anything amusing has ever happened to Samantha in connection with a spoon?

PR: No.

NEXT WEEK: *Sarah Cox, Me and my Apple.*

F·R·I·E·N·D·S REUNION

YES, THEY'RE BACK! The lovable team who made the 1990s and 00s such fun are all returning for a special one-off of their show, "Friends"! They feature:

Tony, the lovable dude with his guitar and his cool Union Jack parties who made audiences laugh and laugh about his mysterious Third Way

Mandy, the smooth operator known for his catchphrase, "I'm a bastard, not a quitter"

Cambo, the thug who just loved to rough up journalists and then point out how terribly his mental health had suffered as a result

And, of course, there was **Gordon**, the figure of fun with the crazy accent who was mostly there to serve people coffee and was never really accepted as one of the gang.

With its catchy theme tune, *I'll be Blair for you*, the series swept the entire world – and particularly the Middle East! – with a combination of jokes, dramatic plotlines, and lethal high-grade explosives. All the cast are now ageing millionaires – but do they still have anything useful to contribute today? *(No. Ed.)*

62

From The Message Boards

Members of the online community respond to the major issues of the day...

Iconic illusion celebrated

As a Reader in Gender Studies, I was interested in the recent centenary of the 'Sawing a woman in half' trick, when jocular remarks such as 'Can you saw my wife in half?' were juxtaposed with the serious views of professional female 'assistants' who argue that they, not the male 'magicians', do the hard logistical work. The original version performed by 'P. T. Selbit' (Percy Thomas Tibbles) involved a woman tethered by ropes, the misogynistic semiotics of which demand further interrogation. – *Dr Sarah Reeves*

Tibbles lived in London during the Whitechapel Murders of 1888 to '1891' and I and other students (we disavow the 'Ripperologist' label) consider him a person of interest. His re-enactment of this butchery on stage, involving blood and other gruesome gimmicks, bore the classic hallmarks of a dormant killer seeking the thrill of publicity. Our critics point out that he was six years old when Mary Ann Nichols, the first of the so-called Canonical Five victims, was slain; but what better way to avoid suspicion than posing as an 'innocent child'? As for the contemporaneous Thames Torso Murders… draw your own conclusions. – *Eternal Vigilance*

This reminds me of my grandfather Maurice Welby, better known as 'The Laughing Hangman' who combined execution with showmanship. ('Give 'em a good send-off,' he would say!) To set the condemned man at ease he would point the 'squirting flower' buttonhole at the chap's eyes then shake his hand using a comedy electric shock device. Hood on, next thing the fellow knew he was falling through the trapdoor with laughter ringing in his ears! – *T.L.Welby*

Maurice visited my school in the 1950s, fixed a noose on the wall bars in the gym and 'hanged' pupils for alleged crimes! Lovely gentleman, he signed my cigarette card of him from the 'Hangmen of Great Britain' series and wrote, 'Stay out of trouble!' My granddaughter sold it on eBay to pay for her eighteenth birthday present (a beautiful tattoo of Marcus Rashford, an NHS nurse, and a unicorn, all sitting on a rainbow). – *Young Smidge*

A 1950s 'Welby Junior Gallows' in original packaging just sold for £1,287! – *Black Cap*

come to stoke we will saw you in half and kick your fucking head in – *stokie steve*

HISTORIC CELEBRATIONS AS SUPER LEAGUE FALLS

WILD scenes of celebration broke out on the streets of London last night, following the toppling of the much hated Super League.

"This is like the French Revolution, the Arab Spring and the Bolshevik uprising of 1917, all rolled into one," said one exuberant fan.

"Tonight, the people have taken back control of football. Vive la Révolution. The demise of the Cabal means we won't be lining the pockets of the much hated billionaire owners of these elite clubs playing in The Super League.

"We can instead go back to following the Premier League, which is a true competition, where every club, no matter how small, can lift the trophy, which is always won of course by one of the elite clubs with all the money and a hated billionaire owner.

"This is a great day for 'people power', as we wrest control of the beautiful game from unscrupulous foreign billionaires and place it back into the hands of unscrupulous foreign billionaires."

PM SAVES FOOTBALL FOR THE MASSES

It's not fair if people can just buy success

'Disgraceful attempt to cash in' says Lineker

Gary Lineker has welcomed the scrapping of the proposed Super League, describing it as a cynical money-making exercise, whilst munching his way through a delicious bag of Walkers Salt and Vinegar crisps.

"These top clubs and players need to be reminded that their reputation is all they have – is that really to be auctioned off to the highest bidder?" Gary asked, tucking into his second pack of deliciously cheesy Walkers Cheese and Onion crisps.

"When it came to the crunch, what were the players going to choose?

"I'd suggest Walkers new Roast Chicken and Sage flavour, which has plenty of crunch and then some," opined Gary, donning a chicken suit to (cont. p94)

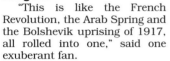

DYSONS – A GUIDE FOR THE CONFUSED

Bagless   **Taxless**

ENGLISH FANS DISAPPOINTED BY CLUB BOSSES

by Our Top-Flight Football Correspondent **Nye Eve**

FOOTBALL fans have reacted with shock and dismay at the news that the people in charge of the modern game are motivated by the prospect of earning hundreds of millions of pounds.

"I had no idea," said one Chelsea fan. "I was absolutely certain that Roman Abramovich got into football due to the memory of treasured boyhood kickabouts, using jumpers for goalposts, drinking orange squash at half time, and wandering home through the twilight with muddy knees to a dinner of tripe with his ten siblings.

"Now I find out he bought the club using the billions he earned during the post-Soviet era by acquiring a large oil company at a knockdown price. I'm simply appalled."

A Manchester United fan added, "Until now, I assumed the Glazer family had reached their net worth of £3.6 billion by selling pie and mash on the terraces, or possibly by licensing agreements for amusing and offensive chants about opposing teams and their players' mothers.

"Now I learn that Malcolm Glazer earned his money through real estate, relentless leveraging of small investments and junk bonds. You could have knocked me down with a feather."

THE aborted European Super League saga should serve as a timely warning to us all of the danger of foreigners buying up British national institutions.

The spectacle of J.W. Henry grovelling to Liverpool fans shows what can happen when foreign nationals get above themselves and try to exploit the man in the street for their own greedy commercial interests.

No US-based billionaire, who doesn't give a damn about the lives of ordinary Brits, should ever be allowed to hijack any element of our culture, and turn it into his own money-making plaything.

If such a thing were to happen in say, journalism, the ramifications would be too awful to… Oh, hang on… Yes, Mr Murdoch. Sorry, Mr Murdoch… I'll get my coat.

POETRY CORNER

Lines on the 200th Anniversary of the *Manchester Guardian*

Congratlatiouns
To the *Grauniad*
For your historic
Archivement.
(Subs, don't check)

Yes, you have
Reached 200!
"Is that readers?"
Asks Keith's mum,
Who says she thinks
The paper's got a
Bit boring recently
And would rather
Buy the cup of coffee
Than donate online.

But this is unfair –
Let's all lift a glass
And have a moan,
It's what you would
Have wanted.

E.J. Thribb (17½ typos)

"Groomed online? What do you mean?"

HEIR OF SORROWS
A Short Story Special

by Dame Sylvie Krin, author of *Duchess of Hearts* & *You're Never Too Old*

THE STORY SO FAR: The death of Prince Philip has been a severe blow to the House of Windsor. Prince Charles has retreated to his beloved principality of Wales. Now read on..

THE rain lashed mercilessly on the slate roofs of the cottage in the village of Llandrover, on the outskirts of Lloonytuyn in the Belisha Beacons, as Charles looked mournfully at his breakfast of leeks. Now was the time for contemplation on the future of the whole monarchy malarkey business, brought into sharp focus by the events of the preceeding week.

On the table was his notebook with a page headed "Slimmed-down Royal Family" and a list of names underneath in spidery hand-writing. And after some of the names there was an ominous question mark… Princess Eugenix and Princess Beatitude… Zara Tara Boomdeay-Phillips-Tindall… The controversial Duchess Markle of Sparkle… Prince Edward of Potato and his wife, the Queen's new confidante royale, the Countess of Westeros… Who would survive the necessary cull to usher in the modern Carolingian Age? For this was how his era would be defined and how at his own funeral he would be judged… Charles' mind wandered off as the sound of the rain drummed its own melancholy march…

"And still they come to pay their respects," intoned the voice of the elderly Huw Jedwards, as the mourners assembled in Yesminster Abbey. "Throughout his long career of service and duty he was much respected, if not always appreciated, by his people and was perhaps underrated as a moderniser, environmentalist and spiritual thinker…"

The assembled dignitaries took their places in the still socially distanced pews, as the three-person choir sang Benjamin Button's *Jubilee Line Extensione*.

Charles had planned the event meticulously, insisting that there should be no uniforms. This was a diplomatic solution to avoid embarrassing his son Harry Archewelloff ™, the presenter of five international Emmy-Thompson-winning documentaries, including "Aren't My Family Ghastly?" and "Aren't my Family Ghastly 2?". If uniforms had been allowed and Harry had been forbidden to wear his dress uniform of the HouseParty Cavalry (the famed "Blues and Rhythms"), he might well have done something silly and paid a trip to Windsor's Fancy Dress Emporium, "Nazi Uniforms R Us".

Charles shuddered at the thought of his wayward son. But there had been an even more pressing matter of uniforms. And that was whether Prince Andrew should wear the bright orange jumpsuit denoting the rank of Guest at the Yuma State Penitentiary and Correctional Facility ("Have a Nice Stay").

Instead, both princes were soberly dressed in Mourning Coats, and a discreet ankle tag for the former Duke of Yuck. It was only the Duchess of Fergiana who had rather let the side down by appearing dressed as a police woman in fishnet stockings, wearing a sash saying "Slimmer of the Year 2027" and advertising her own brand of lo-cal health drink called "The Juice of York".

But thank goodness for The Duchess of Katebridge, Katherine Middleclass, looking radiant in a chic black Catherine Walkers-Crisp coat dress and wearing her Nobel

Peace Price medal for her work as mediator between the Princes William and Harry.

This had been a remarkable triumph in negotiating skills, which the UN had recognised as a world-beating example of conflict resolution and which had, according to Britain's last remaining newspaper, The Daily Middleton, saved the world from conflagration. It was just a shame that her canonisation by the Pope had not quite come through in time for the ceremony.

And perhaps also it was regrettable that William, the Duke of Katebridge, had chosen to honour his position as the so-called " Prince of Fans" by wearing the away strip of English Super Football Club Liverchestersea United.

But on went the proceedings and the lilting bardic tones of Huw Jedward were replaced by the voice of the even more elderly and all too familiar royal broadcaster Nicholas Witchmagazine, whose unctuous monologue had been the wearying soundscape to Charles' entire life.

"And now the Abbey Clancy Choir are singing the traditional naval hymn *For those in Peril On the Season 94 of the Crown*. And now the Prince's former Valet and Bearer of the Toilet Seat Royal,

Sir Alan Fitztightly, can be seen with his partner and carer, Air Vice Marshal Johnny 'Johnny' Johnson. Sir Alan will now read out the list of the deceased's official and heraldic titles."

And there was Sir Alan, looking a little frail in his rainbow tricorn hat, pink silk garters and pantaloons, but still boldly reading from the vellum scroll.

"Guardian of the Galaxies, Champion of the Wonder Horse, Protector of the Prayer Book, Slayer of the Monstrous Carbuncle, Whisperer to the Plant Kingdom, Defender against the…"

There was a tense moment of silence as the ancient aide-de-camp-coffee struggled to find the right word. But then, blessedly, it came to him.

"Defender Against the Appalling, in a very real sense…"

Charles sighed with relief. And so the list continued, as his roll-call of achievements mounted up into a picture of a life well lived.

"Lord Patron of the Royal Order of Goonery, Highly Commended Watercolourist of the Year 2003 from The Royston Strong Art Gallery in the Royal County of Glossopshire, Apothecary- General of the Royal Society of Homeopathololologists, including the St John's Wort Foundation…"

AND so the list went on, as Charles experienced a sort of out-of-body thingie, as he hovered above the ceremony. It was what his old friend and mentor, Sir Laurens Van Der Postitnote, had written about so often when he was travelling with the bushmen of the Kalamatahari Desert.

Sir Nicholas Witchmagazine gave way to royal expert Dame Penny Dreadful who sombrely announced the Air of Sorrow, an old Highland lament from shores of Lochdoon, beneath the craggy summit of Ben Cumberbatch.

A lone piper, dressed in the traditional Alastair Campbell Shortbread Tartan, began the mournful melody and all eyes were on one person. The Queen. Hang on! thought Charles, panicking in his reverie. That didn't look like Camilla…?

Dame Dreadful continued: "There she sits, the solitary figure of Her Majesty Queen Elizabeth, the longest-serving monarch in the history of the world, who still reigns majestically in this, her Double-Diamond Titanium Multi-Centenaversary year, as her son…"

Charles awoke with a start, as a clap of thunder crashed over the Welsh Valley of Cwm Dynewythme. What a terrible nightmare. And a frightful vision of the future. It was like the Scrooge chappie from the Christmas Carolingian story with the ghosts and what-not…

Charles returned to his list with a renewed vigour. And under the new heading "Royals To Be Retired In Order To Create 21st Century With-It, Modern-Style Monarchy" he added a new name:
"HRH Queen Elizabeth the Second…"

(To be continued)

Boris Johnson MP
● Live   385,000,000 Views

Prime Minister's Question Time Live on Fakebook

👍 Like   💬 Comment

0 people like this

Hoorah!

Another Bozza election **triumph** in the bag, snatching **victory** from the jaws of **defeat**! In the words of St Margaret of Assisi, "**Rejoice! Rejoice! Gloat! Gloat! Gloat!**" I told you the public weren't interested in anything about wallpaper, **sleaze**, PPE, **cronyism,** corruption or who runs the country. In the words of that other great Tory, St Tony of Blair, it's "**Vaccination, Vaccination Vaccination!**" Our **stonking** election tsunami proves conclusively that I am the greatest "One vaccination Tory" **ever**! See what I did there? It's the **Bojo Banter** that the public love. They don't care about **anything** else. They love **me** and that's **all** that matters. See you in ten years' time folks! **Play** that music!

(EXPENSIVE RUSSIAN DIGITAL MUSIC SYSTEM PLAYS RED WALL ARMY CHOIR SINGING "TOTAL ECLIPSE OF THE HARTLEPOOL")

Cabinet Secretary (Simon BriefCase): Technically, you're meant to answer some questions, Prime Minister.

Boris: What's the **point**? Whatever I say or do **doesn't** matter! I could murder your Granny in **broad daylight** and get away with it!

BriefCase: Of course we haven't had that inquiry yet...

Boris: It'll **still** find me completely **innocent**. Oh all right BriefCase, have it **your** way. Let's get some **questions** in before Carrie **insists** on your **resignation**.

Robert Pestilence: Robert Pestilence, ITVeeeeeeeee. Prime Minister, you still haven't answered the question about where the money came from to pay for the refurrrrrrrbishment of youuuuuur flat.

Boris: No one's interested in **that**. That's **yesterday's** snooze. **Yawn, yawn**. No one cares about **decoration**, Pesto – it's **vaccination** that matters - or don't you read the newspapers? **Next** question!

Deth Rigby: Deth Rigby, SkySnooze. So what did Lord Brownnose get in return for his 58 grand? Was it one of those government contracts that you handed out to your chums?

Boris: No one's interested in **that**. That's the **day-before-yesterday's** snooze. **Wake** me up, someone. They don't care about **jobs** for the boys – it's **JABS** for the boys – and girls, obvs. **Next** question!

Jon Snowflake: Jon Snowflake, Channel Four Snooze. What about Lobbygate and the failure to close the borders and the failure to lock down and your willingness to let the bodies pile high?

Boris: I know you're incredibly **old**, Jon, but are you **deaf** as well? I said, no one's interested in **anything** you've got to say**,** grandad!

BriefCase: Shall I launch enquiries into all these scandals? And if not shall I launch an enquiry into why I haven't launched an enquiry?

Boris: Good **idea**, BriefCase. And I think I know **just** the person to **head** the enquiry. **Me**. **Next** question?

Laura Koronaberg: Laura Koronaberg, BBnothingtoC-here News. Do you have a problem with money?

Boris: Yes. I don't have **enough** of it. So if anyone out there's **got** any, you know my phone number, as I **haven't** changed it. Just give me a **ring** and then give me some **money**. No one will know. And even if they **do**, the public **aren't** interested. They can see I'm just a **working** man, **struggling** to pay his bills, **redecorating** the spare room 'cos 'er indoors **insists** – or I'll have to sleep in **there**, with the **dog**. Just an **ordinary** bloke with the **same** worries as everyone else. Just your **normal**, **average** man in the Downing Street who's won a **humongous** victory that puts me on a par with Winston Churchill, The Duke of Wellington and Julius Caesar!

Koronaberg: Now you come to mention it, Prime Minister, could I ask you about your relationship with the truth?

Boris: Like **all** relationships, it can get a bit **tricky**, but I'm **always** faithful to the truth, except if there's **another** truth that's more **attractive**, in which case, I **understandably** commit myself to the **next** truth for as long as it takes for another one to come along. And sometimes the truth **locks** you out of the house, calls you a **liar** and throws your **trousers** out of the window, and you have to go and **live** in your **car**.

BriefCase: Shall I launch a...

Boris: No. Time for **me** to ask another question. Laura, I need some **childcare** on the cheap. **You** spend a lot of time hanging round Number Ten. **You** busy this evening?

Koronaberg: I'm doing the news. Apparently you just won a big election.

Boris: That's a pity. Who **else** hasn't got anything to do at the moment? I know! **Allegra**!

Prime Minister's Former Spokesperson Now Doing Two Weeks' Shift Work on Climate Summit: How dare you! I'm a friend of Carrie's.

Boris: Good point. Don't want the **nanny** to be too **chummy** with the **mummy**. Never works out. Conflict of interest problems down the line. Take it from **me**. Oh I know! **BriefCase**! You're a **civil servant**, you must need a **second** job. There we are. Sorted! **Bosh**! And if Wilfred makes a mess, **you** can clear it up.

Andy Capp-in-Ring

Henry Davies, Tom Jamieson and Nev Fountain

VACCINE WINS ELECTION

"Are there any unpleasant side effects?"

"You'll be out of power for years"

CARE HOMES 'NOT OBLIGED TO GIVE RESIDENTS A REASON TO LIVE'

by Our Elderly Correspondent **Al Zeimers**

THE government has confirmed that the advice given to care homes – specifically, that residents should be allowed out for short walks without the need to quarantine afterwards – isn't mandatory, and that care homes will be given discretion as to how they crush the spirits of their residents into the dust.

"Now that we have forced our elderly residents to live a life isolated and alone in their rooms all through 2020, the last thing we want is to waste all that hard work by giving them a reason to live," said one care home provider.

"We're sure the day will come when normality will return and vulnerable residents will be allowed out freely, but we're urging caution for now and saying this is not the time for hope or joy; let's keep on being spirit-crushingly cruel for a few more months, as that saves us a bundle on staff costs."

BBC SHOCK: ANOTHER EX-DOCTOR WHO STAR OUTED FOR BAD BEHAVIOUR

by Our Dr Who Correspondent **Tim Traveller**

HOT ON the heels of the controversy surrounding Noel Clarke and John Barrowman, another *Dr Who* star has been engulfed in allegations about his inappropriate behaviour on set.

Speaking from his palatial flying saucer in the trendier part of Skaro, Dalek Zeg was clearly angry, as he defended himself in the strongest terms.

"I do concede that, yes, I did exterminate a few people on set," Zeg rasped. "But they didn't give any impression that they did NOT want to get exterminated, other than screaming and trying to run away from me.

"In my particular, powerful clique, extermination is all part of the good-natured horseplay of making a television programme.

"I apologise if I did offend anyone by blasting them into atoms, but you have to realise that it was a different time. We thought nothing of exterminating dozens of people during the day, and then heading off to Groucho's for a few extra exterminations before work the next morning."

Meanwhile, the BBC has welcomed the current controversy. A spokesman said yesterday, "In the past, we have been worried that our sexual monsters have been seen as too white, too male and too heterosexual.

"But as you can see, with Mr Clarke and Mr Barrowman, we are making real progress in opening up opportunities for appalling on-set behaviour in the black and LGBTQ communities.

"Now all we need is for Jodie Whittaker to slap a cameraman's arse and call him 'toots' and we've got the set."

"We're life-long Labour voters – of **course** we're not voting Labour!"

Keir Starmer WRITES

HELLO! All the election results are in. And there's bad news and good news!

The bad news is despite my best efforts at ingratiating myself with the north-eastern peoples of England, which involved, basically, not wearing a coat on a chilly beach, they don't seem to have warmed to me!

I was always at a disadvantage against the Prime Minister, as he's made much more of an effort to blend in with those types, what with his vulgar home furnishings, fights with his "lass" and his large brood of illegitimate children!

That's the bad news. And I take full responsibility for the fact that Angela Rayner was to blame for all the disappointing results.

Now the good news is we're moving forward and we're bouncing back! Angela and I had a difficult and lengthy meeting, and we finally agreed that I should keep my job in the reshuffle.

As for Angela, we have agreed that she should take on a few new titles to go with her role as deputy leader. Henceforth, she is to be known as Angela Rayner, Deputy Leader of the Labour Party, Shadow Chancellor of the Duchy of Lancaster, Shadow Secretary of State for the Future of Work, Defender of the North, Queen of the Great Grass Sea, Mother of Dragons, The Unburnt, Breaker of Chains, Queen of the Andals and the First Men, Protector of the Seven Kingdoms and Lady of Dragonstone. I hope she's okay with those!

Yes, truth be told, I think I did go a bit over the top when I started trying to sack people before all the election results were in, but look at it this way; yes, I did over-react to the Labour party's bad results, but I did compensate by under-reacting to our good ones! So if you think about it, that evens everything out, doesn't it?

Thanks very much for all the advice to be much more left-wing and to be much less left-wing and to be more like Corbyn and to be more like Blair and to come up with new policies like the return of Cool Britannia or for Owen Jones to replace Monty Don on *Gardeners' World*.

I know how sceptical certain quarters of the party were when I said that I would lead the party from the centre and unite both the left and the right. And yet I've managed it. Little more than a year down the line and they all want me to resign. I amaze myself sometimes!

Sincerely, Keir.

DR WHO SET

PUT IT AWAY!

GOVERNMENT 'TRAFFIC LIGHT' TRAVEL SCHEME WORKING WELL

It's all systems stop... or go... er...

A message from the

BILL & MELINDA GATES *foundation*

A number of people have voiced their concern about the future of our philanthropic charity in the light of our impending divorce.

We would like to reassure you that we are committed to spending billions to help the most needy. And there's nobody more needy and desperate than divorce lawyers. They need bigger cars, bigger houses, bigger pools and bigger yachts.

We will not stop until we see an end to the tragic inequality that they suffer in comparison to hedge fund managers, oil tycoons and billionaire software nerds.

It looks like you're trying to write divorce papers. Need some help?

Microsoft's Clippy senses an opportunity

Liz Truss heralds landmark Australian trade deal

AFTER weeks of intensive negotiations, I'm delighted to announce that I have secured a great deal for Britain.

From now on, our supermarkets will be filled with the very best produce from Australia, including: raw dingo meat and chlorinated crocodile and wallaby steaks. But those aren't all the zero-tariff goodies we can look forward to from the Land of the Didgeridoo, there's also: prime kangaroo testicles, juicy wombat anus, and succulent platypus penis.

Yes, it's one in the eye for the Remainer doommongers who'd forgotten our great tradition of export deals with Australians.

Ever since we shipped them to the other side of the world for stealing the odd loaf of bread just because their families were starving, we've had close bonds of friendship. No wonder they've done us such a bonzer deal!

EUROPE: TIME TO TAKE BACK CONTROL AND GO IT ALONE

by Our Entertainment Staff
Neil Points

In the light of Britain's humiliation at the hands of our so-called European friends, it is clearly the end of the road for the Eurovision project and its deluded goal of building a European-wide musical super-state.

Last night, Britain's world-beating export song was given a massive "NON!" by the assorted unelected judges of Europe. This was followed by another populist vote delivering no votes at all to the British contribution.

The time has now clearly come to say goodbye to Eurovision once and for all and forge exciting new individual song contests with other nations like Australia and Israel – negotiated by Lord Frost and hosted by the multi-lingual Amanda Holden.

Only then will Britain be able to operate on a level playing field and once again succeed in the global music industry.

Said Liz Truss, "The money saved by leaving Eurovision will be spent on Lulu, Cliff Richard and Brotherhood of Man. People will be queuing up to have song competitions with us.

"We will no longer be Puppets on a String, but will be the ones Making Our Minds Up, and when we exit Eurovision everyone will be saying Congratulations and Celebrations.

"Anyone who claims that the whole thing will go Boom Bang a Bang is just out of tune, as was the British entry, and…"
(cont. 2094)

Minor disagreement doesn't provoke woke row

by Our Backlash Correspondent
Milly Ennial

AN ONLINE argument has occurred without being described as a WOKE CONTROVERSY by the *Mail*, *Telegraph*, *Times* and *Express* newspapers.

"It's absolutely shocking," said one participant. "I was disagreeing with a friend about something online and nobody stepped in to scream that this shows exactly what's wrong with young people today, or that it simply proves the past is an irredeemable pit of racism and sexism and it should be binned immediately. I don't know what to say."

The other party in the argument said, "I'm staggered and it's deeply unsettling. Nobody has compared us to TERFs or referred us to Ofcom or demanded we have a statue put up to us, or that that statue is then torn down, or involved Stonewall or cited racial trauma. It was just a slight disagreement and we both feel fine about it."

At the time of writing, neither Piers Morgan, Julia Hartley-Brewer, Owen Jones, Charles Moore or anyone else had stuck their bloody oar in to explain why the argument meant the National Trust should be disbanded or why, in fact, nobody needed to apologise for the Empire which was actually fine. Nobody had covered the story on GB News and nobody had compared any participants to Winston Churchill.

Who do you think should be the new Mrs Bill Gates?

Who should replace Melinda Gates and hook up with the world's most eligible bachelor to form a new global philanthropic power couple?

 **Mrs Melania Gates**

Mrs Meghania Gates

 **Mrs Mel B Gates**

Mrs Mel C Gates

 Mrss Mel and Sue Gates

 **Mrs MacKenzie Bezos Gates**

 **Mrs Elizabeth Windsor Gates**

That's Rich List

A HUGE number of people have joined the That's Rich List, the record of humbug that is compiled annually. This year has seen a massive increase in hypocrisy, particularly in the last week, over the Martin Bashir affair.

 ■ Top of the That's Rich List is **Prime Minister Boris Johnson** who has been lecturing the BBC about journalistic ethics, despite being fired by the Times for fabricating quotes.

 ■ Hot on his heels is **Priti Patel**, a welcome BAME entrant to the That's Rich List, who claimed that the BBC had damaged its reputation, after being sacked by the previous Prime Minister for deception and for subsequently being censured for bullying. She complained without a trace of irony that the BBC had buried the investigation, ignored whistle-blowers, and refused to accept any responsibility for its actions.

 ■ **Earl Spencer**, whose family have been on the That's Rich List for many years and have a vast stock of humbug accrued through many generations, made a good showing this year, asking why no one did anything at the time when he did nothing either.

 ■ Not on the That's Rich List once again is **Mr Rupert Murdoch**, the proprietor of all the tabloid newspapers which hounded Diana and which have now rounded on the BBC for its journalistic failings which they now claim led directly to her death – which was nothing at all to do with the press or the paparazzi chasing the Princess through that tunnel in Paris. *(Please don't sack me, Mr Murdoch. Ed.)*

ON OTHER PAGES

Did Bashir drive the white Fiat Uno when he murdered Diana?

Did Bashir kill Michael Jackson with an overdose of painkillers?

Did Bashir murder Dr Shipman and all his victims?

Did Bashir kill Dr Black with the lead piping in the conservatory? *(Now you're being silly. Ed.)*

EXCLUSIVE TO ALL NEWSPAPERS

THANK GOD THE BBC ALONE KILLED DIANA

…and so it's perfectly clear to anyone who was paying attention in the 1990s that the only people responsible for Diana's instability and paranoia was the BBC, whose entire mission during this time was to convince the Queen of Hearts that everyone was out to get her and that her husband had been unfaithful and that she was surrounded by a bunch of backstabbing traitors who didn't have her best interests at heart, and the role our own newspaper played is completely immaterial, and in fact our headlines at the time, such as LOOPY DIANA IS GOING BANANAS or DODI-DIDDLING DI IS A DREADFUL MUM or WE SIDE WITH THE QUEEN AGAINST THIS TRASHY VINDICTIVE HARPY were absolutely nothing to do with Diana's terribly fragile mental health, and furthermore we would like to say that we definitely never printed any invasive photos of Diana, not even those taken with extremely long lenses by paparazzi photographers who were nothing to do with us, and anyone who says different is probably in league with the Satanic Broadcasting Corporation run by a sinister cabal of top executives who are the REAL perpetrators of the car crash which killed her and without which we'd probably still be printing invasive photos of her today… er… er…

ROBERT THOMPSON

GLENDA SLAGG

She's the Fleet Street variant!!!! Geddit??! Hope not!!!

■ EUROVISION – don't you love it??!! OK, so the music is terrible and they take drugs live on TV!?! What's not to like??!!! And wasn't the Italian lead singer divine… mmmmmm… Signor Heavy Drugs *(surely Metal, Ed?)*… I'm addicted to you!??!! Douze points from this judge and that's just for the leather trousers!!!! Just sayin'!! No offence!! Loved the song!!!

■ EUROVISION – don't you hate it??!? Not as much as they hate us!!?! Nul points!!! Just because our singer was a bit on the chunky side and wasn't as goodlooking as Signor Hokey-Cokey from the Italian entry… mmmmmm… *(You've done this bit. Ed.)*. At least poor old James Newman wasn't caught live on TV eating pies!!?! Just sayin'!!? No offence!!! Loved the song!?!

■ AMANDA Holden!!!! OK, so you don't know that "bonjour" means hello!!?! Now it's time for us to say "au revoir", "auf Wiedersehen", "ciao" or, as we say in England, "get lost, Grandma"!!?! No offence!!! Just sayin'!?!! Love your work!!!! And I don't mean what you've had done to your face!!?!

■ SO Max Mosley is no more!!??? Shed a tear with me for the late anti-press campaigner and son of the more famous Sir Oswald!!?! This week, we in the newspaper biz will all be wearing black… though not shirts, obviously, because that would be in poor taste!!!!! As Formula One supremo we mourn your passing – and indeed the lack of passing that made the Monaco Grand Prix such a snooze fest!!!? (Thanks to the guys on the sports desk for this high-octane racing gag!!!?) And, as you are laid to rest and your many achievements are celebrated, let us hope no one brings up the News of the World case and says "spanks for the memories"??!?? Geddit!??!!!!!!

Byeee!!

NHS LATEST
'FISHING GOOD FOR MENTAL HEALTH'

Not if you're a fisherman!

Hancock: arse coverings may have to continue past June 21st

■ Speaking on *The Andrew Marr Show*, Health Secretary Matt Hancock gave the firmest indication yet that arse coverings will have to continue to be worn after June 21st.

"Following the revelations from Dominic Cummings about care homes and elderly patients being shipped out to nursing homes without Covid tests, as I promised, I am going to have to be covering my arse for some considerable time yet," he confirmed. "Possibly right up to the start of the public inquiry in 2022."

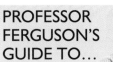

PROFESSOR FERGUSON'S GUIDE TO…

'Cautious hugging'

Britain's top legoverologist, Professor Fuggerson, gives his formerly Sage advice on how to hug safely in Britain's new normal:

1 Arrive at door of married mistress.

2 Look left, look right – check no one's watching.

3 Look through the window – check husband's gone.

4 Double check *Daily Mail* photographer not in bushes.

5 Enjoy safe hugging with someone else's partner of choice.

© *Professor Fuckerson 2021*

Boris Johnson MP
● Live   385,000,000 Views

Prime Minister's Question Time Live on Fakebook

👍 Like   💬 Comment

0 people like this

Something old, something new, something borrowed (the money for the wedding) something blue (the red wall)!

(PRIME MINISTER ENTERS TO SOUND OF RED WALL ARMY CHOIR SINGING "I'M GETTING MARRIED WHILE YOU'RE MOURNING" FROM MY FAIR FIRST LADY)

Boris: And with **one** bound, our hero was **free**! Yes folks, despite a spot of local **difficulty** with a **disgruntled** ex-employee, ie my old mate Dom, the Bozzter simply wheeled out the ultimate **dead cat** distraction strategy and rolled out a **secret** wedding for the papers to **spaff** all over the front pages. And it worked a **treat**. The successful nuptial **roll-out** came in **on** budget and **ahead** of time – a **year** ahead of time, actually, due to Carrie throwing a **wobbly** and saying "You've got to marry me **tomorrow**" after Dom was so rude about her just being my "**girlfriend**", ie top **totty** but not the real **shebang** with all the trimmings. Yes, when your back's to the wall and the ship's **sinking** and the **rats** have left to give evidence to Select Committees, only the **real** statesman can pull a **rabbit** out of the hat. So, I'm sure you've got **lots** of questions to ask about the **service** and the **reception** and the **bride's dress** and I'm **not** afraid to answer them. First one from our **regular** interlocutor, Ms Jo Public. Go, Jo!

Jo Public: Dominic Cummings has accused you of the manslaughter of tens of thousands of innocent people, due to chronic indecision, failure of leadership, dereliction of duty, culpable negligence and criminal incompetence. What do you have to say?

Boris: I'm glad you asked, **good** question. The **reception** was absolutely marvellous. All the papers loved it and most of them put us on the front page. The **dress** came from the **eminent** Greek designer Costalottos, but **obviously** we didn't pay full whack, because **I** was paying. So Carrie borrowed it on the **cheap** and returned it without **any** wine stains on it at all, **hardly**. She said she was keeping the **dress** for two days and I said, "That's how long I **intend** to keep my vows." Top wedding banter from the Bozzter. **Next** question, from Ivor Question…

Ivor Question: Aren't you ashamed of yourself, failing to support the children of this country, not that supporting children is your thing really is it, with your botched Education Catch-Up package?

Boris: Thanks for asking and **yes**, the guest list was **limited** to 30. That's because of **regulations** laid down by Carrie and **not** because I don't have any **friends**. Which I **do**. And it was a **lovely** party. It wasn't a big **affair**. Well, it was, obviously, but it's bad **form** to bring that up at a wedding. So, we all sat on straw bales and drank **cider** from a bottle. Partly to fit in with the **rustic** festival vibe, but mostly because **I** was paying. **And** by the way, the straw bales matched my **hair**. Very Glasto! Very glamping! Very **cheap**! What I call "no cash and Carrie". More top wedding **banter** from yours truly. And the wedding cake was **lovely**. It was of course in several **tiers**. I think it was four, or **maybe** three. Guests were advised **not** to move between tiers. But the important thing was, I **had** the cake and **ate** it. Next question is from Ms Geri Atric – ah ha! Sounds like she was one of the **old** Spice girls! Ding-dong! I **love** Union Jack dresses! Best worn at **half-mast**!

Prime Minister's Brand New First Lady (formerly Senior Girlfriend and Very Special Advisor): Watch yourself! You're a married man now!

Boris: And your **point** is?

Prime Minister's Brand New First Lady: Let Ms Atric ask her question and stop being sexist and ageist.

Boris: OK, I'll let the **old bag** have her say. Geri?

Geri Atric: When are you going to sack Matt Hancock for lying repeatedly, particularly about care homes where you sent thousands of infected patients out of hospital to spread the virus amongst the most vulnerable?

Boris: We drove away in the Prime Ministerial **Uber**, for which **I** paid, but it's 40% off at weekends, and no **surge** pricing, thankfully. We had a big sign "**Just Carried**" on the back, which was a **boffo** joke, dreamt up by **yours truly** when I should **arguably** have been in a COBRA meeting. The car had **several** cans attached, by my dad, Stanley, the First Father. Some were the cans that I keep **kicking** down the road - Heathrow, Hinkley Point, HS2, etcetera, plus the very **big** can that Matt Hancock is going to be **carrying** soon enough. Then it was straight off on our **mini-moon**, which **I** paid for in its **entirety**, due to **Premier Inn's** two-for-one Covid Quarantine **Special** and we shared a corridor with a delightful family from **Bangalore**, who were staying there **without** leaving their rooms for two weeks as it was **so** comfortable. Nothing but the **best** for Carrie, who I'm proud to call my **latest** soulmate.

Boris: Next question – Thomas Doubting…

Thomas Doubting: I'm still concerned about your wife's current role in Downing Street. "First Lady" sounds a bit ironic. "94th Lady" sounds more accurate. Can you clear up what is now her official title and what are her duties?

Boris: From now on, she will **not** be known as Princess Nut Nuts, which was a **typically** derogatory sexist nickname given to her by the **disgraceful** person who was my chief advisor, **confidante** and friend. She won't be known as the Third **Wife**, because that sounds a little bit like the third **wave**, which isn't going to happen, obviously. No, the **latest** Mrs Johnson will now of course be referred to by her official title of **Prime Minister**.

(PRIME MINISTER AND NEW HUSBAND LEAVE TO SOUND OF RUSSIAN ORCHESTRA PLAYING VAN TAM MORRISON'S HIT SONG "BROWN-EYED OR BLUE-EYED OR GREEN-EYED GIRL, I'M REALLY NOT FUSSED")

"Gerry's not ready for hugging again yet"

Astonishment worldwide

■ There has been astonishment worldwide after the agreement by G7 finance ministers to set a minimum Corporate Tax rate that could result in companies making billions in profit having to pay some tax.

"It is extraordinary to think that this agreement could mean these companies will actually pay some tax," said one Wall Street analyst.

"Ensuring companies that make huge profits pay some tax is a wild idea, why didn't people think of it before?" said another analyst.

"It's almost as if these companies have to obey the same rules as everyone else when it comes to paying their fair share. It truly is a mind-boggling concept," said a *(cont. p94)*

POPE CALLED IN SHOCK

Was the PM's wedding legal?

Is Boris Johnson a Catholic?

Those reasons why Michael Gove did not have to self-isolate on return from Portugal in full

1. He is a member of the government and thus no rules apply to him.
2. He has no friends so it doesn't matter.
3. He sweats hand sanitiser.
4. He is a fish and therefore immune from Covid.
5. He is Covid.

Selfish holidaymakers condemned

DOWNING STREET has condemned selfish travellers determined to take unnecessary overseas trips despite amber travel warnings being in place, highlighting the shocking case of one B. Johnson:

"Mr Johnson was so determined to travel to India that he refused to cancel his trip until the very last possible minute, meaning he's only gone and ruined summer for everyone.

"People like Boris are just so impossibly selfish, so desperate for their moment in the sun, they don't care how many lives they ruin in the process."

New Reformed Catholic Church Service of Holy Matrimony for Use in Exceptional Circumstances

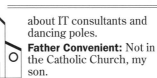

Father Convenient: Welcome, everyone, to Westminster Cathedral. And may I say how delighted I am to officiate at this…

Groom: Get on with it, Padre, the papers are about to go to press.

Father Convenient: Have you come here to enter into Marriage without coercion, freely and wholeheartedly?

Groom: Is that a joke? She's got me by the nut nuts?

Father Convenient: Are you prepared, as you follow the path of Marriage, to love and honour each other for as long as you both shall live?

Groom: Can you stop these gags and get on with the ceremony?

Father Convenient: Have either of you been married before?

Groom: I have a couple of times, but they were C of E.

Father Convenient: Oh, they don't count.

Groom: That's what I always felt.

Father Convenient: Could you now read this bit of paper?

Groom *(reads out)*: I, Boris Alexander the Great de Piffle of Peffle Johnson and Johnson, take you, Carrie, for my lawful wife, to have and to hold, from this day forward, for better, for worse, for richer, for poorer, in sickness and in health, until death do us part *(stops reading)*. Cripes, that's a pretty tall order! Are you sure this is right?

Father Convenient: Yes.

Groom: Well, I've probably done this marriage thing more often than you have and I'm sure there's a get-out clause about IT consultants and dancing poles.

Father Convenient: Not in the Catholic Church, my son.

Groom: Blimey, I seem to be a bit unprepared, haven't read the detail…

Congregation *(all)*: What's new?

Groom: You lot can shut up, if you want the free cider afterwards.

Father Convenient: There will now be an exchange of rings.

Groom: So, I give Carrie a ring – and I get a ring from Dave Cameron.

(Groom's phone rings. Groom answers.)

Groom: Can't talk about supply chain finance now, Dave, I'm in church… Getting married… Stop laughing.

Father Convenient: I now declare you: man and current wife.

Groom: Phew! You've forgotten the bit about there being any just cause or impediment. The Bozzter was a bit worried there might be a chump at the back saying, "How long have you got?"

Father Convenient: We don't do that bit in the Catholic Church.

Groom: I knew there was some reason I chose you rather than Finsbury Park Mosque. Right! Got Wedding Done. Sorted.

Number Ten Photographer: You may now kiss the bride.

Groom: Why would I want to do that? She's my wife now.

Father Convenient: Time now to end with the Lord's Prayer.

Groom: Thank God for Lord Brownlow.

Congregation *(all)*: Amen.

"It's Boris Johnson's pre-nuptial confession – the priests are having to take it in shifts"

Wallace and Gromit statue announced to great joy

by Our Claymation Correspondent
A. Ardman

FINALLY, a statue has been announced which everyone across the entire country can get behind. A tribute to the much-loved comedy pair of Wallace and Gromit is not only a joyful piece of public art to unite the nation, but also a tribute to the brilliant, hard-working animators who did so much to bring the nation's children perfect moments of ingenious, innocent and delightful comedy.

Who could possibly object?

....

On other pages

▨ **Wallace denounced as middle-class white male with no idea of what life is like for ordinary people**

▨ **Wallace's use of language like "crackers" deemed inappropriate**

▨ **Gromit's use of silent treatment deemed a microaggression**

▨ **#Wallacemustfall campaign gathers momentum because of "what he did to that penguin"**

▨ **Wallace torn down and thrown into river for wearing wrong trousers at inappropriate moments**

GCSE Maths

IF THE Recovery Commissioner for education proposes a comprehensive £10bn catch-up plan for UK pupils left behind in the pandemic, but we end up with only a piecemeal £1bn programme spread over three years, who suffers?

A Poor children attending failing schools

B Poor children who don't attend fee-paying schools

C Poor children who don't have pushy middle-class parents

D All of the above

DIARY

BOB DYLAN AT 80
THOSE COLUMNISTS WRITE

PAUL MORLEY: Bobby Dylan speaks to us today just as he will speak to us tomorrow and spoke to us yesterday, as well as the day after yesterday, which is today, though by tomorrow today will be something else, something that defies all dating, something mysterious yet strangely comprehensible. Under Trump, context was flattened, language crumbled, and the "nothing lasts forever" that Dylan had articulated with a sense of beauty and hope as well as grief and loss would be replaced with a crueller, lonelier "nothing lasts forever", a dark ages he could see coming – because he could see into the past, which he knew needed to be surpassed, where fates and destinies and a world of polarities had been set in motion – but which he tried to outwit, jumping into the fray, dodging bullets, however distant and unconcerned he seemed, telling the truth and lying through his bardic hat, scaring himself with his own desert places, but doing the work he needed to do, and that's what really makes you think, though even the word "think" has been redefined by Dylan in ways we cannot comprehend without thinking what thinking now means in this, and every other, context.

CAROL MIDGLEY: I only have to hear a Dylan song to know it's a Dylan song because, well, he always sounds so like Dylan, which is understandable, I suppose, 'cos that's in a way who he is. Fave Dylan song? No contest. "There's Two Wheels on My Wagon". Was that one of his? Breathe not a word to my other half, but I've always had this thing for Cherokees. And in my humble opinion, "Where Do You Go To My Lovely" is one of his all-time best, for what it's worth.

SUZANNE MOORE: This man at 80 knows what he is. He knows what he does. And he always did know what he was. Because what he was is what he did and what he does is what he is. But what do we know of this man at 80? What we know is also what we don't know, because the Dylan we know is also the Dylan we thought we knew before we realised we didn't know a single thing about him. That's the nature of the man: intensely knowable yet at the same time intensely unknowable.

As told to
CRAIG BROWN

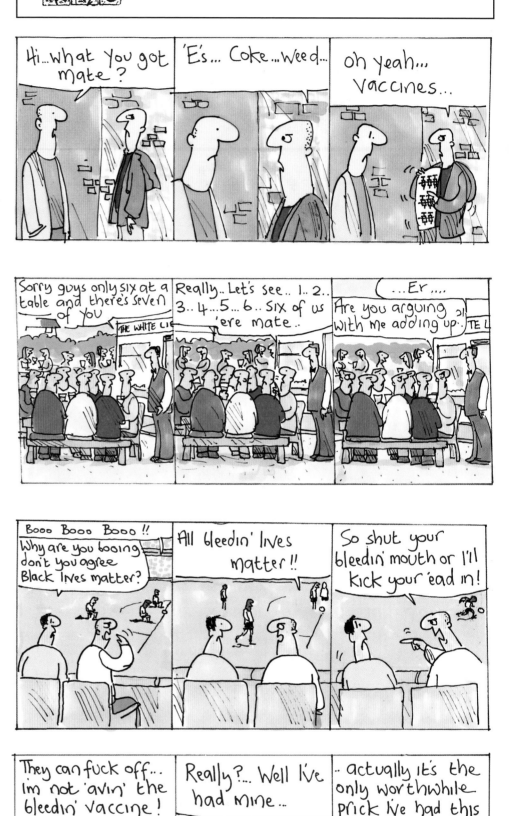

WETHERSPOONS STAFF SHORTAGE

I'm desperate, I'll hire anyone

Wetherspoons boss calls for more EU migration
Satire to sue Tim Martin

by Our Pub Staff **Arthur Lager**

Wetherspoons boss, Tim Martin, has urged Boris Johnson to introduce a visa scheme for EU workers, as his pubs struggle to recruit staff.

This was immediately followed by the news that Satire would be suing Martin.

Said a clearly angry satirical spokesman, "Tim Martin cannot be allowed to get away with passing off such a piece of timeless satire – where a prominent Brexiteer discovers he actually needs the EU workers he campaigned so vociferously to have sent home – as his own work."

He continued, "Up and down the country, satirists are losing their jobs, as there is no way they can compete with the Swiftian levels of satire coming out of Tim Martin's mouth."

A spokesman for Wetherspoons said Tim Martin would vigorously defend Satire's action, pointing out that he'd been a ludicrous figure spouting fanciful nonsense long before these comments and would remain one long after.

■ **New Wetherspoons Happy Hour** – just listen to Tim Martin for an hour! Be happy!

Film highlights
Battle of the Bulging Wallet

How's your hearing?

Half past three

Remake of the famous Second World War tank warfare classic. This time, the British Army drives its new US-designed Ajax armoured fighting vehicle against the enemy, but cannot exceed 20 miles an hour because the crews get tinnitus and they have to stop the battle every 90 minutes to change personnel. Watch the enemy quake in fear as they realise that the British Ajax vehicles can't fire on the move and cannot manoeuvre over small objects – "including bulges", as one cockney driver amusingly quips! You will be amazed at the special effects – particularly the disappearance of £5.5 billion into the manufacturers' pockets to produce the armoured vehicle they call "the Pantser". *(That's enough. Ed.)*

EYE RATING: Terrific battle, which the evil dictators win.

THOSE 'SWEET' HIDDEN MESSAGES MEGHAN CONCEALED IN HER CHILDREN'S BOOK, 'A BENCH OF GRIPES'

■ Princess Diana's favourite flower was the "forget-me-not"

■ Meghan is Princess Diana

■ Don't you forget it!

■ Oh yes, Charles is a rubbish father

■ And so was his father

■ The royal family are all rubbish.

■ Aren't I sweet?

From The Message Boards
Members of the online community respond to the major issues of the day...

Logo controversy

Guys, I see Amazon amended its new logo, which was a patch of serrated packing tape over the familiar curved arrow, thus resembling a Hitler moustache above a smiling mouth! I must admit I laughed when I saw it, but my teenage daughter called me a white supremacist and boycotted Amazon for a week, meaning I had to order her vegan hair conditioner through my account! – *Bogbrush*

I suffer from alopecia barbae and can only grow facial hair on a small area directly under my nose. When I did Movember people called it a Hitler moustache, which inspired me to do a mural of Hitler riding a unicorn over an NHS rainbow, with doctors, supermarket workers and Amazon operatives underneath. My neighbours liked it so much they did an extra minute's clap just for me! – *Phil Trum*

Hitler in fact favoured an expansive Kaiserbart moustache but this imperial style was incompatible with a gas mask, so he was ordered to trim it while serving in the Deutsches Heer during the Weltkrieg. If more people knew this, they might judge him less harshly and see that the toothbrush is actually a very practical design which enables the correct wearing of a face covering. As for people complaining about 'little Hitlers' prosecuting people for not wearing masks – I can assure you that if Der Führer were in charge today, they would be facing something a bit stiffer than a £200 fine! – *Legion of the Damned*

wtf!!? first his mum calls him adolf hitler then hes ordered to grow a hitler tash? thats never gonna end well 😅 – *Hunny pot*

Scientists now know that the philtrum plays a crucial role in determining facial structure during embryonic development. Given Hitler's interest in physical characteristics, it is ironic that he chose to obscure this particular area with a facial 'fig leaf'. Or is it more than mere coincidence? Could it be that he instinctively knew he must hide this key to his true self? Was the fraudulent cosmopolitan shapeshifter aware that his 'Aryan' façade was a barber's blade away from exposure and *This post has been shortened by the moderators – new user name*

My young son had never heard of Hitler, and I had to explain what a bad man he was. Now he screams in terror when he sees an Amazon van, and not just because of the pollution from their idling engines. – *Emily*

hair hitler with his one bollock woud be a great empowering roll model for cancer #testiclercancer #workethic #notoracism #helpforheros – *Darling Deneyz*

Great stuff guys! – *Bogbrush*

POETRY CORNER

In Memoriam Edward de Bono, physician, psychologist, author, inventor and philosopher

So. Farewell
Then Edward de Bono,
You were famous
For lateral thinking.

Now, sadly, you
Are horizontal
And no longer
Thinking outside
Of the box.

E.J. Thribb
(17½ thinking hats)

CAMPUS

"Would you back a consent test? It's a simple 'yes' or 'no'"

BROADCASTING HISTORY MADE
GB NEWS LAUNCHED

We apologise for the technical problems – many of you can see and hear us perfectly

GB News focuses on controversial gesture

In the wake of the Black Lives Matter movement, a new gesture has been gaining enormous popularity and is sure to inflame recent conflicts over social justice and the so-called "woke culture".

"It's called 'Taking the Neil'," said one expert. "All you have to do is go on GB News, spout a load of mad opinions to a completely supine interviewer, take a cheque on your way out, and that's it.

"The beautiful thing is that it can mean so much – taking the Neil shows you are clearly taking a really impressive stand against lockdowns, the EU and about 500 other things that seem to make people very angry these days.

"The worrying thing is that it may lead to other gestures, like 'jerking the knee', where you instinctively react against something just because it's been on Great Brillo Snooze."

Embarrassing names make GB News a laughing stock

by Our Media Staff
Ivor Made-Up Name

THE new national news channel, GB News, was the object of ridicule this week, as its launch was marred by a string of childish names making their way onto the screen.

Viewers were staggered to hear introductions to presenters such as "Andrew Neil", and "Dan Wootton".

"This is simply not funny," said GB News viewer, Mike Hunt. "It's not clever and it's not amusing.

These are not names that anybody could take seriously."

Another furious viewer, Mike Oxlong, agreed. "I do not turn on my television and expect to be told to watch somebody called 'Laurence Fox'. This joke has gone too far, it's really pathetic."

A Mr Hugh Janus from Pratt's Bottom added, "I definitely heard somebody introducing 'Allison Pearson of The Daily Telegraph' as if that could be a real thing. Grow up, GB News, before I report you to the regulator OffFuck."

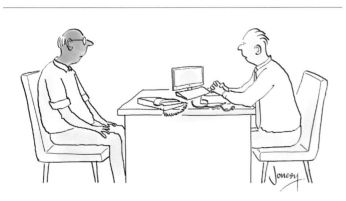

"It isn't too much sun, Mr Compton, it's too much GB News"

Worrying new signs of property babble

by Our Housing Correspondent
Lee S. Holder

THE country is widely reckoned to be experiencing its clearest signs yet of a "Property Babble", where nobody talks about anything except house prices.

"It's really concerning," said one industry expert. "If you look at the times people normally bang on and on and on about house prices, it's been rising at a steady rate for several years. But in the last year it's shot up by 10-15% across the country. London's experienced smaller growth because nobody talked about anything else there anyway, even before Covid, but now it's affected the North-East, Cornwall, and other formerly cheap areas."

Another pointed out, "The worst thing is that often out-of-towners come to deprived areas and only talk about their charming new cottage and how the value has gone up in the last few years, which literally sucks all the oxygen out of the discussion and means that locals don't get a chance to have their own endless boring discussions, because none of them can afford to buy a home in the first place."

G7 celebrates coronavirus success

THE meeting of leaders from the developed world last week announced their delight at the immediate success of their coronavirus initiative.

"I think we've really made a difference to the spread of the disease already," said President Biden. "People were sceptical about what we could achieve, but we've proved the doubters wrong."

The president pointed to the huge spike in cases in Cornwall following the decision to fly in leaders, their staff and security teams from all over the world to a small location, in a part of the United Kingdom that had previously got off lightly.

"It's important that all the world should be levelled up, and treated equally," said the US president, "and hopefully Cornwall will now have as many Covid cases as Delhi."

(Rotters)

THE DANIEL MORGAN MET CORRUPTION SCANDAL

Who will question Cressida Dick

Who we would like to see question her

Nothing to happen urgently as a result of damning new report which shames nation

DOWNING STREET says a damning report which shames the nation, revealing corruption and underhand practices in public procurement/Tory donors/the police, will result in nothing whatsoever happening urgently.

"We need to act by doing nothing with urgency, as that's what the public expect," said a Downing Street source.

"It's not enough just to be seen to be doing nothing, we have to actually do nothing.

"It would be so easy to just sweep all this under the rug because we're 15 points ahead in the polls... so that's what we're doing."

Let's Parlez Franglais!

Numéro 94
La Guerre des Sausages

(A la barbecue finale du Summit de G-sept sur la plage de Corbis Bay, le Prime Minister de Grande Bretagne, states-homme mondiale et diplomate extraordinaire, menace le Président de France avec un fork)

Boris: En garde, Monsieur le Froggy! C'est la guerre maintenant! Acceptez-vous les snorkers britanniques ou else!

Macron: Mais c'est le treaty about Northern Ireland que vous avez negotiated et signed!

Boris: Did je? Vraiment? Je ne me souviens pas les details – c'est un très longue document et très boring et je was probablement distracted par Madame Arcuri et les leçons de technologie informatique... nudgez nudgez, winkez winkez!!!

Macron: Vous n'avez pas read it, n'est-ce pas?

Boris: Parlez about le pot et le kettle! Vous pensez que Northern Ireland n'est pas un integral morceau du Royaume United?

Macron: Bien – is it? C'est difficile à tell avec le border imaginair dans la mer et les protocols qui ne font pas de sense!!

Boris: Quoi je will say is ceci: keepez-vous les mains off nos bangers, Monsieur Wannabee Napoléon! Je suis exactement comme le Duc de Wellington, Winston Churchill et Madame Thatcher, toutes rolled ensemble! C'est mon moment de Falklands, sauve avec les produits de porc instead of les missiles d'Exocets. We shall combatter vous sur la plage de Cornwall! Et dans les streets de Belfast! Nous ne surrenderons pas jamais!!

Macron: Typique perfide Albion! Vous êtes bonkers!

Frau Merkel: Qu'est-ce-qui happen here?

Boris: Oh non! Les allemands entrent la guerre sur le wrong side!!

Frau Merkel: Achtung! Hände hoch Engländer – for you, the sausage war is over!

President Biden: Calmez-vous down tous! C'est un summit important, pas un food fight!!

Boris: Food Fight!!!

(Le PM jette une saucisse à la tête de Président Macron)

Macron: Je suis blessé! Je bleed!

Boris: Non, c'est le ketchup, vous blouson grand de la jeune fille!! Et vous, Madame Merkel, prenez that! Avez-vous some mushy Peas in Our Time!! Ha ha ha!!

(Il jette des pois-hâchés dans la direction de la Chancellor allemande)

Boris: La Grand Guerre Saucisses sera won sur les playing-champs d' Eton!!

Macron: C'est pathétique. Mais ce n'est pas la guerre.

(Le Summit continue sur les sujets borings de climate change, le roll-out globale des vaccines et les taxes pour les géants technologiques zzzzzzzzz)

© The Late Kilomètres Kington 2021

NORTHERN IRELAND: THE MAIN MISSING MEAT PRODUCTS

- Chicken "no-get"s (frozen)
- Ongoing beef burger
- Blocked pudding
- You-lose sausage
- Missing links
- A complete stuffing (rage & onion)
- Turkey swizzlers
- Gaggis
- Chicken DUP-pers
- Sausage rules
- Encumbered-land sausage

Soup of the Day   Day of the Soup

POLICE LOG
Neasden Central Police Station

08.36 hrs All officers assemble for briefing on today's FREE NEASDEN march along the High Street, in which a number of respected local civic groups ("Neasden Twinned with Palestine For a Calmer World", "Neasden 5G Lizard Neighbourhood Watch" and "Neasden Justice For Fathers And For Maddie Too") will be walking the streets to the town hall to make their case for the cautious roll-back of Covid restrictions.

09.14 hrs Officers witness a number of calm and respectable Neasden residents following a journalist from the Neasden Argus through the streets at a running pace, in what they naturally presume is a fun charity event. The new Neasden Policing Conduct Pledge ("Mind Your Language") prevents them from intervening, as the journalist repeatedly screams "Help me, you stupid bastards, these people are mad," so they restrict themselves to maintaining order in an observational capacity and threatening the journalist with arrest for foul language. Senior officers note that if the journalist is subsequently beaten to death, they will be in a prime position to arrest wrongdoers as they leave the scene. Station answerphone reveals 37 messages from someone claiming to be a journalist from the Neasden Argus in fear of his life, which are deleted as being a microaggression against station answerphone capacity.

23.38 hrs Neasden Police Press Office issues leaflets about how successfully today's march was policed, pointing out that nobody was chased at all, and even if they had been, no officers from Neasden witnessed anything. All officers return to station to begin recording video pledges that the Neasden service is definitely not institutionally corrupt and anyone who says it is, is likely to get their head kicked in.

ROW OVER RIP-OFF PCR COVID TESTS

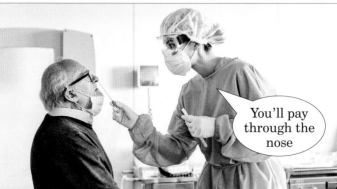

You'll pay through the nose

NHS gets cross

THE ENTIRE National Health Service got very cross today when they found out that they were receiving a medal and a letter from the Queen rather than a decent pay rise.

The official announcement by Buckingham Palace surprised doctors and nurses throughout the country, who had been hoping for a more than 1 percent increase in their pay packet. They received instead a small piece of metal on a ribbon, to be shared between 1.5 million people.

Said one disappointed health worker, "It's a lovely gesture, obviously, but sadly I can't pay the bills with a decoration – even one with such a distinguished history as the George Cross."

She added, "Actually, I'm not cross. I am livid."

LLOYD WEBBER ATTACKS GOVERNMENT OVER WEST END RESTRICTIONS

Don't make a song and dance about it!

Sarah Vain

on Sarah Vine's divorce

BOO-HOO-HOO! So Sarah Vine is splitting up with her other half! Excuse me for not shedding a tear but, let's be honest, they weren't the most lovable of couples. And as for her boring old marriage, well, she didn't half bang on about it in her column!

I'm sorry, Sarah, no one wanted to know about how Michael didn't pull his weight around the house and wasn't up to scratch as a husband – whatever that means! Urghhh! "TMI"!!!! That's "Too Much Information" for those of you don't have children who shout this at you when you write about them and the mess they make in their bedrooms!!!

Ok, so Govey didn't do as much hoovering as he might have done, but he was running the country, dear. Which you were quite keen to brag about in your column, if we are being honest. Just saying! No offence! Love your work!

But to be brutally frank, Sarah, which I know you would want, why do you think the *Daily Mail* gave you a column in the first place? It wasn't for the make-up tips and the handbag insights, was it? No, it was because Mr Vine was in the cabinet and you could give us the lowdown on Dave and Samcam and the goss on Boris and Carrie!

So forgive me if I don't get out the tiny violins and stifle a snigger when you ask for privacy. Come off it, Sarah! *Daily Mail* columnist requests privacy? What next? Pope asks for a Hindu funeral? Bear asks for an indoor toilet?

And your husband's no better is he? He's the man who told us we could LEAVE a relationship and expect everything to remain the same! Govey told us we would remain friends with our former partners and that it would all be easy and we would even be richer! By £350 million.

That's not how it works, mate! As you're about to find out! In spades! Or maybe spads!

Now I must go and write a piece about my niggling doubts about Harry and Meghan's marriage! But good luck to you, Sarah, as you embark on the world of Sad Singledom and don't think I won't be watching from the sidelines and wishing you all the best in what I hope is the car crash of your life. No offence! Just saying! Love your work! You're the one who put the ME into MEAN!

©*Sarah Vile 2021*

"Do you have any more supportive mattresses?"

BED SHOP

YOU'RE A WALKING PIECE OF CRAP

R&J

British Museum loses its marbles

by Our Archaeological Staff
Perry Cleese

IT'S OFFICIAL! The British Museum has completely lost its marbles and appointed former chancellor George Osborne to be its chairman.

Commentators are all agreed that the appointment is conclusive proof that the museum has gone totally bonkers and needs to be saved from itself.

Said the Greek Heritage Department, "The British Museum clearly cannot look after itself and needs to send all its artefacts to Athens at once before Osborne privatises them and sells them off to Tory donors."

Defenders of Osborne say he was chosen on the grounds that he has a lot of experience with ruins and has a successful track record of reducing numerous British institutions to piles of rubble.

Said one delighted governor, "It's not just the Evening Standard

that he turned into history, but also the British economy and the North of England."

Said another, "The British Museum has been having problems, but with George in charge, those problems will soon be over – along with the museum."

George Osborne already has eight jobs, but is said to be delighted to take on the challenge of the British Museum, declaring, "Who says I never created any jobs ? I've got loads."

Lord Elgin was unavailable for comment, with friends saying he was too busy turning in his grave.

FIRST DAY COVER-UP

POST OFFICE

TO COMMEMORATE the commencement of the statutory enquiry into the Post Office's Horizon IT scandal, we present this first day cover-up of stamps showing key moments of that memorable chapter in history.

The four stamps will depict ex-CEO Paula Vennells ignoring the plight of jailed postmasters while sitting in a chair, ignoring the plight of a jailed postmasters while sitting in a different chair, ignoring the plight of jailed postmasters while standing up, and ignoring the plight of postmasters whose lives were destroyed, while wearing a blouse.

Treat them just like Paula treated her staff: tear them from their friends, throw them inside the confines of a deep, dark metal box, and then just walk away for someone else to let them out!

For once, there's something first class about her!

MATT 'N' GINA'S POLITICAL AFFAIR

EXCLUSIVE TO ALL NEWSPAPERS

MARTHA HANCOCK IS WHO WE SHOULD FEEL SORRY FOR, AS WE HARASS HER

by **Philippa Space**

IN ALL the acres of coverage of Matt Hancock and his lover, the one person who should have our sympathy, as we chase her down the street screaming questions at her, is of course his long-suffering wife and the mother of his three children, Martha Hancock.

We can only imagine what is going through her head and the strain she is under as her marriage of 15 years ends so painfully, because we've had no answer from her yet, no matter how many of our reporters camp outside her house bellowing questions through the letterbox.

This woman has done nothing wrong and yet seems to be the one who looks near breaking point as she attempts to get through our scrum of reporters and paparazzi to reach the car with her children.

So yes, let's have nothing but sympathy for Martha Hancock, she deserves time and space now. Time and space to decide to which one of the hacks hiding in her shed she will give her first exclusive interview.

SECURITY BREACH LATEST

Who wanted to get rid of Matt Hancock?

MI5 narrows shortlist of suspects down to 60 million people.

The Eye's Controversial New Columnist

The columnist who is angry that he hasn't got his own series on Disney Plus

This week I am very angry about the news that they have developed a flying car that has successfully flown between two Slovakian airports. They do not seem to acknowledge my role in the development of this invention. I have been doing extensive research in this field and, in the course of my investigations, I have successfully managed to put trains, books, Lego bricks, plush Winnie-the-Poohs, ice lollies and soiled nappies all in the air for several seconds. Building up to phase two, I decided on a suitable car, which was a talking Lightning McQueen with four phrases and glowing eyes. I then performed modifications on the car, which involved smearing Nutella on it to ease the drag from crosswinds. In March of this year, I launched the car, and during its flight it travelled from my hand, stayed several feet in the air without need for petrol or electricity, and made a successful landing on the cat. I am very angry about them leaving my name off this invention and rest assured that if they develop a flying cat (which was a serendipitous discovery caused by my research) they will be hearing from my *(cont. p94)*

Flying cars by 2030

"What's this idiot's problem?"

Boris Johnson

Home | Create

Boris Johnson MP
● Live   385,000,000 Views

Prime Minister's Question Time Live on Fakebook

👍 Like   💬 Comment

0 people like this

(PRIME MINISTER ENTERS TO RUSSIAN SOUND SYSTEM PLAYING RED ARMY CHOIR SINGING FUNEREAL VERSION OF "I'M FREE" BY THE WHO-ARE-YOU-KIDDING?)

Boris: **Greetings**, folks! Yes, it's the **day** you've **all** been waiting for – the day I promised was **irreversible**. Not a **red**-letter day. Even better, even safer – an **amber**-letter day! July 19th is **"Freedom Day"**!

(RED ARMY CHOIR SING "HALLELUJAH", SUDDENLY CUT OFF BY...)

Professor Scareyouwhittyless: We told you not to say the F Word!

Boris: That's what "Freedom Day" is **all** about. I'm **free** to say it! And that's just the **start**.

(PING! PRIME MINISTER IGNORES PHONE)

Boris: Here are some of the **other** freedoms you can now **embrace**. But not too **closely**, obviously. You will be **free** to stay indoors. **Free** to work from **home**, should you want to continue to do so. **Free** to wear a **mask**, if you so choose. **Free** to frown at others **not** wearing masks, if you think it's **appropriate** and they're not **bigger** than you. **Free** to catch Covid-19. **Free** to share it around. **Free** to visit A and E. **Free** to throw off your **face** mask and change it for an **oxygen** mask. **Free** to blame anyone else for this mess apart from **me** because from now on it's your **own** responsibility!

Sir Patrick Unvallanced: Prime Minister, you're also free to change your mind about "Freedom Day".

Professor Scareyouwhittyless: Which we implore you to do.

(BORIS'S PHONE STARTS PINGING MADLY)

Boris: Hold on a second – I'd better **check** that. Don't worry, **nothing** serious, it's not **Arcuri** or **Cameron**. Just the **NHS App** telling me I've been in **contact** with 60,000 possible Covid carriers at Wembley.

Professor Scareyouwhittyless (taking a step back): Oh my God, we're all going to die...

Sir Patrick Unvallanced (to Boris): So are you going to do the right thing?

Boris: Absolutely, Boffin B. I'll do what **everyone** else is doing when they get pinged – I'll **delete** the NHS App.

(PINGING STOPS)

Boris: There! **Sorted!** The pingdemic is **over!** It's Freedom Day! **Freedom** from the NHS App! **Freedom** from boring old self-isolation! Time for me now to **open** up to the country, but only in a very **safe** and responsible way. Here's a question from a Captain Sensible. **Damned** good military man. **Fire** away, Captain...

Captain Sensible: You keep talking about people using their common sense, but can we trust the public's common sense, given that there was a man in Leicester Square sticking a flare up his bottom?

Boris: Absolutely. **Top** bloke! Give that man **honorary** membership of the **Bullingdon Club**! And just to be clear, by "**common** sense", I don't mean "**Commons** sense". "Commons sense" dictates that it's okay to stick your **tongue** down the throat of your **SPAD**, whilst being filmed by a secret camera in your office's smoke alarm. That is **not** to be recommended, and is even **more** dangerous to your career prospects than removing your underpants and placing a **flare** up your **jacksie**. Next! It's a Ms Carla Blind. **What's** your question, Carla?

Carla Blind: Speaking of football supporters – what are you going to do about the terrible racist messages?

Boris: Now. **Serious** face. Let me **assure** you, Carla, that I will **not** stop

until I have **named** and **shamed** the person who's to **blame** for these foul outbursts of vile abuse. The responsibility **clearly** falls at the door of the person at the **top**, who's stoking the **fire** and creating an atmosphere in which these **appalling** views can flourish. And **I'm** not scared of stepping up to the plate, holding **my** hand up and **pointing** the finger at Mark Zuckerberg. **Not** forgetting Jack Dorsey. They will **not** be allowed to attend **any** football matches in future.

Carla Blind: Unless of course they break in, having stuck a couple of hundred quid into the hands of a steward.

Boris: Which is the sort of **cash** for **access** that should **only** be done through the **proper** channels. If Johnny Gatecrasher would like to play **tennis** with me in return for a **generous** donation, then I'm sure that could be arranged. Just use your "**Commons** sense". Now, as it's Freedom Day, I'm **free** to clear off, before anyone checks **my** history and notices any out-of-context racist **slurs** in my old articles. **Escape** to victory! **Onwards** to liberty!

(PRIME MINISTER STARTS TO LEAVE – BUT IS MET AT THE DOOR BY THE HEALTH SECRETARY. PRIME MINISTER EMBRACES HIM)

Boris: What ho, the **Saj**! How's my **new** Minister for **Health**?

Sajid Javid: Unhealthy. I've got Covid again. And now maybe you have too.

Boris: No **sweat**! Thank **God** I turned off the app.

Sajid Javid: No, Prime Minister, you need to self-isolate.

Boris: **Pish** and **nonsense**! I have a **cunning** plan. I've checked the **rules** and I've found a **special** rule that says the rules don't apply to **me**.

Jane Calamity, Captain Sensible, Carla Blind and others: Boooooo!!!!

Boris: **Yikes** and **double** yikes! Disgruntled public alert! What I **meant** to say was: of course I'm doing the **sensible** thing and holing up for **ten** days, so I'll be **completely** out of touch.

Jane Calamity: So what's new?

Boris: **Phew**! Think I got away with it. What a **Phew-turn**! Now where **was** I? Oh yes, **forwards** to freedom!

(PRIME MINISTER EXITS)

That successful NHS Chief application letter in full

Dear Mr. Javid,
I am not
Dido Harding.
    Yours,
    Amanda Pritchard

"What's the betting it's going all the way to Troy?"

ROBERT THOMPSON

BANG! BANG! DON'T TAKE IT TOO LITERALLY SIR

JULY 19 END OF ALL RESTRICTIONS

WORLD EXCLUSIVE FIRST INTERVIEW

'IT'S WONDERFUL TO HAVE MY FREEDOM BACK'

by Our Lockdown Staff **Libby Tarian**

IN A WORLD exclusive first interview on Freedom Day, the coronavirus has spoken of its joy that the shackles are finally off and it can enjoy the freedom cruelly denied to it by 15 months of rolling lockdowns.

Relaxing by his pool, the virus looked clearly relieved at the end of restrictions.

"You have no idea how much I have missed popping into a pub filled to the rafters!" he gushed. "And as for nightclubs, God, how I've looked forward to strutting my stuff again! I see a dance floor and I light up. I just love the positivity that comes from sharing a damp room full of sweaty people forgetting all their inhibitions and just living for the moment.

"Freedom Day could not come a day too soon for me. People need to abandon their masks, go out and just breathe in that air! Doesn't that feel good? That's the taste of freedom and I'm determined to go out there and do what I want, when I want.

"Life isn't about being cooped up indoors hiding, life is for dying... er, I mean living."

Those handy planet-saving tips in full by *Allegra Stratton*

Want to save the planet? DON'T WORRY. You absolutely DON'T have to do anything really drastic like cutting down on meat or dairy, taking fewer flights, or do anything as reckless as giving up your car. Here are a few brilliant suggestions which will do practically as much good, but which you'll hardly notice!

1 If you are a man, shave only one half of your face. If you are a woman, only shave your legs from the knee up. This will dramatically lower your hot water and shaving-foam carbon costs and probably save a few pandas.

2 Spend two minutes a day breathing half as often as you normally would. This means you will be expelling a bit less carbon dioxide and will probably make up for a transatlantic flight or two!

3 Try switching your normal toothpicks for toothpicks made of bamboo. Toothpick use is believed to be a substantial part of the modern carbon footprint and cutting down here will work wonders.

4 When your are driving your two-ton car 200 metres to the shops and back, make sure you keep the air-conditioning on a LOW setting instead of a HIGH one. Car air-conditioning systems on an unnecessarily high setting are doing real damage to the ozone layer and coral reefs.

5 When you're out at a cocktail bar, ask the waiter to remove a single olive from your martini. This will save olive transportation costs and this can HUGELY impact your *(That's enough incredibly stupid lifestyle changes. Ed.)*

SAGE WARNS ABOUT EFFECTS OF LONG JAVID

by Our Pingdemic Expert
DIDO HARPINGDEMIC

Leading scientists in Britain were today united in expressing concern at the latest development in the coronavirus pandemic – the existence of Long Javid.

Said one, "Javid is bad enough when you experience him the first time and many early sufferers thought he had gone away for good. But now, over a year later, Javid's back, causing havoc to our public healthcare system and it looks like he's here to stay."

The future implications of Long Javid are as yet unknown, but already thousands of Britons are reporting feelings of fatigue, depression and a constant pain in the neck.

The scientist continued, "We have to face facts and acknowledge that we're going to have to learn to live with Javid. The best we can recommend is that the public wear masks over their eyes whenever he appears on TV."

That Southern Water CEO's apology

On behalf of my company, Southern Water, I'd like to apologise for my earlier apology for leaking raw sewage into the sea.

TOILET DUCK

It now appears that my apology was also full of shit. When I said "putting the environment front and centre is what matters to all of us", I was clearly talking out of my arse.

TOILET DUCK

Unfortunately, a large amount of crap made it into my statement without being properly processed and filtered out. When I observed that we owed it to our customers that our company, Southern Water, should be "fully transparent", I should have mentioned that that transparency did not apply to the water we were pumping into the sea. Or, as it's now known, "the wee".

TOILET DUCK

Our customers have every right to poo poo my earlier statements, which stank, but rest assured that, despite the £90 million fine, we are still flush with cash. It was just a plop in the ocean.

Yours sincerely,

A TURD

A. Turd
CEO, Southern Water Closet

BEZOS ANNOUNCES PLANS FOR SPACE TRIP

The toilet and food conditions will be incredibly primitive, of course

Will it be worse than one of your warehouses ?

POETRY CORNER

Lines on the 100th anniversary of the Chinese Communist party

So. Congratulations
Then China's
Communist Party,
You are 100
Years old.

I wonder what
You want for
Your birthday?

Oh, that's right –
Taiwan.

E.J. Thribb
(17½ Uyghurs left)

Lines on the Football Match Between England and Scotland in the Group Stage of the European Championships

'Twas in the year of 2021, delayed from 2020,

That there should have been drama and thrills a'plenty,

For this was the great clash of the Auld Rivals at Wembley,

A fixture that made grown men in replica shirts go trembly.

Not since Euro 1996 had these teams faced up on the pitch

In a match long-awaited by fans from Crowborough to Crianlarich.

The match was billed as being "once in a generation"

With Brave Caledonia and Proud Albion meeting nation to nation.

In the great quarter-packed Stadium the opposing teams gathered

And on the television the pundits and ex-players all blathered,

A tartan army invaded London and went to Leicester Square,

There were men in kilts with bagpipes and cans of lager everywhere.

The capital was festooned with these traditional Scots regalia,

Though only a few fans got drunk and showed off their genitalia.

And so the battle was hyped up by one and by all –

This would be indyref two, except with goals and a ball.

And what happened in the event ? It was a nil-all draw.

As a poet this seems quite a clear metaphor.

There was more chance of sighting yon monster Nessie

Than seeing a goal in this contest so messy.

For 'twas neither Bannockburn, nor indeed Culloden,

And no decisive result was coming any time sudden.

Perhaps, as in politics, so it was played out in sport?

No one was the winner – aye, there's food for thought!

I realise of course this may not be how Ms Sturgeon spun it

And she may have decided that it was in fact Scotland wot won it,

But I am afraid that in this case I will have to disagree

With the lookalike Krankie so bold and so wee.

© *William McGonagoalless*

Mary Ann Bighead on
...being taken less seriously than men

IN MY brilliant new book I look at the most important issue of the day: why am I always undervalued, and never given the credit that I deserve?

Ever since I left my top school and went to a top university, where I excelled before being given a top job on the *Times*, I have always been underestimated.

It is a fact that I am brilliant and the men I come across are all useless – yet still the jealous misogynists imply that I am a bighead and have an over-inflated opinion of myself. As a result, they attempt (and fail) to mock me, by giving me the silly nickname "Mary Ann Sieghart".

It's yet another example of men trying to keep all women – not just me – in their place and merely proves that they are not nearly as a clever as I am, since, as I may have mentioned, I am not just a world-renowned pundit, but also a top columnist and visiting Professor at King's College London, Trustee of the Scott Trust, as well as Visiting Fellow of All Souls College, Oxford.

Which all goes to prove the point that I am NOT a bighead, and in a just world, I would be given the opportunity to write an article about how unfairly I've been treated, like the one you're reading now (which you probably aren't even reading because it wasn't written by a man!).

A Scottish Doctor Writes

AS a doctor, I am often asked, "Doctor, have I got Covid?"

The simple answer is, "Yes – of course you have, now get out of my surgery." What happens is that the Scottish football fan, or patient as they're now known, goes down to England wearing full tartan army uniform, including kilt and tam o' shanter, but no underpants and, more importantly, no mask. He then fails to observe any social distancing whatsoever, and comes back full of beer, kebab and Covid. This is known as "football fever" or *delirium idioticus maximus*, to give it its full medical term.

A positive side effect of football fever is that the patient can say the Scots didn't come back from Wembley empty handed. The negative side effect is that the patient is now in bed, in isolation, with nothing to watch on TV but England going through. Football fever leads to a subsequent spike in coronavirus infections in Scotland, which is then ignored by all politicians.

If you think you're suffering from the Delta variant after travelling to England to watch Scotland, you're absolutely right. Please stay at home and don't come anywhere near me.
© *A Scottish Doctor*.

LATE SCORE
Covid – 19, Scotland – 0.

Former contestants look back at Love Island experience

by Our Entertainment Staff
Bea Kini and **Phil Speedos**

A COUPLE have told of their mental anguish after appearing in the first ever series of Love Island.

Set in an Eden-like paradise, the experience turned out to be less than perfect.

Explained Eve, "I got really good vibes off Adam. As well as his rib. I didn't want to, like, put all my eggs in one basket, but there was only, like, one basket."

Said Adam, "Eve was hot, she was wearing virtually nothing – well totally nothing actually."

The first challenge the Love Islanders were set was to resist temptation. "I mean, who would have thought that snake would turn out to be, like, a total snake," recalled Eve.

"He told me to, like, take a bite and well, one thing led to another and we, like, coupled up and cracked on."

After being evicted, the pair continued to be celebrities for a while, regularly appearing on page one of the Bible (the Sun having only just come out for the first time), but the media soon lost interest in them after they begat top influencers, Cain and Abel, who themselves hit the headlines after featuring in a notorious murder case.

"I was buzzin' when it all started," said a chastened Adam, fully-clothed in a fig leaf, "but now I really regret taking part. The fall of mankind put a real strain on my mental health."

The show's creator, God, defended the contestants' aftercare, saying, "I have always given contestants free will. What the numpties do with it is their own business."

"Of course we won't treat you like a piece of meat"

ENGLAND'S FOOTBALL HEROES

1. LATE SUBSTITUTE

They think it's all over...

...let's pretend it is!

2. AWAY PLAYER

♫ I'm not coming home ♫

3. GOING ALL THE WAY

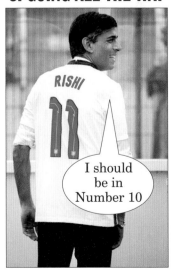

RISHI 11

I should be in Number 10

ENGLAND TEAM 'CAN TAKE HOPE FROM EURO 2020 VICTORIES'

COMMENTATORS say that, despite losing to Italy, England can take real positives away from their victories at Euro 2020, with stunning wins over Germany, Denmark and Priti Patel.

"It was their victory over the Home Secretary that will stay long in the mind. There was some lovely movement right across Twitter and Priti was quickly outflanked by both Mings and Rashford, who teamed up nicely to leave her leaden-footed as they attacked on Insta," chuckled Gary Lineker, as he ate a bag of crisps.

"They held the line impressively – that Priti was creating an environment where racism thrived and, under all that sustained pressure, it was only a matter of time before Priti's jumping on the football bandwagon turned into a massive own goal for her."

Gary Vinegar continued, "If the England lads can take that form into the 2022 World Cup, you have to say there's no politician on the planet they'll be scared to take on."

EURO 2020 SCANDAL

How did these so-called fans get into the stadium?

THERE was fury from well-respected football hooligans, who had spent hours climbing fences and running from police and stewards, after they witnessed some chancers with no interest in football just waltzing into the stadium.

"It's a disgrace," said one yob. "You can see he's just pulled an England shirt over his suit so he can pretend to be a football fan. He's clearly managed to wangle his way in scot-free with his lady friend, taking a seat which should have gone to someone who really needed it

because they've been drinking Strongbow since eight in the morning."

The fears are that the presence of this couple could ruin Britain's bid to stage the World Cup in 2030.

A Doctor Writes

AS A doctor, I am often asked, "Doctor, I have a burning sensation in my anus, what do you think it could be?"

The simple answer is, "You have a flare stuck up your arse. Now get out of my surgery, you drunken idiot, before you burn it down."

© *A doctor.*

♪ PINGING IN ♪ ♫ THE RAIN ♪

"I'm good at opening things up"

"How much has he paid to sit next to me?"

TOP TEN WAYS TO AVOID BEING CAUGHT BY THE 'PINGDEMIC'

1. Turn your phone off.

2. Wrap it in three layers of tinfoil just to be sure.

3. Drive ten miles from home then throw your phone down a drain so nobody can contact you on it and tell you to isolate.

4. Sell your house, in case you get pinged through the walls due to your sick neighbours.

5. Leave your family and move to a remote croft in the Scottish Highlands without telling them, to ensure you can keep everyone away.

6. Grow a beard more than three metres long to ensure nobody can get close enough to ping you.

7. Live a new life off the land, speaking to nobody. Return to the wild. Eat raw rabbits you have shot from a distance with a bow and arrow so the rabbits can't ping you either.

8. Have your ears surgically removed.

9. And your head, just to be sure.

10. Er... that's it.

That Mohamed Amersi/Prince Charles Intimate Dinner Menu in Full

Entrée

Brown-nose Windsor soup

A lot of dough balls

– ❋ –

Donor kebab

Squids proquo

Greased Palma Ham

Assortment of meets, served with carrots and gravy

Duchess (of Cornwall's nephew's) potatoes

– ❋ –

Bread pudding

Choice of Sweeteners

– ❋ –

Price: £15k to have dinner with Prince Charles or £30k not to.
Apply:
B. Elliot,
c/o Quidsintotally

TORY GROUP 'DENIES INFLUENCE'
by Our Conservative Correspondent **Quinn T. Cential**

A shadowy group of rich Tories who meet in secret to discuss policy has denied having any influence over government policy.

The mysterious group, known, only as the "cabinet", is rumoured to have meetings with the Prime Minister and the Chancellor, where they discuss matters over coffee and biscuits.

"All the decisions about government policy are taken in meetings between the Prime Minister and Ben Elliot's 'Advisory Board' of rich Tory donors," insisted a cabinet member.

"While the Prime Minister might occasionally run ideas by us so we can rubber stamp them, our group has no formal role in the decision-making process.

"This is quintessential Boris at his very best. Bringing together rich businessmen in secret to make sure he gets the best bung for his buck. The public can rest assured that Britain still has the best democracy that money can buy."

DAILY EXPRESS
BREXIT TRIUMPH

BRITS were jumping for joy this week, when they went to their local supermarkets and found them magically free of food.

"I've been battling with my weight for many years," said Mrs Madeup Lady.

"I can never resist temptation in my local Tesco's. I always weaken and buy food, but now I have that little extra help to keep to my diet! Thanks, Brexit! If I could vote for you again, I would!"

Mr Complete Fabrication added, "I'm always cluttering up my fridge with fruit and bottled water, but now, thanks to the great gift of Brexit, I can stop buying all that nonsense, clear it out and give it a good clean! I might even defrost it."

Dr Daley Express, an expert in food, said, "Eating food can cause all sort of health problems, including cancer, flatulence and tooth decay.

"Far better to avoid it. I would say if you meet anyone with an unhealthy addiction to food, they're probably a Remainer."

PINGDEMIC LEADS TO FOOD SHORTAGES

"I'm shelf-isolating"

"Oh God... now Ahab's following me on Twitter"

NEW COVID GLOSSARY

Pandemic Everyone gets Covid-19

Pingdemic Everyone gets "pinged" on their phone and told to isolate, despite not having been anywhere near a Covid sufferer

Pingu-demic Parents of young children go mad after hearing the same theme tune every five minutes for days on end

Pongdemic Everyone plays amazing new video game (NB last happened in the 1970s)

Pangolindemic The next disease we're all going to get from eating something we shouldn't, thanks to nobody having learned any lessons from the last time

Pundemic Tidal wave of stupid and irritating jokes being made by people who are stuck at home due to bloody Covid rules
(That's enough stupid jokes. Ed.)

THE EGO HAS LANDED
WORLD CELEBRATES FIRST BEARD IN SPACE

Richard, I know you'll travel a long way to avoid tax, but this is *ridiculous*

CLUBBERS FURIOUS OVER VACCINE PASSPORT PLAN

by Our Nightclub Correspondent **Ray Von**

CLUBBERS have expressed dismay at the government's plans to allow only people who are double vaccinated into nightclubs from September.

"How do I know this vaccine is safe? It could have anything in it," said one clubber, buying two Es off some bloke his mate's sister's boyfriend went to college with.

"There's a lot of stuff online about all the chemicals Pfizer put in it and about the side effects."

"I don't want to put anything in my body I can't be certain won't damage me," said another clubber, happily accepting a line of coke from a girl she'd just met in the toilets.

Many other clubbers with heavily dilated pupils dancing until dawn agreed that taking the vaccine could have huge health implications further down the line.

ENGLISH – AFGHAN PHRASEBOOK

ENGLISH	AFGHAN
Thank you for your help	⇨ *We're off now*
If there's anything we can help you with, just let us know	⇨ *I should warn you, the UK's a bit full at the moment*
We'll set up a process to relocate you in the UK	⇨ *Have you met Priti Patel?*
There may be a transition phase before your relocation	⇨ *There may be a hiding phase from the Taliban for a few years*
We absolutely guarantee the safety of you and your loved ones	⇨ *Make that decades*
See you again soon, buddy	⇨ *Sorry, who are you again?*

TALIBAN RESURGENCE

Stone me!

SPACE TOURIST INFORMATION

There's nothing there

TOKYO OLYMPICS
FIVE TO WATCH

Delta (India) Has been setting records all this year. Can anyone catch him? Yes – everyone.

Gamma (Brazil) Promises to race through the streets of Tokyo at remarkable speed. Has recently been overtaken by Delta, but refuses to be written off and says he'll be back stronger than ever.

Alpha (United Kingdom) The plucky variant from Kent looked unbeatable until a performance-reducing drug became available (AstraZeneca), but has still got what it takes to leave you gasping.

Beta (S. Africa) The rainbow nation's top virus looks set to run and run, and won't be beaten easily, proving that when it comes to pandemics, coronavirus is a marathon not a sprint.

Lambda (Peru) Having trained in the Andes, the Peruvian variant is brilliant at peaks, but has he peaked too soon?

(That's enough variants. Ed.)

ME AND MY SPOON

THIS WEEK

DOMINIC CUMMINGS
AS INTERVIEWED BY
THE BBC'S LAURA SPOONSSBERG

Do you have a favourite spoon?

Yes, I do. Unlike Boris Johnson, who couldn't make a decision to save his life, I had to choose all the spoons. He would have chosen forks or knives. He's a complete idiot.

Were spoons important in Downing Street life?

The Prime Minister's girlfriend wanted flashy, expensive spoons without asking who was going to pay for them. Gold spoons from Lulu Ladle. In cutlery terms, she was nut-nut-crackers. I hated her and her total refurbishment of the kitchen utensil department.

As the most senior Spoon Adviser, or SPAD, as they're known, did you try to shake up the Number Ten cutlery drawer?

Of course. All the spoons were useless. They'd been there too long, but Carrie just wanted to get in her favourite spoons. I wasn't having any of it. Her behaviour was unethical and illegal, spoonwise. Did I mention I hated her?

Do you have any spoon-related regrets?

Look, we were in the middle of a spoondemic and difficult choices had to be made. And Boris made all the wrong ones.

Could you give me an example?

Well, you know all this. I leaked it all to you before...

Yes, but this is on the record...

Okay. He wanted to go and have tea with the Queen and share a silver spoon with her. And I said, "You're mad! What if your spoon is infected and kills her?" But he said, "Who cares? She's over 80. She's dispensable."

Is that actually true?

You decide.

So that's a No, then.

Hey, I'm a weirdo, maverick spoon disruptor who likes to stir things up in a conventional utensil world.

I have no idea what you're talking about.

That makes two of us.

Can I end this cosy chat by asking you whether anything amusing has ever happened to you in relation to a spoon?

Watch this! I always used to do it when I left an important meeting of COBRA, or Cutlery Oversight Briefing Room A.

(Cummings mimes throwing a spoon over his shoulder and crouches down as the imaginary spoon explodes)

So that's another No, then.

NEXT WEEK: *Simon Rattle, Me and My Rattle*

WORLD IN PICTURES

NEW IRANIAN HARDLINER WINS ELECTION

It's a hung parliament – or it will be if they disagree with me

SLIM JONG-UN REVEALS DIET REGIME

I've been starving myself – it works for the rest of the population

NETANYAHU FURY AS ISRAEL ACCUSED OF 'GAZA SLAUGHTER'

Why are they blowing things up out of all proportion?

That's our job

SAUDI PRINCE PLANS NEW NATIONAL AIRLINE

We hope to cut the flight times into little pieces

DIARY

'HER HEART FOR A COMPASS' BY SARAH FERGUSON, DUCHESS OF YORK

CHAPTER 1

"It falls to me to inform you that your mother and I have identified a suitable husband for you," sniffed The 7th Duke of Burlington. "You are engaged herewith to Lord Coldfish of Leching – and let no more be said on the matter!"

Lady Sarah had never felt so completely alone nor so utterly wretched. Impetuously, she threw back her rebellious mop of red hair, letting it tumble wild and loose down her back.

She felt all the bubbles drain from her personality. In the past, all her friends had told her how bubbly she was. "But now I have never felt so totally unbubbly!" she sobbed.

Would she ever possess a sufficiency of bubbles to pen another adorable, much-loved tale about Budgie the Coach-and-Four to gladden the hearts of little children the world over?

"Here I am, a beautiful, young, 19th-century aristocrat with a heart of gold and a gift for making everyone feel so, so special – yet I myself am so utterly lost!" she sighed, sighingly.

And with that, she fled through the back door of her family's hugely impressive multi-million-pound Mayfair mansion, worth literally millions in old money, complete with 15 en-suites, luxury wall-to-wall carpeting and state-of-the-art crystal chandeliers, and ran for all she was worth.

CHAPTER 2

"Any old iron! Any old iron! Any-any-any old iron!" Where was she? Blinded by tears, she had run runningly through the streets of London. Her ballgown, sewn from the finest French silk, was in tatters.

"Wh-wh-where am I?" inquired Lady Sarah of a one-legged beggar with an eyepatch, a parrot, two teeth and a heart of gold. The poor man had lost his other leg, through no fault of his own, in the Charge of the Light Brigade, a failed military action involving the British light cavalry led by Lord Cardigan which had occurred earlier that year.

All around her, cheery, sooty-faced chimney sweeps kicked their knees up, stepping in time.

"You're in London's famous East End, dearie!" replied a passing prostitute, selling flowers from a grubby wicker-work basket. "Who will buy my sweet red roses? Two blooms for a penny!"

"Ripe pears, ten-a-penny and nar mistake!" shouted a street urchin. "Good luck will rub awf when I shakes 'ands wiv you!" Seeing a lady of such delicate appearance in their midst, a goodly number of very poor but happy children gathered around, in the hope that 'Er Ladyship, as they delighted in calling her, would read them one of her marvellous stories, leading to rapid improvements in their mental health.

CHAPTER 3

Lady Sarah had barely begun to read when she was assailed by a Victorian pickpocket in a top hat. "The wretched fellow has made off with my precious handbag!" she exclaimed, exasperatedly.

Luckily, at that juncture, the unruly vagabond was tackled by a handsome stranger, who returned the precious handbag.

"Might I perchance introduce my good self heretofore?" he quothed. "Lord Adam de Vere, second son of the Duke of Sutherland, at your service."

He moved closer, and yet closer. Their lips met. Hungrily, they kissed, and, as they kissed, his tongue touched hers and her tongue touched his, and soon their two tongues grew entangled in each other's mouths. "Surely," thought Lord Adam, "we shall forever be bound together."

"Your Lordship," sighed Lady Sarah, extricating herself. "You have perchance been inordinately accommodating, for which I am indeed most gratitudinous, but though our relationship is by now, I fear, perchance considerably advanced, I regret I am no longer the impulsive young woman I once was. Though my heart is indeed racing, our love can never flourish, given the harsh reality of our respective circumstances, so let us bid our farewells – and think, perchance, no more of what might have been!"

CHAPTER 4

Breathless and confused, and giddy with love, she brushed the tears from her eyes and made hither to London's famous docks, to embark forthwith on a voyage to America. The Atlantic Ocean was very, very rough and very, very wet, but thankfully she was not obliged to swim, as she had been most gratefully accommodated on board a sea-going vessel.

"This here be a ship – and a very fine ship at that, Your Ladyship," said the swarthy Captain, as he gazed into her eyes of deep burgundy.

The soft pressure of his lips on hers made her want to swoon. Their tongues met and clenched, finding a warm spot towards the back of her mouth where they might huddle together for comfort like babes in a wood, perchance.

"That was indeed a most elegant sufficiency, My Lady," exclaimed the Captain, essaying a smile and wiping his mouth with the discretion of a true gentleman.

"Oh, but it must not be! I fear our love can never flourish, given the harsh reality of our respective circumstances!" replied Lady Sarah, sobbingly. And, with that, she tearfully threw herself head-first into the frantic ocean, only to emerge, absolutely soaking wet, two days later, at the foot of New York's famous Statue of Liberty – a neoclassical sculpture 151 feet high, given by France in 1886 to the United States in celebration of American independence.

CHAPTER 5

"Lady Sarah! This is a most unexpected surprise! How do you do?" It was Lady Astor, who was, forsooth by chance, strolling aristocratically around the statue. "Have you met my handsome eldest son, Randolph, who is, as luck would have it, heir to our distinguished family's multi-million dollar fortune?"

Sarah gazed deep into Randolph's eyes, which so closely matched her hair. They kissed, deep, starving kisses, kisses deeper than the very ocean upon which she had voyaged so recently, though not quite so damp. Their tongues met, introduced themselves to one another and embarked on a waltz together around their respective mouths.

"Oh, my dear Randolph! It is not to be!" Sarah sighed, as their two mouths parted with a bitter pop. "Alas, our love can never flourish, given the harsh reality of our respective circumstances! Tragically, I am most speedily running out of pecuniary resources! But – hark! – I have just had a most splendid idea! I know of a mysterious American financier, much given to holding out the hand of compassion to titled folk down on their luck. Yes! Methinks I shall prevail upon the goodly Mr Jeffrey Epstein Esq. to put things right – and then all shall be well!"

As told to

CRAIG BROWN

Daley Mail

FRIDAY, JULY 6, 2021

YES, IT'S THE GOLDRUSH!

by Our Tokyo Correspondent **Lunchtime O'Lympic**

THE race for an Olympic record hoard of gold is on – with the Daley Mail leading the way!

No sooner had Tom splashed his way to Olympic glory than we were splashing him all over the paper, in the hope that someone would buy it! And that was just the start!

From then on, the hunt for gold began, as equestrians, rowers, gymnasts and swimmers all joined in helping the Daley Mail fill its coffers with the Olympics' most precious metal!

And after a long, hard year of writing depressing pieces about Covid, it's just what the nation wants to see – a happy, cheering proprietor, laughing all the way to the bank – and weeping tears of sheer joy at the sight of his newspaper sales.

So, come on Britain, get behind Team GG (Geordie Greig) and put the Daley Mail on the top of the podium – ahead of the Daley Express, Daley Mirror, Daley Telegraph and The Sunday Toms *(That's enough "Going for Gold". Ed.)*

News in brief

UK's gold medal rush could lead to huge uptake in people thinking about taking up sport

■ Team GB bosses say Britain's gold rush at Tokyo 2020 could lead to a massive increase in the number of people briefly thinking about taking up sport, equalling the record set after our successes at Rio 2016 and London 2012.

"We're excited that millions of people will be inspired by our gold medal-winning athletes to briefly think about getting up off the sofa and taking up a sport, only to phone for a takeaway instead while bingeing on some new Netflix show," said one *(cont. 2094)*

Russia taught lesson at Olympics

by Our Bad Sporting Staff
Ivor Syringe

THE International Olympic Committee hailed its ban on Russia competing at the games as a great success in its battle to stop cheating in sport.

"The fact that Russia, or the Russian Olympic Committee as no one calls them, is only a humiliating third in the medals table and has only won a desultory 50 medals, is clear evidence that our policy is working. Other countries will think twice about doping when they see the impact of these sort of draconian sanctions."

Said one delighted Russian athlete, "You won't catch me taking drugs because I'll be moving too fast!"

The Olympic Committee said, "This is a very difficult matter to get right. We are caught between a ROC and a third place."

*"When are **you** going to start hanging around skate parks?"*

Exclusive to all newspapers

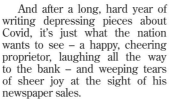

TOKYO 2020

OLYMPICS COVERAGE

It's **MAGIC MONDAY!**

It's **TREMENDOUS TUESDAY!**

It's **WONDERFUL WEDNESDAY!**

It's... **TREMENDOUS THURS**... oh no, we've done that one... ummm, it's **TREMENDOUSER THURSDAY** *(That's not a word. Ed.)*

It's **FANTASTIC FRIDAY!**

It's **SUPER SATURDAY!**

It's **SUPER**... umm... **TASTIC**... yes, it's **SUPERTASTIC SUNDAY**... *(You're fired. Ed.)*

The Daily Fablegraph

=== 6th Century BC ===

Sporting contest hit by shock athlete withdrawal

by Our Sporting Correspondent
E. Sopp

THE WORLD of fables was thrown into disarray last week, when one of the biggest names in animal-based morality stories unexpectedly pulled out of an important athletics competition.

Much-fancied sprinter, the Hare, was going head to head with the Tortoise before sensationally deciding he needed to sleep and that rest was more important than winning.

The Hare has always been a very confident performer on the big stage and was expected to comfortably beat the Tortoise, whose personal best of seven hours was considerably slower than the Hare's one minute 37.94 seconds over the same distance.

The Tortoise had been resigned to medal in second place, with a disappointing silver, whilst the rarely-beaten Hare, or GOAT (Greatest Of All Time), as he calls himself, was odds-on favourite to take gold.

However, at a dramatic press conference, the Hare announced that during the initial stages of the event, he had made the decision to take a nap, as he was feeling "tired of the whole thing" and could no longer bear the weight of expectation on all four of his shoulders.

"I'm not having fun anymore," he said, nibbling on a sponsored carrot, "and I can't cope with the responsibility to the whole world, which is watching my every move. I'm not in a good place right now. I'd rather be under a tree, asleep."

The Tortoise sent a message of sympathy, saluting the Hare's bravery in facing up to his issues, and thanking him very much for presenting him with the gold medal on a plate.

There was more controversy when the medal ceremony overran, as everyone waited for the Tortoise to climb onto the winner's podium.

DIANA MEMORIAL UNVEILED

At last we are united. We both think it's terrible

I expect Charles is seeing another statue

THE ALTERNATIVE VOICE

DIANA MUST FALL

by **DAVE SPART**

The totally sickening celebration of the imperialist royal colonialist collaborator and stooge, the so-called Princess Diana, by putting up a statue of her in the grounds of Kensington Palace, marked a new low in the history of British oppression and was a deliberate affront to the entire BAME population, not to mention the entire exploited working classes who loved her so much, er… er… putting on a pedestal this typical iconic white upper-class elitist heterosexual woman, whose ancestors were directly involved in slavery or at least knew someone who was, and whose entire wealth was built on the subjugation of the labouring classes over centuries of British plutocratic dictatorship, er… er… this utterly nauseating and inflammatory not to mention highly popular tribute to the so-called People's Princess, er… er… must be immediately pulled down and thrown in the nearby Diana memorial fountain, er…er… only then will society be rid of this offensive reminder of a history we all want to banish into the dustbin of, er… er… *(cont. p94)*

ANSWERS TO LAST WEEK'S OLYMPIC QUIZ

1   Freestyle Knitting

2   The gold medallists were identical triplets from San Marino

3   BMX underwater 800 metres. 4 x 4 mixed relay

4   Adam Peaty's moustache was 10mm too short

5   Clare Balding, Clare Balding and Clare Balding

6   An Ollie twistie backflip with a double-pike board-hold trouser press

7   The British horse punched the German trainer

8   The 49-class Omnium Freestyle Artistic Dressage Speed-Climb

9   Yemen who will host the 2094 winter Olympics

10 Clare Balding, Clare Balding and Gaby Logan

WHAT WILL BORIS CALL HIS NEW BABY?

- Thingummy
- Cripes
- Which one are you?
- Er…
- I think that's a private matter

CONSPIRACY UPDATE
MISSING BBC SPECIAL

It's been a momentous week for conspiracy addicts everywhere, as we all travelled to the BBC to protest against the sinister invisible lockdown imposed on us by the government… Only to find the BBC has completely vanished and there are just a lot of luxury flats and restaurants in its place! A real mystery!

TRUTH-IS-OUT-THERE4356's Day-Glo website is first off the blocks with this theory:

"If you look at a map of London and draw a triangle around it, you will see that a huge triangle magically appears! This fenonema is liek the BERMUDA triangle. But the diffrence is it swollows up TV STATIONS. It took TV-AM in 1992, and THAMES TELEVISION in 2003. The BBC has now been taken and it's only a MATTER OF TIME before VIRGIN MEDIA is next."

DRWhodiedformetoday%45323 has his own take on the mystery. His grim-looking Facebook page says:

"It is obvious that the BBC is HIDING because it is preparing to get rid of Doctor Who after that lady leaves, and it is getting ready to avoid the hoards of angry fans storming it in protest. That is why, in readiness, I am changing my website from CANCEL DR WHO NOW! to SAVE DR WHO NOW!"

QANON fan MAGA435 is most alarmed at this development. Typing his tweets from his jail cell he posits this theory:

"The Communist Democratic party is moving the BBC to the US, so that it can infect the hole of America with its wokeness. Once it is estabilized on our shores, the wokeness will spread like wokefire. I urge all armed militias to develop a vaccine against it. I wont take the vaccine myself, because I eat stake meat and do kung fu, but the more vunerble members of society will need it."

But let's give our glorious leader PiersCorbyn #haveplacardwilltravel the last word from his dodgy megaphone:

"The BBC has not gone anyway. The telepathic deception ray has worn off so we now see the BBC for what it is – A SERIES OF RESTAURANTS AND APARTMENTS owned by a ZIONIST CARTEL. #resist #takebackcontrol #moremonopolymoneyplease

Terrifying stuff. But I have to admit, my mushroom burger was delicious! The mystery continues!

Sports superstar joins debate on mental health

AT a packed press conference, one of the world's leading sportsmen highlighted the problems facing top athletes in the pressure cooker of the sporting arena.

"Earlier this week I was beside myself with worry, not knowing what the future held. I was in floods of tears, but then those tears turned to tears of joy. It's hard to explain," said Paris Saint-Germain's new signing, Lionel Messi, "but maybe money has got something to do with it."

A leading psychiatrist said, "Messi's experience shows how important it is to be given a million pounds a week to ensure a more positive outlook on life. His rollercoaster ride of emotion is clearly linked to a life-saving injection of vast amounts of cash into his bank account. We really need to pay more attention to footballers' mental wealth." *(Rotters)*

"I'm guessing this is your first attempt at Beef Wellington"

@Vilmirimo

Daily Mail

FRIDAY, 20 AUGUST, 2021

CHANGE IN EXAM SYSTEM A DISASTER

by Our Educational Staff
Ed Mistress

Daily Mail readers are furious at the standard of photographs of fruity girls getting their A Level results, after the change in the system of assessing their results.

Under the old system, the fruity girls were depicted jumping into the air with delight.

But now, thanks to Gavin Williamson's disastrous intervention, the girls, though still fruity, are depicted inebriatedly slumped on the pavement.

One educationalist called it a clear sign that standards are falling – as, indeed, are these fruity girls.

BEFORE

AFTER

On other pages

● Fruity girls now face an anxious wait to see if they'll be pictured in the Mail throwing up during Freshers Week at the university of their second choice **p2**

● Universities offer students £10,000 to defer vomiting for another year. Said one vice-chancellor, "Our toilets are all full of puke, and our clearing system simply can't handle it" **p7**

● A Levelling up: Students from poorer backgrounds encouraged to get just as drunk as those from private schools **p94**

Teacher assessments show consistency

by Our Education Staff
Ed Master

Despite the difficulties of the past year, teaching staff across the whole country have admirably risen to the task of matching grades with achievement.

Said one teacher, "It actually wasn't as difficult as some people have been saying, and there has been uniformity across the board in marking Gavin Williamson's exam performance. Every teacher agrees that he's an A***."

On hearing his result, Gavin Williamson was relieved, saying,

"This is much better than my predicted result. The way the last few terms have gone, I thought the teachers were going to rate me a C***."

He continued, "It just goes to show how accurate the grading systems are. I was predicted to fail, and I did so with flying colours."

Thanks to so-called "grade inflation" this year, it looks likely that next year's A Levels will be marked numerically.

Mr Williamson is set to be graded a Number 2 and will certainly not make it to Number 10.

A Level question

If 45% of A Level students received A or A* star grades after exams were cancelled due to Covid and teacher assessment was used instead, does that mean:

A) The students sitting A Levels in a year massively disrupted by long periods of home schooling rose to the challenge of a nightmare year and worked tirelessly to maximise their potential and achieve excellent grades?

B) The cancellation of exams meant that, despite students not working anywhere near as hard as they would in a normal year, teachers were free to award ridiculously high grades that make a mockery of the exam system?

Answer: *A or B depending on which paper you read.*

University of Neasden

New course for October 2021

M.A. in Treading Water Studies

A two-year course open to recent graduates looking at the merits of procrastination, deferral and decision-avoidance strategies in the context of an employment downturn, with particular reference to the unavailability of long-distance travel options due to the global pandemic parameters.

Course fees begin at £94,000.

Successful applicants will be restricted to all those who apply.

Contact:
The Vice Chancellor,
Sir Hugh Check,
University of Neasden
(formerly Wollydoodlealltheday Poly)

Nigella to change name of dish

NIGELLA LAWSON has agreed to change the name of one of her dishes from "Slut Red Raspberries in Chardonnay Jelly" to "Ruby Red Raspberries in Chardonnay Jelly" after complaints that the name sexualised the recipe.

"The last thing I would want to do is blur the line between sex and cooking," said a horrified Nigella, delicately fingering a couple of overripe plums.

However, Nigella was quick to reasure her legions of fans that, while she may have stepped over the line this one time, she had no plans whatsover to rename any of her other signature dishes, including her famous "Creamed Butter Knobs", "Big Breasted Chicken Surprise" and "Perfectly Stuffed Courgettes". *(That's enough recipes. Ed.)*

"Well, now you're getting your jab"

TALIBAN RETAKE AFGHANISTAN

AMERICAN TROOPS EXIT

Mess-up accomplished!

ISLAMIC EMIRATE RETURNS

We've turned the clock back 20 years

It's a lot more than that

BIDEN DEFENDS WITHDRAWAL

So we are all agreed – I did the right thing

TRUMP SUPPORTERS 'FINALLY ACCEPT RESULT'

■ THERE were jubilant scenes across the US today as Trump supporters finally accepted the 2020 election result and agreed that Joe Biden was their president, after his humiliating foreign affairs disaster in Afghanistan.

"We had no idea that Joe could be every bit as inept and out of his depth, blundering about on the world stage, as Trump was.

"If we'd have known he was this useless, we'd have supported him earlier," said one redneck wearing a stupid hat.

"It turns out that Joe is a good old boy like Trump, isolating America and making us a pariah on the world stage. Who knew he had that in him?" said another delighted Trump supporter, cheering on Biden while burning down a vaccine centre.

"Joe is one of us, a total embarrassment. We love you, Joe! Biden just needs to dump that saggy old wife of his and marry a 30-year-old former Playboy bunny with big titties and he can stay president forever," said a cheering Trump voter, drinking bleach to ward off the Delta variant in *(cont. p94)*

AGHANISTAN

BRITAIN'S MEDIA REACT TO THE CRISIS IN AFGHANISTAN

The Daily Telegraph

THIS is the worst crisis since Suez, apart from all the other ones where we said it was the worst crisis since Suez, apart from the Suez crisis itself, when we said it was the worst crisis since Afghanistan in 1842

The Guardian

Why is the West pulling out of Afghanistan when we have been telling them to pull out of Afghanistan for the last 20 years?

THE SPECTATOR

Why are we so horrified that the Taliban are telling Afghan women to cover their faces when our own Covid fundamentalists are telling British women to wear masks?

★ Morning Star

WE SALUTE our sisters in Afghanistan for their noble and indeed literal sacrifice in the cause of proving that Western Imperialism has been crushed and defeated by the historic forces of extreme Islamism *(surely Marxist-Leninism? Ed.)*

DAILY EXPRESS

WHY are we worrying about Afghanistan when Geronimo is about to be cruelly murdered by the Taliban Health Police?

Daily Mail

Why has the pathetic EU and Ursula von der Leyen utterly failed to stop the Taliban takeover of Kabul and the fall in UK house prices this week?

Sun

CAN Spurs' Harry Kane manage an orderly exit from Tottenham as the regime collapses into chaos around him?

GB N

We have a number of emails supporting the Taliban's efforts to prevent further illegal immigration to this country by so-called asylum seekers. We have some other rude emails from Mr Ivor Huge-Penis and Mr Andrew Neil, which are, frankly, childish.

EveningStandard

AS KABUL falls, we have sensational pictures of George Osborne's new baby – did the Stork Deliveroo it?

Trump fury over Afghanistan

IN the wake of the Taliban's capture of Afghanistan, former President Donald Trump has rushed out an angry statement denouncing the group.

"These Taliban guys have completely ripped me off and I'm going to sue them," Mr Trump fumed yesterday.

"It was my idea to storm a nation's capital using extremist, women-hating crazy guys with bad facial hair and carrying guns. They even stole my slogan. I hear they say 'Make Afghanistan Great Again'."

On hearing that Mr Trump was planning to sue them back to the Stone Age, Taliban leaders danced in the street and shot their weapons into the air.

Coming soon

Miss Kabul

Heart-rending musical about the fall of Kabul in 2021 and the non-love affair between the Afghan population and occupying US troops. Based on the opera Madame Saigon, Miss Kabul lasts for three hours – the time it took the Americans to scuttle out of the capital in helicopters. By the authors of Les Miserable Bearded Bastards.

EYE RATING: Miss Kabul will run and run – like the population to the airfield.

TALIBAN BARBIE

BERNIE

BLACK AND WHITE FLAG

WHITE FLAG

Boris Johnson MP
● Live   385,000,000 Views

Prime Minister's Question Time Live on Fakebook

👍 Like   💬 Comment

0 people **like this**

(PRIME MINISTER ENTERS TO RUSSIAN SOUND SYSTEM PLAYING RED ARMY CHOIR SINGING TALIBANY WYNETTE'S FAMOUS HIT "AFGHANISTAN BY YOUR MAN")

Boris: **Greetings**, folks. **Serious** face time. I've just come out of a G7 Zoom **summit**, called by **myself**, to discuss the **very**, **very** serious face issue of our **withdrawal** from Afghanistan. Now, you **may** say withdrawal's **not** my forte. It's all about **timing**. Knowing **when** and **how** to pull out…

First Lady (on smart phone, via SeriousFaceTime): Get on with it. I'm listening to you.

Boris: So, this G7 meeting was **perfectly** timed to consider what had happened **after** it had. And **we** decided that we would support the good people of Afghanistan in **every** way **except** by supporting them. And President Biden listened **intently** to every word I said, with his eyes **closed** in concentration. In fact, I'm going to ring him **now**, just to show you how **special** our special relationship **still** is.

(PRIME MINISTER SPEED-DIALS HOTLINE)

Boris: Hi Joe, it's **Boris** here… **Johnson**… **Prime Minister**… Of the **UK**… No, **not** Ukraine… No, not **ukulele**, that's not a country, Joe… **Sorry**, have I just woken you up? I must have got the time difference **wrong**. Is it mid-morning over there?… No, of course, **sorry,** I'll go via the switchboard next time. **Bye!**

(PRIME MINISTER ENDS CALL)

Boris: So **there** you have it. A **forceful** exchange of ideas by **top** international statesmen on the **pressing** issue of the day. The special relationship in **action**. And I **know** all about special relationships. I've had **loads**. And **every** one is special for a bit, until they **end** in disaster. Usually **expensive** and with **crying** children being **handed** over. Which is why I'm going to use **all** my experience to sort the **crisis** in Afghanistan. Top of the agenda is the **mercy** mission to sort flights for those **most** in need, who've **loyally** worked hand in hand with the British government, and I'm **delighted** to tell you that Dominic **Raab** has safely landed from Crete, after **chaotic** scenes at the airport in **Heathrow**, and being under **fire** from the Tabloidiban. Good news **there**. Feelgood story with a **happy** ending. And of course I'm **not** going to fire Dominic for being a **terrible** Foreign Secretary who's **always** on holiday during a crisis. I mean, we'd **all** be in trouble then, wouldn't we?

First Lady: Get on with the real victims.

Boris: Yes. **Double** serious face. People in Britain know who have **really** suffered in this crisis. And that's the brave **cats** and **dogs** who have worked **so** hard in Afghanistan to rebuild their country, which is why we have made it a **priority** to fly out 200 cats **and** dogs, providing they have the right **papers** and that the Afghan hounds of the Taliban **don't** mind.

First Lady: It's not funny.

Boris: Right, because if **anything** went wrong with the plane, it would be **raining** cats and dogs. **See** what I did there? Top **banter** – or you could call it **Talibanter**!

First Lady: Get on with the pet rescue.

Boris: **Whatever** you say.

First Lady: And don't forget to tell them that I never tell you to say stuff.

Boris: Right. Yes, Carrie **never** tells me to say stuff. That's Afghanistan **sorted**.

So the matter's now **closed**. Like the **sea** when Dominic tried to go paddle-boarding, whilst keeping a **close** eye on events in Kabul from the **beach** in Crete. **All** part of our **flip-flop** foreign policy. Wear flip-flops! You see, **even** in a crisis, Bojo can come up with some reassuring **banter** to calm the **nerves**.

Simon Briefcase: I don't think this is helping morale, Prime Minister.

Boris: But, triple serious face, do some **boostering**… amazing **achievement**… the **greatest** evacuation since **Dunkirk**… **heroic** action by our boys… something to be **proud** of… saved **thousands** of lives… welcome Afghan refugees… particularly if they're **lorry** drivers… anyone with a **HGV licence** come on in… Britain will do **everything** in our power… ie not a great deal… we'll shift **heaven** and **earth** to achieve **something** or other… and, yes, we'll be **back** – though we won't be, obviously… and we'll work with our allies, including, er, the **Taliban**, so long as they feel they can **trust** me… or is it vice versa… whatever, it'll all be **fine** in the **long** run… or long run **away**, as I call it er… er…

(PRIME MINISTER EXITS TO SOUND OF RED ARMY CHOIR SINGING POPULAR AFGHAN FOLK SONG "HELP!" BY THE BEATENS)

JOHNSON'S GOVERNMENT SPENDS £163,000 ON UNION FLAGS

🌴 BIBLICAL TIMES 🌴

Friday 3 September 2021

'Get My Fucking Animals Out Of Here' – Noah In Foul-Mouthed Rant

BY OUR MIDDLE-EASTERN STAFF HARRY MOUNT ZION

Prominent animal rescuer, Noah, caught in the middle of an unfolding catastrophe last night, hit out at officials trying to prevent the evacuation of the last of earth's animals from the disaster zone. Noah, who runs the charity Noahzat, swore at bureaucrats who were delaying the departure of his Ark.

Said a furious Noah, "If you don't help me, you will all fucking drown… you'll be finished… you will never work again or indeed breathe again, as the waters will rise up and consume you."

Noah's relief operation was heavily criticised by local politician, Tom Twobytwogendhat, for not including any humans, apart from his family, and for leaving large numbers of civilians to their fate at the hands of religious extremist, God.

A spokesman for the Almighty said, "Give it a bit of time, say 40 days, and we think that everything will have quietened down, due to everyone being dead, and that it will then be time for an olive branch to be offered and

(That's enough Noah. Ed.)

THOSE AFGHAN EVACUEE NAMES IN FULL

UNPOPULAR	POPULAR
Mohammad	Rover
Abdul	Fido
Bibi	Lassie
Gul	Ginger
Sayed	Socks
Ghulam	Patches
Fatima	Smudge
Ahmad	Hammy

CLIMATE SUMMIT RAISES HOPES FOR FUTURE OF PLANET

by Our Environment Correspondent **Gus Boiler**

GOVERNMENT minister for the environment, Alok Sharma, hailed the Glasgow eco-convention as the last chance not to sort out the global problem of catastrophic climate change.

He said that the much-heralded "NotMuchCop 26" would see a gathering of the world's top politicians flying in to discuss pressing green issues and the urgent necessity for action before doing nothing.

Mr Sharma continued, "We expect NotMuchCop 26 to deliver nearly as little as the Paris Agreement, CopOut 25,

where the major world powers agreed to do net zero by the time of NotMuchCop 26. Which we have done. Meeting the zero target easily."

He immediately published his plan for action, called: "Deeds not Words" – a thousand-page document, outlining all the speeches yet to be made – concluding that there would be more hot air emitted into the atmosphere in Glasgow than even China can manage.

"It's great to have Britain in the driving seat of the diesel car that is NotMuchCop 26," Mr Sharma added.

"I just thought, 'Why not?' while we've still got the chance"

RISHI SUNAK TAKES THE SPOON TEST

Favourite spoon?

Wow, man, that's a tough one. I like all spoons really. They're great.

Soupspoon or teaspoon?

You're killing me. Soup is good, but so is tea. I like to use the soup spoon to eat soup, but then again the teaspoon is good for stirring tea.

Wooden or silver?

I think that, in the light of the forthcoming spending review, I shouldn't comment on this sort of issue.

Animated cutlery – Forky from Toy Story or The Spoons from Beauty and the Beast?

I haven't seen a lot of films recently, but I am told that films are often very good and ordinary people enjoy watching them.

What was the last spoon you enjoyed using?

Now you've got me, man. I think I used a dessert spoon, but that's not to say that I don't enjoy using other spoons greatly, which I do when the occasion arises.

What's the naughtiest thing you've ever done with a spoon?

I'm about to stab Boris in the back with one... whoops... my SPADS...

You mean Spoon Advisers?

Yes, they told me not to mention the stabbing bit and to keep it as bland as possible.

Do you like your nickname Dishi Spoonak?

Yes and no.

Thank you very much, Prime Minister.

Saving planet from terrifying heat death 'Might cost a bit of money' shock

A STAGGERING new study has revealed that there may have to be TAX RISES if we want to prevent our grandchildren living on an uninhabitable earth, breathing through oxygen tanks, wading through a flooded hellscape and fighting each other for tins of food.

A spokesman for the Conservative Party's Climate Action Group said, "This is obviously completely unacceptable to Conservative voters. Nowhere in the last manifesto did we say anything about the world ending, and hard-working voters shouldn't have to face any consequences for the last 200 years of insane expansion we've enjoyed, thanks to the industrial revolution and all its lovely, lovely oil."

POETRY CORNER

**In Memoriam
Peter Corby, inventor of the Corby Trouser Press**

So. Farewell
Then Peter Corby.

You used aeronautical
Warming technology
From Concorde.

Yes, you were flying
By the seat of
Your pants.

Now you have died,
Aged 97.

We don't know
What you looked like,
But my guess is
You didn't have
Any wrinkles.

Sadly, where you
Are going nobody
Wears trousers.

E.J. Thribb
(Hotel Room 17½)

Advertisement

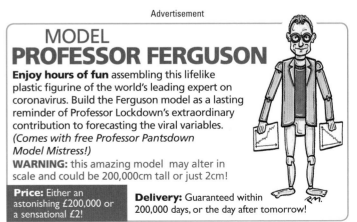

EXTINCTION REBELLION BRINGS LONDON TO STANDSTILL

by Our Protest Staff **Lester Square**

THE climate change protest group, Extinction Rebellion, created massive disruption across the capital yesterday as protesters blockaded roads and occupied traffic hubs in key locations.

Workers throughout London complained that their normal routines had been thrown into disarray by the activities of the eco warriors.

Said one furious home worker, "It was a nightmare. Usually I am watching the news as I fix myself a sandwich and a cup of tea in preparation for a Zoom call with Phil from Accounts and then suddenly the screen was full of these Extinction Rebellion protestors.

"I mean, they literally took over the whole news bulletin, leaving no space for the Paralympics or the cricket. Have they no concern for ordinary people working from home?"

Said another, "As soon as the XR mob came on, I found myself

glued to the television and I couldn't get away. I got no work done whatsoever and I posted no memes of cats being amusing for over two hours."

Extinction Rebellion defended its disruptive antics, with a spokesman saying, "We planned to stop the London traffic entirely, but unfortunately there wasn't any traffic due to the pandemic.

"We are, however, sorry that the WFH community have been inconvenienced, but it is important that we remind all those staying at home and having a Microsoft Teams brainstorm with Deidre from Human Resources that travelling is a very bad idea and that they should all stay at... er... hang on..."

"Not the best bridge to glue yourself to"

Covid protection wanes as everyone pretends it's over

by Our Covid Correspondent
A.S. Fixiate

A major new study has revealed that Covid vaccine protection wanes just at the point everyone in the UK pretends that the pandemic is over and enjoys a great summer of festivals, house parties and overseas holidays.

"With 30,000 cases a day, and deaths this week rising to over 180 in a single day, it's clear that vaccine protection wanes somewhat when everyone ditches their masks, gets wasted and forgets about social distancing while they party and have a great

time, as Boris Johnson encouraged them to do," said the study.

"Over 4,000 Covid cases alone have been linked to the Boardmasters Festival in Cornwall. Who could have possibly known that teens partying in a holiday resort could result in loads of Covid cases? Apart from everyone.

"The UK now selfishly needs to start administering a third booster jab for everyone, when most poorer countries haven't even given their people a first jab, so that we can carry on enjoying ourselves and pretending the worldwide pandemic is all over."

WHO WAS THE GREATEST:
Lenin or McCluskey?

THE EYE tackles the big question that's kept fans arguing for the best part of 50 years.

Pro McCluskey:
Yes, Lenin was good, and had all the ideas, but it was McCluskey who turned them into crowd-pleasing hits, with feel-good anthems like *A Hard Day's Unite*, *Back to the USSR* and *Hey Judas! Don't Cross the Picket Line*.

Pro Lenin:
Yes, McCluskey had the popular touch, but it was Lenin who was the real driving force, with genuinely radical ideas like 'Revolution' and 'Revolution Number 94'. The tragedy was that after Lenin died, McCluskey just became more middle of the road with his group 'Left Wings' and releases such as *Bland on the Run* and *Oh, Jeremy Corbyn...*

(That's enough. Ed.)

School news

St Cakes
Covid term starts today, it will run for two weeks until the start of home-schooling when all pupils are sent back to their kitchens. PCR Lateral-Flow (Ripoffs) is Head of Testing. Swabs will be held at assembly every day. Michelle Pfizer (Vaxxers) is Head of Bubbles. Pupils will sit the Oxford AstraZeneca entrance exam on November 3rd and again on January 4th and probably again on February 19th, with a booster exam to follow. Mr Zoom Frozen, formerly Head of IT, will now be taking all classes in all subjects until further notice, ably assisted by new full-time staff, Mr and Mrs Parent. School production of Alexandre Dumas' classic *The Man in the Linen Mask* has been cancelled due to the lead actor having a medical exemption and not having to wear one. The Nightingale Sanatorium is closed as a result of the current matron shortage. The bursar is delighted to announce that, in the light of the pingdemic, school fees will be doubled and non-payment will result in your child being sent home, if they're not there already.

NIGHTCLUB IN GOVID OUTBREAK SHOCK

It's all going very well... the pandemic, Brexit, Afghanistan...

He's raving!

WAS AFGHANISTAN PULL OUT A COMPLETE DISASTER?

- Is Biden a Catholic?
- Do Afghan bears hope to be rescued and flown to the UK where they will be resettled in Pen Farthing Wood and allowed to defecate in peace?

BIDEN DEFENDS AMERICA FIRST OUT POLICY

I said I would bring our boys back

The Daily Hellegraph

Friday 3 September 2021

New-Look Leader Reassures World

by Our Religious Staff **Lucy Fer**

THE bearded frontman, who is now in control of one of the most dangerous realms in the firmament, last night played down fears that from now on living there would be Hell.

Mr Beard Al Zebub told reporters from the Bible that there was an awful lot of "misinformation and speculation" about conditions in the underworld.

"Things are very different now," he said, poking a naked sinner with a trident.

"Hell is very modern these days and we have changed a great deal from the old medieval images of Fire and Brimstone. Now it's a more 21st century Brimstone and Fire."

He paused briefly to throw a miscreant into the fiery pit of eternal damnation and commented, "So long as you obey the rules, you will be absolutely fine. Hot, admittedly. And occasionally boiling in flaming oil. But essentially our vision of Hell is one of a progressive, modern, inclusive infernal Kingdom. I mean, really, you'd think from what you read in the Bible that we're all devils!"

He laughed fiendishly at the thought of this absurd misrepresentation and continued, "Really, it's a joke. Although jokes aren't allowed here, obviously, and result in being barbecued for eternity on a spit."

Mr Beard Al Zebub arrived in the capital of Hell, Pandemonium, in a handcart to be greeted by enthusiastic cheers of despair from the assembled multitude of the damned.

Vaccine immunity decreasing shock

by Our Medical Staff
Dr Tim Shipman

THERE are fears that, following the successful roll-out of the vaccine, the actual protective quality of the anti-viral serum is reducing rapidly.

It may be possible that the immunity of the government is now seriously compromised and that what was hailed as the saviour of the Johnson administration will no longer prove effective.

Said a spokesman for the government, "Initially, the vaccine roll-out stopped all criticism of the government. Whatever was thrown at them, they simply defended themselves with the vaccine. But increasingly we have noticed that this is not working."

Attacks on the government over food shortages and the Afghan withdrawal are breaking through, and the vaccine is no longer guaranteed to stop any harm.

JOY AS RUSH HOUR RESUMES

by Our Transport Correspondent **MAURICE MINOR**

AS OFFICES open their doors again, evidence is growing that a confident and largely vaccinated population is returning to work.

As traffic returns to pre-pandemic levels, the rush hour has made a welcome return, with everyone rushing to get in their cars.

Said one commuter, "It's just great to get back to normal, inhaling the fumes of the stationary truck in front of me whilst I sit in a three-mile tailback. To think I could be sitting at home enjoying my late breakfast and getting things done."

Another motorist agreed, saying, "I never realised how much I'd missed fiddling with my radio trying to find a traffic update whilst inching along in first gear."

There had been fears that the lorry driver shortage would dilute the rush-hour experience by removing several vehicles from the road but, happily, many people who would normally use the train are still too scared to do so, and are adding to the much-missed congestion.

"It's not the new technology, it's just that we don't have any drivers"

UK obesity crisis turns corner

by Our Obesity Staff
Duncan Donuts

THE government today hailed a breakthrough in the nation's war against obesity.

Said one junior health minister, "The population's weight problem has been putting a huge strain on the NHS, but at last there's light at the end of this really rather wide tunnel.

"News that McDonald's are unable to serve milkshakes, that KFC and Nando's have run out of chicken, and that Greggs can't offer as many pies as usual is bound to have a positive effect on British waistlines."

Claiming a triumph for the government policy of having no lorry drivers, she continued, "It's only a matter of time before there's nothing to eat in the supermarkets either.

"If that doesn't help the nation tighten its belt and start living on a healthier diet of, say, air and grass, then I don't know what will."

TORY HQ SHOCK!

And this is where we keep the manifesto

HOW BORIS'S PLAN SOLVES SOCIAL CARE PROBLEM FOR YOUNG PEOPLE

- Tax them so highly they can never afford to buy a house
- When it comes to the time they need social care they'll then have no house that they're forced to sell
- Er…
- That's it

Tory MPs' dismay

■ Tory backbenchers have privately reacted furiously to Boris Johnson's £12bn plan to reform social care, lambasting it as being a shocking proposal which finally levels with the British people about the massive cost of a properly funded social care system.

"What the hell is Boris playing at? He wasn't elected for any of this serious, grown-up policy nonsense?" whinged all horrified Tory backbenchers.

Ministers outraged

■ Several senior unnamed ministers say they plan to express their outrage at the proposals to hike National Insurance payments to pay for social care reform by not resigning or voting against the measure in the Commons.

"I am incandescent with rage and I will be expressing my anger by sensationally not resigning and furiously voting in favour of the measures I vehemently oppose," said a senior Tory *(cont. p94)*

Replacement bus

Keir Starmer WRITES

HELLO! I have embarked on a radical course of action that may alienate a few of my fans. I know it seems controversial, but I've made my mind up! I have decided to oppose the government!

"But, Sir Keir," I hear you cry, "surely that's not your job? From what I understand, your job is to support the government and come up with the odd minor caveat from time to time?"

And my reply to that is, yes, you're absolutely right! But there are some principles that mean I have to draw the line, and the government putting up National Insurance to pay for social care is one of those principles!

Finally, here is an issue we can all get behind! If there is one thing that we in the Labour party all agree on it is this: working people on low incomes should not shell out their hard-earned cash to subsidise those on much higher salaries!

So onwards!

Ahem. I have just taken several phone calls from every Union leader that gives the party money, pointing out that "working people on low incomes shelling out their hard-earned union dues to subsidise those on higher salaries" is the absolute guiding principle of the Labour party, and if that principle falls apart then the Labour party ceases to exist.

So… backwards!

What we can all agree on, is that working people on low incomes should not give their money to some things, but definitely to others!

I think we can fit that on a poster come 2024!

Sincerely, Keir.

Corbyn finds new political home

by Our Political Correspondent **Noah Newtaxes**

IN A MOVE which has surprised many at Westminster, Jeremy Corbyn has abandoned his attempts to be readmitted to Labour, announcing instead that he has joined the Tory Party.

"What was becoming increasingly clear to me was that the high-tax, high-spend Conservative Party shares my values forged in the socialist movement of the 1970s," Corbyn told reporters.

"But what really swung it for me was the Tories finally going behind in the polls. Any party with policies that unpopular is the party for me.

"Seeing the Tories wipe out all the gains they'd made in the red wall seats, virtually overnight, with unpopular tax hikes to fund essential public services, convinced me that Boris's Tory party members truly are my comrades in arms who will keep the Red Flag flying here."

ZOOM BOSS ANNOUNCEMENT BREAKS THE IRONY METER

We have a big problem. Too many of our staff are working from home

WHAT YOU WILL HEAR ON THE VIRTUAL ABBA REUNION TOUR

Those songs in full

1. Gimme Gimme Gimme
2. Money Money Money (It's a Rich Band's World!)
3. Thank You For The Money ♪
4. The Singers Take It All
5. I Do, I Do, I Do, I Do, I Do Take Credit Cards ♫
6. Chequetita ♪
7. Waterloot (Couldn't Escape Us If You Wanted To) 𝄞
8. Owing Me! Owing You!
9. Voulez-Vous (Un Ticket Overpricé)?
10. Mamma Mia! Here We Go Yet Again! ♪

All from the classic GrABBA album 'MORE GOLD PLEASE'.

EMMA TO BE GIVEN NEW YEAR'S HONOUR!

> But she didn't pay Prince Charles

> ...or donate to the Tory party!

RADUCANU VICTORY SIGNALS END OF THE BBC

by Our Media Staff **Des Perate**

AS Emma Raducanu slammed her winning ace past her opponent, there was no denying who was the biggest loser on the night.

The coverage by Amazon Prime and Channel 4 left BBC bosses wringing their hands in despair, as our so-called national broadcaster once again failed to show a British tennis player winning a Grand Slam final.

Said one seasoned commentator, "When Emma lifted the trophy before a TV audience of millions, I can't have been alone in wondering how many more Wimbledon championships Andy Murray might have won had he not been burdened with the BBC following his every move."

Up and down the country, viewers were left fuming that the BBC had not bought the rights to the US Open at a huge price, so that they could complain about wasting licence-payers money.

Said one irate viewer we've just made up, "I was livid that the BBC did not spend billions of pounds to show lots of adverts for Amazon Prime, which it's not allowed to do. The whole thing was a complete disaster for the BBC. Surely it's time they were replaced by a better service run by the proprietor of a newspaper like, I don't know, yours."

Emma's golden future

by Our Celebrity Staff **Bill Dupp**

SHE has the world at her feet, a world that is her oyster, every ball she strikes a potential pearl.

Gorgeous, glamorous, successful Emma Raducanu looks set to be a dazzling star in the nation's sporting firmament for many years to come. We can only hope that she fulfils all her early promise and doesn't succumb to the darker trappings of fame.

How sad it would be if she were to bow to the pressures of our 24/7 media world and end up being photographed, tumbling out of a nightclub or vomiting in a gutter, by the paparazzi.

How tragic it would be if her life were to slide downhill and become the subject of lengthy pieces speculating on her mental well-being and her inability to handle life in the glare of publicity.

How mortifying it would be for journalists like myself to have to report on her fall from the pedestal on which we so well-meaningly yet misguidedly placed her.

For now, we can only wait, keyboards at the ready, for the editor to give us the call, "New balls please".

THOSE TENNIS HEADLINES

The Sun
EMMA IS A SINGLE(S) CHAMPION, FELLAHS, SO GET READY TO COURT OUR NEWEST TOP TENNIS TOTTY!

DAILY EXPRESS
BREXIT DOOM-MONGERS PROVED WRONG AGAIN, AS U.K. EXPORTS OF TENNIS TO AMERICA SKY-ROCKET

theguardian
Raducanu win proves that government immigration policy is shameful

Daily Mail
RADUCANU WIN PROVES THAT GOVERNMENT IMMIGRATION POLICY IS A TRIUMPH

THE TIMES
Phwoar! Could sexy Emma be the next Kardashian?

The Daily Telegraph
Raducanu earnings to be hit hard by unnecessary national insurance tax rise

Court Circular

HRH Prince Andrew will not be appearing in Court. This morning he will be in attendance with himself behind the sofa. This afternoon he will officially open a number of cupboards and decide which of them to hide in. He will not be meeting Mr Buck NonceHunter III, the acclaimed lawyer from New York, who will attempt to present His Royal Highness with an invitation to attend a gala trial in his honour, in recognition of his Duke of York awards scheme mentoring young American women in the Peedoh islands. He will instead meet officers of the Royal Reputation Protection Service led by Sergeant John Jobsworth who will tell Mr NonceHunter that HRH is not in and definitely not hiding behind the sofa or in a cupboard. They will then assure the NonceHunter team that the speeding vehicle racing out through the back gate towards Balmoral is a pizza delivery man returning to his base in Woking. The Prince's Legal Advisor-in-Waiting, Mr Fudge, from the firm Fudge, Dodge and Dither, will then inform the press that the summons from Mr NonceHunter was incorrectly served according to the protocol laid down by Debrett's. It should have been served, using a fish knife from the left and on a silver jubilee platter, by the second son of a Marquess on a Thursday.

NEW ANDREW SHOCK

> A young girl winning in a New York court? Now I'm sweating!

94

CHANNEL BOATS LATEST

Any tennis players there?

BORDER FORCE

Lines on the occasion of the annual SNP Conference

'Twas in the year twenty twenty one, a year to remember,

That Ms Sturgeon announced her plans for Scotland in September.

And what was her priority in the crisis facing poor Caledonia,

With the virus rampant, NHS straining and critics getting moanier?

What should a wise and responsible First Minister do?

Why, announce plans at once for a new round of Indyref 2!

What other policy is there when the Covid cases spike,

Thought the embattled but undaunted wee krankie lookalike.

(That's quite enough. Ed.)

© *William McGonagall 1867*

Daily Telegraph Friday 17 September 2021

Letters to the Editor

The failures of BBC Drama

SIR – Those of us who are proud to call ourselves "sardines" and who have served our time as submariners in Her Majesty's Royal Navy, have been watching the BBC's drama *Vigilant* with increasing irritation.

Whoever wrote this fandango of fanciful fabrication should be keel-hauled underneath a submarine or made to walk the plank from the conning tower!

The catalogue of inaccuracies is typical of the BBC, or Bunch of Brainless Civilians, whose disrespect for the armed forces knows no bounds. As anyone who has been in a Class 94 Diesel-powered Tristar Hunter Gatherer Submarine could have told them, the periscope is a good 3cm longer than depicted and the thermo-nuclear torpedo tubes are painted yellow and blue NOT blue and yellow and, worst of all, the baked bean tins are NEVER kept in the for'ard galley but in the Sloop Mess in the stern bulkhead.

Such landlubber errors make it nearly impossible to watch the events on HMS Vigilant (which the producers certainly weren't) with any degree of credibility.

As for the depiction of the female police officer. I can only say that when I served on HMS Codpiece at the height of the Cold War, the idea that a woman could join "the smellies" (as "sardines" were affectionately known then) is completely ludicrous and would have resulted in a mutiny.

In my experience, sailors are extremely superstitious and we would never have tolerated a woman below decks unless it was Petty Officer "Sandy" Beach in drag, taking the part of Little Miss Buttockup in the Gilbert and Sullivan opera *HMS Pinochet*, to amuse the men when we spent four years under the arctic ice cap.

Rear Admiral Sir Horatio Gussett CBBC, ITVC (brother of the more frequent *Telegraph* **correspondent Sir Herbert Gussett)**
Dundeterring, Rum Cove, Plymouth Unsound

An HGV Driver Writes

Blimey, I mean I know there's a shortage of qualified people to do the jobs, but this strikes me as madness, mate. You can't take short cuts, well, you can't in this lorry – you'll end up knocking holes in the village post office! But they're just making it too easy to become a politician. I mean, in the old days you had to serve your apprenticeship, but nowadays you barely need any experience at all, and they fast track all these youngsters who don't know anything and have never worked in their lives. It's nothing short of dangerous to put them in the driving seat. I mean, someone who doesn't know what they're doing in charge of a great big country? That's a disaster waiting to happen. The wheels could come off! I mean, they talk about roadmaps but most of them have no idea where they're going. Probably end up driving us all off a cliff. Makes you think! I probably shouldn't be texting this while I'm driving. ☺

NEW HGV DRIVER EXAM TO BE MADE EASIER

It's a crash course!

THIS WEEK

HILARY MANTEL

Do you have a favourite spoon?

Well, it used to be a British spoon, but now I'm embarrassed by British spoons and their reluctance to share a cutlery drawer with foreign spoons. The knives are out for foreign spoons in a way which I find truly ugly and I want nothing more to do with British cutlery.

Perhaps your favourite spoon is a royal spoon?

I find the very concept of a royal spoon absurd. Why are people so interested in them?

But you have made a career from writing books about one particular royal and his spoons.

Henry VIII was a special case – famous for having six spoons. He had an eye for spoons, indeed his fondness for spooning was legendary, though Anne Boleyn's head was removed with a very sharp and big knife.

So if not a British spoon or a royal spoon, what kind of spoon is your favourite?

Well, I'm currently going through the family's old silverware to see if I can find an Irish spoon. The spoon doesn't have to be Irish – any piece of european cutlery will do.

It sounds like you've reached a fork in the road. Has anything amusing ever happened to you in relation to a spoon?

I once displayed a heraldic Tudor spoon on the ledge above the fireplace at Hampton Court and called it a mantelpiece Mantel Piece.

I did say "amusing"… Never mind.

NEXT WEEK: *Michael Fawcett, Me and My Faucet.*

GOVERNMENT DENIES OCTOBER LOCKDOWN PLANS

"You make the sourdough and I'll stock up on toilet roll"

95

HEIR OF SORROWS
A Short Story Special

by Dame Sylvie Krin, author of *Duchess of Hearts* & *You're Never Too Old*

THE STORY SO FAR: Charles is reeling after a newspaper revealed a scandal over "cash for access" and an inquiry into the honours system was announced. Now read on..

"WHERE are my soldiers? One can't function without one's soldiers." Charles, heir to the throne and Honorary Colonel of 17th/94th Dragoonshow Guards looked despondently at his steaming boiled egg, unsupported on the breakfast table by any complement of neatly cut toast-and-butter fighting men.

Sir Alan Fitztightly shimmied into the room in a fragrant cloud of Hugo Swires Cologne.

"I don't want to complain, Sir Alan…" Charles began.

"First I've noticed," interrupted Sir Alan, waspishly.

"…but there is a problem on the eggy soldier front and I may well have to write a stiff letter to Cook."

"Of course, sire," replied his aide-de-glamp wearily, "we all know you've been under a lot of pressure, what with the unfortunate business of the CBE for Mr Mustapha Gong…"

Charles was immediately on the defensive.

"Now look, I had no idea about Mr Gong's intentions. I thought he was a genuine philanthropist who had a real and keen interest in the restoration of Dumfreebies House and the upkeep of Castle #Meytoo…"

Camilla rolled her eyes and another home-made cigarette from her pouch of Old Holborntobequeen Tobacco.

"Funny how many middle eastern businessmen have a passion for clapped out Scottish ruins," she rasped, removing a flake of tobacco from her cruel tongue.

"By which I don't mean you in a kilt."

Charles ignored his consort, who was in a particularly ill humour that morning after reading the new chapters of Harry and Meghan's biography, *Finding Money*, in which she had been criticised yet again by Lalaland's power couple who had just produced a new podcast about the importance of niceness, forgivingness and welloffness.

"You shouldn't have re-employed that ghastly valet of yours, Michael Fawner, to run your charity. I told you he was a bad 'un."

"But he was so loyal to oneself. And he squeezed toothpaste immaculately," Charles protested.

Sir Alan intervened,"That was his job, sir. He was Custodian of the Colgate, Spearmint Carrier Royal and Plaque Remover Poursuivant."

"Well, I think you are wrong about Fawner. I am sure he will come out of this entirely innocent."

"Whiter than white?" suggested Sir Alan, giggling.

"With a hint of minty freshness?" added Camilla, joining in the morning room mirth.

FORTUNATELY, at that moment, the phone rang and Sir Alan picked up the bakeofflite receiver.

"It's a gentleman about an inquiry."

The colour drained from Charles's ears and he stammered, "Yes, yes, of course we must co-operate entirely with any inquiry. What does he want to know?"

There was a pause and then Sir Alan announced, "He wants to know how much a knighthood costs and whether you will take cash and is Camilla for sale, as he fancies another wife?"

Charles grabbed the phone furiously and remonstrated with the caller who was not from the Government Standards in Public Life Committee at all, but was in fact Mr Bigczek, the Chief Executive of the Belarubles Strategic and Tactical Engineering Technologies firm, Armswegottem Plc.

"Now look here, Mr Bigczek, I don't know where you got the idea from that you could just fork out some dosh and I would give you the Order of the Victorian Raspberry, but...

"...ah you were told by Mr Fawner... I see... well, I am afraid that Michael was speaking out of turn and, besides, I have no idea who he is... so thank you very much for your call, but the Prince of Sales... er... Wales... is out at the moment, so could you please leave a message after the tone... Wheeeeeeee!!!"

The Duchess of Rothmans and the First Flunkey Factotum collapsed in hysterics at the embarrassment of the Heir to the Game of Thrones and their cruel laughter rang down the echoing corridors of Claret House and out over the Mall. Would Charles's reputation recover or would it be clouded for ever, like the stormy skies looming over Quickbuckingham Palace...

(To be continued...)

"No, it's not my lockdown dog – it's my husband"

96